'In *Exploring the Natural Underground*, Bingham examines the transformative power of dreaming, accessing and exploring the hidden dimensions of our Earth. Deeply contemplative and philosophical, this book is about the power of hidden dimensions which inspire new ways of living, being and imagining, together. It is an "existential leap" indeed'.

María Alejandra Pérez, *West Virginia University, USA*

Exploring the Natural Underground

This book explores the enigmatic world of the natural underground, viewing it as a site of leisure and a primary sphere of anthropotechnics. It reshapes the old language of caving into new ideas that broaden the possibilities of the sociology of caving.

After outlining a novel methodological approach that can be used to understand new leisure trends and cultures in present modernity, *Exploring the Natural Underground* offers a comprehensive investigation of the societal context in which caving takes place. Thereafter, it goes on to argue that the natural underground can be used as a means of escaping some of the unavoidable influences of consumer capitalism in the way that it stimulates imaginations, senses and emotions differently.

Marking a turning point in the way that the natural underground is understood and the degree to which sensory dimensions of leisure are valued, this book will appeal to anybody interested in caving, as well as scholars and students of leisure studies, the sociology of leisure, the ethnography of leisure and human geography.

Kevin Bingham is Higher Education Lecturer in the Department of Service Industries at Barnsley College in the United Kingdom. He has published in the fields of leisure studies, sport and sociology.

Routledge Critical Leisure Studies
Series Editor
Tony Blackshaw
Sheffield Hallam University

The modern world is one that holds an intense fascination with the activities we place under the heading 'leisure'. Rather than simply being the opposite of 'work', 'leisure' today can be seen as a form of social and cultural life in which 'work' and 'leisure' intersect and mutually inform one another.

This series is a forum for agenda-setting research that examines our contemporary world of leisure. It places a strong emphasis not only on mapping current developments in individual and collective leisure activities, but also on challenging our understanding of these from different perspectives. Providing detailed empirical and theoretical accounts, this series explores the critical issues that underpin people's leisure lives at the beginning of the twenty-first century.

While this series is devoted to leisure, many of its books touch on other subject fields, contributing to interdisciplinary studies and appealing to readers from across the social sciences and the humanities.

Available in this series:

Leisure Communities
Rethinking Mutuality, Collective Identity and Belonging in the New Century
Edited by Troy D. Glover and Erin K. Sharpe

Digital Wellness, Health and Fitness Influencers
Critical Perspectives on Digital Guru Media
Edited by Stefan Lawrence

Transforming Leisure in the Pandemic
Re-imagining Interaction and Activity during Crisis
Edited by Briony Sharp, Rebecca Finkel and Katherine Dashper

Exploring the Natural Underground
A New Sociology of Caving
Kevin Bingham

Information Classification: GeneralInformation Classification: GeneralFor more information about this series, please visit: https://www.routledge.com/Routledge-Critical-Leisure-Studies/book-series/RCLS

Exploring the Natural Underground

A New Sociology of Caving

Kevin Bingham

LONDON AND NEW YORK

First published 2023
by Routledge
4 Park Square, Milton Park, Abingdon, Oxon OX14 4RN

and by Routledge
605 Third Avenue, New York, NY 10158

Routledge is an imprint of the Taylor & Francis Group, an informa business

© 2023 Kevin Bingham

The right of Kevin Bingham to be identified as author of this work has been asserted in accordance with sections 77 and 78 of the Copyright, Designs and Patents Act 1988.

All rights reserved. No part of this book may be reprinted or reproduced or utilised in any form or by any electronic, mechanical, or other means, now known or hereafter invented, including photocopying and recording, or in any information storage or retrieval system, without permission in writing from the publishers.

Trademark notice: Product or corporate names may be trademarks or registered trademarks, and are used only for identification and explanation without intent to infringe.

British Library Cataloguing-in-Publication Data
A catalogue record for this book is available from the British Library

Library of Congress Cataloging-in-Publication Data
Names: Bingham, Kevin, author.
Title: Exploring the natural underground: a new sociology of caving/ Kevin Bingham.
Description: Abingdon, Oxon; New York, NY: Routledge, 2023. | Series: Routledge critical leisure studies | Includes bibliographical references and index. |
Identifiers: LCCN 2022060319 | ISBN 9781032294766 (hardback) | ISBN 9781032294773 (paperback) | ISBN 9781003301752 (ebook)
Subjects: LCSH: Caving–Social aspects. | Escape (Psychology) | Senses and sensation.
Classification: LCC GV200.62 .B56 2023 |
DDC 796.52/5–dc23/eng/20230202
LC record available at https://lccn.loc.gov/2022060319

ISBN: 978-1-032-29476-6 (hbk)
ISBN: 978-1-032-29477-3 (pbk)
ISBN: 978-1-003-30175-2 (ebk)

DOI: 10.4324/9781003301752

Typeset in Goudy
by Deanta Global Publishing Services, Chennai, India

For my daughter, Kaitlyn Lily Bingham — my next adventure.

Contents

List of figures	xii
Acknowledgements	xiii

1 Introduction: First Encounters with the Kingdom of the Dark   1

Introduction 1
The Kingdom of the Dark 3
A Short History of Caving and Cave Exploration 6
Control and Authority over the Natural Underground 14
An Outline of the Book's Content 18
References 20

**2 Descenders, Static Line and Some Methodological
Considerations: Choosing 'Tackle' for the Job**   23

An Introductory Interlude 23
Introduction 27
Auto-ethnography vs Auto-hermeneutics 28
*Research Design: Hermeneutic Sociology and Sociological
    Hermeneutics 32*
On Being an 'Uncommercial Traveller' 34
Some Additional Notes on Travelling Underground 38
References 39

3 The Underside of Modernity   42

Introduction 42
Life on the Surface 43
The Call of the Caves 50
Foggy Lenses and Broken Screens 53

x   Contents

Summary 60
References 61

4   The Poetics of Caving: Rediscovering Intimate Things   63

Introduction 63
The Intimacy of Caving 64
Scotopia 68
Systems of Scotopia 71
Summary 88
References 89

5   Unsilencing Fear in the Natural Underground   92

Introduction 92
Facing a Dialectical Dilemma: Culture of Fear and Fear Avoidance 93
Giant's Round Trip 96
Searching for Fear through Edgework 99
Unsilencing Fear through Limit Experience 102
Summary 107
References 108

6   Life and Death Underground: Mortality, Immortality and Other Survival Strategies   110

Introduction 110
Living with Death 110
Into Each Life Some Rain Must Fall 115
Survival Strategies between Rocks and Hard Places 118
Summary 125
References 127

7   An Uncommercial Traveller's Guide to the Art of Sublimation   129

Introduction 129
When the Differend Speaks 131
Pleasure and Pain: A Recipe for Seduction 139
The Art of Sublimation 147
References 148

Contents xi

8   Journeying to the End and Back: Reaching a Choke   150

The Maze Cave: Versed in the Art of Sublimation 153
References 156

Index   157

Figures

1.1	The mysterious opening	4
2.1	The rocky crawl	24
2.2	First glimpses of the dunes	25
3.1	An unprepared Mcnally learns to abseil	48
3.2	Lamenting the loss of a phone	56
4.1	The entrance to Lancaster Hole	64
4.2	Mayhem consulting the maps while we rest	78
4.3	Stalagmites and stalactites inside the Graveyard Series	79
5.1	The entranceway to Giant's Hole	96
6.1	The last photo taken before we had to make a hasty exit	116
6.2	The entrance to Jackpot (P8) in normal conditions	119
7.1	The entrance to Titan	133
7.2	Contemplating the journey back up, all 141 metres of it	140
7.3	Jamie suspended beneath Mayhem	145
8.1	The Kingdom of the Dark	153

Acknowledgements

For lots of reasons, I would like to begin by thanking my wife, Jenny. Without your continued support, encouragement and patience, this project would not have been possible. I'm sorry our rear porch is now a storage for caving gear ....

I would also like to thank Professor Tony Blackshaw for suggesting I write this book, and for the invaluable guidance you've given me over the years.

A special thank you goes to my good friend, Ford Mayhem. There's no one I'd trust more in the kingdom of the dark.

To James Mcnally, Rizla Rider, Luke Hellewell, Jim Figg and Jamie Daly – a big thanks are due for allowing me to write about our time spent underground. You all contributed to making my task of exploring the natural underground possible.

Finally, I extend my thanks to Lliam Dickinson for supporting the project from beginning to finish.

Chapter 1

Introduction
First Encounters with the Kingdom of the Dark

Introduction

Growing up there was always something about underground space that interested me. I was intrigued by the idea that there might be a second world lurking beneath our feet, a paradoxical world of wonder ready and waiting to be explored. Perhaps my interest was closely linked to a childhood spent in the shadow of the Durham Coalfield, a coalfield that stretched from the natural boundaries of the North Sea and the River Tyne all the way to Consett on the West border of the county and Bishop Auckland to the South. Perhaps. Then again, perhaps not.

In truth, I grew up largely ignorant of Durham's infamous mining past for the Industrial Revolution that led to the large-scale exploitation of coal in the area was well and truly over when I was a child. Following the Second World War, the industry underwent rapid decline and by the 1950s and 1960s most collieries had ceased operating (Beynon and Hudson, 2021). The last colliery in Durham Coalfield – Wearmouth – closed in 1994 when I was five years old. My childhood, then, was spent mostly in the lacklustre surface world of Newton Aycliffe, a realm of grey concrete and modern brick, an expansive industrial landscape mostly comprised of factory units, and some surrounding woodland and fields, a far cry from the mysterious world below. It was not until we were teenagers that we truly discovered the magic of the underground, a stimulating world of lost mines and hidden drains and culverts.

And yet, underground places were at the forefront of our imaginations long before our first real encounter. As children, we enjoyed hunting for abandoned pillboxes on the outskirts of Newton Aycliffe's Industrial Estate, old shuttered concrete fortifications that once protected munitions being stored at Heighington railway station (Creaney, 2020). In our imaginations, these structures were secret entranceways to a vast subterranean labyrinth. For a long while we convinced ourselves they were lost entrances to an intricate bunker complex, or a large natural cavern like those occupied by evil villains in old James Bond films. We even speculated that they might lead to an old chemical waste facility beneath a large synthetic resin factory a few miles from where we lived. Much to our disappointment, however, when we finally did muster enough courage to peek

DOI: 10.4324/9781003301752-1

inside one of the old pillboxes, we discovered none of our elaborate underground networks seemed to exist. The structures, unlike our imaginations, were empty.

Our anti-climactic discovery did not deter us for long. If anything, it only raised our interest in the underground, especially our yearning for finding a means of accessing the subterranean world we *knew* existed. It was during one long summer break from secondary school that we decided we would try again, this time by attempting to construct our own underground bunker. Borrowing a couple of old spades, a sledgehammer and a rusty wheelbarrow from my dad's shed, we set up camp in a nearby wood and for the next six weeks set about digging a hole. Our plan seemed simple enough. We would tunnel into the earth horizontally, excavate some soil to make a larger chamber, construct a floor using a couple of bags of sand and cement we had 'borrowed' from someone else's dad and line the walls with some old fence boards. Easy.

It was not long at all, however, before our lack of knowledge and skill was realised, for in the first two weeks our entranceway grew steadily into a single gaping hole in the ground. No matter how hard we tried, we could not fathom how to stop it from collapsing. So, after much frustration and confusion, we decided in the end that it would be much easier to simply carve out a 4-metre-deep hole and then cover it with a plastic tarp (again, 'borrowed'). We continued to dig for another month until we finally had a hollow deep enough. In the end, it was so deep we were forced to cut a dozen thick steps into one of the walls so we could climb in and out. Needless to say, we were impressed with ourselves. Sadly, though, our plans never progressed much further. The day after completing our magnificent creation would mark a weeklong wet spell which brought with it more than enough rain to transform any vision of a secret bunker into a murky woodland pond. This of course marked the end of a disappointing summer, the bitter taste of defeat serving as an unpleasant reminder of how much time and energy we had wasted.

Notwithstanding all the frustration and regret we felt at the time, what our experience also marked was the beginning of an important relationship, an embryonic relationship that would eventually grow to become an important part of our lives. We did not know it at the time, naturally, but this is the moment our journey into the underground first began. We had tried to sample a special type of elixir, one comprising the excitement, magic and, I would also add, the misery that is found only when you discover a way of undoing the surface. Our yearning for more was now greater than it had ever been. Sadly, though, Newton Aycliffe is not well known for having any caves or underground fortresses so the closest we ever got to anything remotely subterranean for a long while was Middridge Quarry, an open-air site well-known for containing interesting fossils.

Fast forward a few years and my same burning curiosity for adventure, and of course that of some close friends, led to our discovery of a new form of leisure known as urban exploration (also known as 'urbex'), which, as I have explained elsewhere, involves exploring human-made structures and environments (Bingham, 2020). Although it was abandoned buildings and ruins that had initially captured our attention, it was not long before our bizarre new interest led us underground. It was always inexpressibly exciting when we found buried ruins, tunnels and chambers, far more sensational in fact than any 'derp'.[1] There was something about being underground that was especially thought-provoking and mysterious, and what we realised very quickly is that there are signs of another world beneath our feet almost everywhere. From cellars in the backs of abandoned pubs to old air raid shelters, mines, drains and culverts, we discovered there were all kinds of subterranean places waiting to be explored, a whole new world carved into the darkness below by human hands and a little imagination. This was our first *real* introduction to the underground, a taste of that special elixir we had once almost sampled, albeit it was a notably artificial one, but it was an introduction to things that cannot happen or be seen on the surface nonetheless. It was also how we eventually stumbled across the extraordinary world of the natural underground.

The Kingdom of the Dark

Dressed head to toe in dust-stained waterproof clothing from years of exploring drains, culverts and abandoned mines, we entered the arched entrance of an age-ing Victorian culvert. A thin trickle of brown stream water was our guide, leading us forward into the unknown. All the while the rumble of traffic and the sound of general chatter from the street above followed us.

Inside, the walls of the tunnel were constructed of large black stones at the base, changing to red bricks further up which gave the impression that the lower section of the tunnel was badly water stained. Like other Victorian culverts we had explored, this one was carefully crafted and ornate. It had an imposing parabolic arch that made it difficult to think of anything other than the great innovation, wealth and craftsmanship that must have been required to create such a monolith. The passage had direction and purpose, allowing water to flow directly and predictably beneath the city so that it would not impede further progress and development. It was another reminder, like all those other magisterial reminders on the surface, that the noise of urban life is intense and designed to be as noticeable as possible.

A harsh metallic thud reverberated throughout the tunnel, the suddenness of the sound immediately stopping us in our tracks. Realising very quickly that it was caused by a vehicle passing over an iron maintenance cover, our small group pressed on as we were interested to discover where the old culvert would end. We continued to walk for 50 metres or so, our footsteps echoing loudly against the solid brick walls, until we were interrupted by an unexpected opening low down on our right-hand side. The opening was a deep scar in the stonework, a natural tear in the earth that had been impossible to conceal with human effort. Within there was a blackness that somehow managed to completely absorb our torch-light. There was something spellbinding about this dark fissure, something in its silence that was good on our city-blunted senses. Curious to learn more about the

4 First Encounters with the Kingdom of the Dark

Figure 1.1 The mysterious opening.

mysterious aperture, one by one we wormed our way inside. The gap was barely able to accommodate a human body, but we managed to slide through the passage which soon spilled into a larger cavernous space. We had entered some kind of natural cave where the laws and rules of human creation no longer seemed to apply (Figure 1.1).

For a start, the sounds of the cityscape had disappeared. For the first time in a very long time, we could hear nothing. With the exception of a faint drumming sound which turned out to be our own raised heartbeats, complete silence filled the chamber. The smell was very different. It had an earthy freshness to it, poles apart from the familiar dank-smelling culvert we'd left behind. The space also had a sensuous appeal that spurred the imagination to run wild. The chamber we had entered had no logical structure, nor a clear path. Instead, there were several routes ahead, all unique in shape and size. It felt strange as well, for a fine layer of mud that had the texture of playdough coated the floor, the walls and even the ceiling. This was the moment we had entered a new world for the first time and there was something about it that made us want to venture further. We did not know it at the time, we were urban explorers after all who felt at home in the great cityscapes of present modernity, but what we had stumbled across is what Bruce Bedford has described as the 'strange, awesome and often exotically beautiful kingdom of the dark' (1985: 6).

For years me and the lads I spent my youth growing up with found enjoyment 'urbexing' together. We eventually went on to call ourselves WildBoyz, which I realise may sound odd to an outsider. Yet, there was more to us than the curious name. What WildBoyz ('the Boyz') represented was a unique leisure world we constructed for ourselves. It was built around the phenomenon of urban exploration and an illusion of 'deviance' (Bingham, 2020). In short, what we created was a temporary escape from day-to-day life, a space of compensation which after borrowing Michel Foucault's (1984) concept of heterotopia I went on to refer to as heterotopic social space. This is space that involved knowing how to balance being a *skholēr* and a *khôraster*. In other words, we were people who not only sought a warm sense of belonging with likeminded others but also had a parallel desire to become performative 'artists of life' (Blackshaw, 2017).

Unfortunately, though, impermanence is the hallmark of the twenty-first century (Bauman, 2000). To borrow the great philosopher Heraclitus's way of putting it, 'no [person] ever steps in the same river twice ... for it is not the same river and [they are] not the same [person]' (cited in Winkler, 2016: 52). This rings true for 'the Boyz' and over time, as members of the collective have parted ways, 'the Boyz' heterotopia has lost its vigour and intensity, so much so the group meet only very sporadically these days. Except for Mayhem, Rizla and very occasionally Rags, the rest of the group have all but surrendered their freedom to the responsibilities and ordinariness of everyday life. Nevertheless, just as Octavia Butler has famously pointed out, 'in order to rise from its own ashes a phoenix first must burn' (2012: 309). I would argue that this is precisely what happened to 'the Boyz' and from the ashes emerges something new, a group that has decided to turn their attention exclusively to underground exploration. What our new group has discovered is that while the old heterotopia may have ended, we might perhaps have stumbled across something even better. What we have found is the *natural underground*, a place that has always intrigued human beings because it is steeped in mystery and the spice of true adventure. To borrow Bruce Bedford's (1985) way of putting it, what we discovered is the great kingdom of the dark.

What is special about this kingdom, as Ralph Crane and Lisa Fletcher (2015) reveal, is that it is one of the last sources of opportunity for original discovery and exploration in the twenty-first century, especially since it requires physical human presence to navigate the dark passageways that are constantly changing and transforming. The natural underground is a confusing, labyrinth-like reality then that is at odds with how things work on the surface world. Even more important, though, is that the natural underground is not just different geologically, it is also starkly different in an ontological sense for this is a world where people can leave behind prescribed roles and sensibilities. It is here, as the remaining 'Boyz' and I have come to realise, people can explore newly discovered emotions, senses and identities that have otherwise been repressed or become absent in the humdrum of everyday life. This view, therefore, challenges the all-too-common assumption that there is an apparent pointlessness to underground exploration (Gillett, 2007). Of course, underground exploration can in the end boil down to nothing more than a dead end, but to view it in this way, as something that is fundamentally meaningless, is to ignore the true significance of an alternative

6 First Encounters with the Kingdom of the Dark

dimension. In other words, what the remaining 'Boyz' have learnt fundamentally is that something remarkable lies within the natural underground. In it, they have found the irresistible call of the *dark*. And so, it is my task now, reader, to tell you all about it.

What remains to be said in this chapter, however, before my sociology of caving can begin is a little more about what other scholars have said about the natural underground. This discussion serves to strengthen my argument that from a sociological standpoint caving is something that has typically been under-investigated and overlooked. It will also allow me to expand on the idea that control and authority over the natural underground, and of course much of the literature produced about it, has for too long been dominated and controlled by a strict legislating culture.

A Short History of Caving and Cave Exploration

The subject of caving and natural underground exploration is by no means an under-researched area. In fact, many scholars have taken to investigating it and, as a result, there exists an extensive and diverse body of work that helps us explore and understand the phenomenon. To achieve the task of ensuring this book makes a valuable contribution to the existing literature, I begin by unpacking how caving has typically been examined and understood and where subsequent gaps in knowledge begin to emerge. It is my intention that the ideas presented in this chapter will begin to set out my thesis. In turn, this will allow the reader to better understand and appreciate the direction I have chosen to take – an interpretation of caving that focuses on the natural underground as a synchronic environment, an environment that can be entered at any time for an existential experience that is sometimes social but always deeply personal. As it will be argued towards the end of the chapter, it is my belief that there is room for a more sociologically developed investigation of natural underground exploration that can contribute to the existing body of literature.

Underground Adventure

One of the main ways the natural underground has traditionally been understood, especially in the early years of its development when it was still gaining traction as a form of sport or leisure, is through the simple idea of *adventure*. As the well-known cave archaeologist Edmund Mason explains in his 1977 book *Caves and Caving in Britain*, it was the challenge and adventure of being underground that first drew his interest and appreciation. The likes of Arthur Gemmell and Jack Myers (1952), David Heap (1964), Dave Haigh and John Cordingley (2017), Des Marshall (2019), Michael Taylor (2020) and, most recently, Graham Proudlove (2021) all share similar views, and it is their books in particular that are successful in articulating the excitement and adventure of underground exploration from first-hand perspectives.

There are of course many others, people I have not mentioned above, who similarly discovered the adventure of caving. As Pierre-Olaf Schut (2006) reminds us, underground exploration gained an increase in attention during the nineteenth century as awareness and curiosity of its existence was suddenly realised. The bourgeois traveller Édouard-Alfred Martel is a good example of such an individual from this period whose attention was drawn to the natural underground, specifically the dark caves in Cévennes. Although Martel had a scientific interest in cave exploration, more so as he realised the cultural atmosphere of science during the nineteenth century was synonymous with progress and status, he had been a dedicated adventurer since early childhood and so might also be described in his early years as having been a tourist in search of everything adventurous, from picturesque landscapes and natural beauty to uncovered mysteries (Schut, 2006). It was arguably this raw, primaeval sense of adventure and wonder before science that drove Martel to commence his first underground trip into the Dargilan Cave. It was this same sense of adventure that brought Martel to Gaping Gill in North Yorkshire. And it was here, much to the disappointment of British explorers, that he became the first person to make the − 109.7 m descent to the bottom where he was able to accurately sketch a map of the cavern (Lovelock, 1969).

Another explorer famous for having a strong appetite for adventure is Norbert Casteret. He is known as one of the greatest precursors to caving and wrote a large number of autobiographic books detailing his underground explorations. According to Trevor Shaw (2004), Casteret might be described as the archetype of a 'dedicated sportsman' for he was especially well known for his boldness and being involved in a series of dangerous trips underground. Certainly, from diving naked into siphons with only water-resistant candles and matches at his disposal to fearlessly descending free-hanging ropes hand over hand into unexplored pits, Casteret reveals all kinds of first-hand accounts of adventure across his years of caving (Lovelock, 1969). To paraphrase Shaw (2004), what sets Casteret apart from most other cavers is his obvious enthusiasm and passion for underground exploration, both of which are clearly articulated across all 47 of his books.

It will be many years before explorers exhaust their underground playgrounds, for there is much still to be discovered (Crane and Fletcher, 2015). There are, without a doubt, many more adventures waiting to be had. However, the days of adventuring for the sake of adventure, of facing danger in leather caps, woolly jumpers and ties, and of blindly chasing natural curiosity, appear to have reached something of an end because the symbiotic relationship between underground exploration and technological innovation has changed drastically over the course of the twentieth century (ibid). That is to say, the old ways with their pencil-drawn maps, carbide lamps and hemp ropes have gradually been replaced by LED headtorches, survey software, specialised clothing and nylon. What these changes mark in effect is the end of the romance of adventure tales and the beginning of a speleological movement. To be clear, this is not to suggest that all

8 First Encounters with the Kingdom of the Dark

adventure underground has ceased. As the likes of Marshall (2019) and Taylor (2020) show, it has not. My point out is merely that the idea of adventure for many cavers has transformed.

The Speleological Crusade

All the technological advances in caving that occurred in the twentieth century were designed with one key aim in mind – to extend the possibilities of underground exploration. Known as the scientific study of caves, the practice of *speleology* gained popularity in the twentieth century, especially in Britain, several European countries, Cuba and North America, and from then on various speleological associations and societies were established (Pérez, 2021; Mattes, 2020; White and Culver, 2019). The broad aim of these groups was to understand the physical properties, histories and different life forms that exist inside caves. In addition, they also set out to understand the processes that create natural underground spaces.

The so-called 'founding father' of speleology is generally known as Édouard-Alfred Martel, the same Martel mentioned earlier, and his original version of the discipline emerged as what he described as a 'sporting-science' (Cant, 2006). In other words, although Martel's interest in underground exploration began with an interest in adventure, he later went on to found the *Société de Spéléologie*, the first organisation dedicated to the scientific study of caves in the world, and quickly became a pioneer of cave exploration, documentation and study. With this in mind, it should be noted that speleology emerged first and foremost as a 'field sport', one belonging to members of the gentry, and in this world participation in muscular exertion and physical activity were both regarded as a distinguishing mark of a gentleman and a means of acquiring disciplined perceptions of the world as a scientist (Pérez, 2015; Cant, 2006; Hevly, 1996).

Before the discussion continues any further, it is worth noting that although Martel is known widely as the pioneer of modern speleology other individuals and caving societies in the first half of the nineteenth century were already laying the foundations for a scientific study of caves in Slovenia, Austria-Hungry and Italy. The mining official, Antonio Lindner, for example, was one of those involved in its evolution. Aiming to solve a water shortage in Trieste, Lindner set about searching for underground water noise after bouts of heavy rainfall (Mattes, 2020). Eventually, his research led him and his team to a subterranean river 329 metres below ground, a cave depth that had never before been reached (ibid). This feat marked the beginning of a new three-dimensional focus for cartography and shaped cave study as a newly emerging field of scientific interest. This was a type of study, however, that only involved the right kind of explorers, and it was these individuals who quickly seized control over the idea of vertical geography.

In order to descend, the new conquerors of the natural underground not only required specialist equipment such as 'knebel' devices, specialist ropes, tree-trunk ladders and diving equipment, they required practical knowledge and superior bodily skill to be able to navigate unexplored passages and chambers (Mattes, 2020). In other words, self-appointed explorers reinvented themselves as physically strong, disciplined underground 'scientists' and experts – a new elite essentially – and this enabled them to distinguish themselves from the less capable masses such as common travellers and lowly 'cave tourists' (ibid).

Following a similar interpretation of 'cave study' as that developing simultaneously in Europe, consistent with the idea that it was becoming a scientific activity positioned between a range of interweaving and overlapping academic fields and of course sport, in Britain the first Speleological Association was formed in July 1935. This was the British Speleological Association (BSA). The central aim of the BSA was to bring caving enthusiasts together and provide opportunities to share knowledge, engage in coordinated research projects, and offer support and advice to all members (Palmer, 1937). In Britain especially, speleology was renowned for operating on the fringes of other academic disciplines, relying on their knowledge, methods and practices, but the creation of the BSA marked the start of something much more reputable. Although speleology still had no dedicated departments in British universities at this time, and the BSA was more of a loose group of enthusiasts and amateurs than it was scientists, the association served to grant speleologists in Britain a sense of collective identity for the first time (Cant, 2006). In the first few years of its existence, the BSA first set about ensuring all its members were active in the field (speleology was viewed as a 'sporting-science' after all which meant 'armchair' scholars were not gladly received). The organisation then went on to compile literature on British caves, produce a series of cave surveys and maps, hold a conference at Buxton Town Hall and publish a quarterly magazine named *Caves and Caving* (Cant, 2006).

Despite its early successes, the influence and control of the BSA gradually declined in the mid-1940s and new organisations such as the Cave Research Group (CRG) were established (Gunn, 2004). The key concern and stimulus for creating new organisations came down to the argument that speleology was not being practised as a true science (BCRA, 2005). In other words, while both organisations had a specific type of individual in mind when thinking about the ideal speleologist – that the individual should be sociable, disciplined, enthusiastic, hard-working, knowledgeable and generally 'of a good character' – it was the role of sport that became the source of discord (Cant, 2006). For the BSA, speleology was viewed as a 'sporting-science' and it was the duality, the combination of both activities, that gave their work scientific legitimacy (Cant, 2006). However, for the CRG good speleology was something different, and to improve the image of the discipline as one legitimised by orderly, systematic and objective processes, it was decided that subjective elements (i.e. personal narratives and enjoyment) had to be removed (BCRA, 2005). Sport was viewed as something done primarily for fun, and too much fun in the minds of CRG speleologists was not appropriately scientific. What this change in perspective marked then was a shift to reconstruct speleology in Britain so it was more in line with other conventional scientific practices.

The transition towards what might be described as speleological elitism, where caves are typically accessed and explored not for the love of adventure but for surveying, making observations and collecting samples, did not just occur in Britain and Europe. As María Pérez (2015) points out, in the 1970s, the same tensions surrounding speleology's sport-science duality surfaced in Venezuela. Here, it was the embrace of a minimalist ethic together with a geologic imperative that drastically altered the dynamics and compositions of exploration teams. According to Pérez (2015), it became the task of certain speleologists in Venezuela to push exploratory and survey efforts in the country, making sure field notes were taken on every visit, that notes were converted into detailed maps, that thorough trip reports were written and that samples were carefully and accurately analysed. In other words, many members of the Venezuelan Speleological Society (SVE[2]) had their sights set on establishing themselves as members of a respectable scientific organisation and they subsequently rejected any form of caving that was devoid of scientific aims (Pérez, 2015; Sociedad Venezolana de Espeleología, 2006). According to this mindset, only certain individuals were worthy of being speleologists, people who strived to be highly disciplined, skilful, athletic and capable of working as part of a team (Sociedad Venezolana de Espeleología, 2006). These were individuals willing to dedicate their entire attention to:

> the very diverse and uncommon study of hypogean fauna (biospeleology); ... climatological conditions, temperature, humidity, underground currents (speleohydrometerology); ... varied photographic techniques (speleophotography); etc., ... [and] geological, archaeological possibilities and exploratory techniques.
>
> (Tronchoni, cited in Pérez, 2015: 238)

It is fortunate, however, that attitudes and beliefs are never truly set in stone in what we might call the 'liquid' modern turn, and there have been many instances where the likes of Tronchoni have transformed in an ontological way. What this means is that they have been willing to question doxic understandings and challenge former beliefs. This of course is one of the key advantages to living in a mobile present where people are guided by 'weak ontologies' that have neither a solid foundation nor involve deep commitment (White, 2000). As White argues, since the world has become more fluid and individuals more accepting of different perspectives ontologies have become contestable. This means twenty-first-century individuals are better able to reflect on their observations of the world and their sense of who they are, how they want to live their lives and how they view other people (Bauman, 2000). Indeed, as interviews that took place towards the end of his life reveal, Tronchoni's stance towards exploratory cavers became more relaxed. In fact, Tronchoni went so far as to suggest that certain attitudes have, to some extent, jeopardised caving. What he pointed out is that elitism not only risks limiting the scope of both science and exploration in and of caves, but it can hinder the recruitment and retention of new cavers (Sociedad Venezolana de Espeleología, 2006).

A Subterranean Turn

Notwithstanding concerns that the act of exploring caves may have become too scientifically orientated, there is a growing body of evidence that supports my point about the changing nature of life and leisure in the twenty-first century. That is to say, since the turn of the new millennium, some investigations of subterranean space have shifted their focus and are now including the diverse thoughts and ideas of individuals who have other interests and perhaps less concern for science (see della Dora, 2011; Hurd, 2003). In addition, new studies have emerged which reveal there has been a blending of knowledge as concerns around subsurface geology, homogeneity and the right kind of scientific practice have amalgamated with neoteric interests in social, cultural and political influences and the growing heterogeneity of subterranean spaces (Mattes, 2020). What this body of work demonstrates is that the twenty-first century marks the beginning not only of a major 'subterranean turn' that broadens scholarly appreciation and understanding but also the beginning of an era where scholars are willing to take seriously new themes and ideas that have previously been overlooked (Squire and Dodds, 2019). Some of the key scholars to investigate social practices and political dynamics linked with or tied to the natural underground include María Pérez, Johannes Mattes, María Zurita, Paul Munro and Sarah Cant.

Beginning with Pérez (2021, 2015), what is evident is that by drawing on her extensive ethnographic work on cave expeditions in Venezuela and Cuba, she approaches the topic of caving through a range of different lenses. Some examples include intimate geopolitics, volumes and vertical geography. Using these lenses, what Pérez has been able to do is critically examine relationships between space and power. In other words, by drawing attention to social dynamics, political influences and masculinist heroics that shape underground environments what she reveals is that caves are embodied, experienced and constructed in a multiplicity of different ways. Another scholar whose work has been pivotal in exploring the extent to which strong personalities and masculine ideas of caving have had a major influence on the development of British speleology, especially the formation of its dual character that was noted earlier, is Sarah Cant. To briefly summarise her paper, what Cant (2006) argues is that the personalities of certain leading speleologists (such as Eli Simpson) are responsible for creating antagonisms, arguments and fixed ways of thinking about caving.

Turning to other important and relevant contributions, the work of Johannes Mattes, particularly his study *Reisen ins Unterirdische* (Travelling into the Underground), also demonstrates that there has been an important 'subterranean turn' with the scholarly focus being channelled in a new direction. In this study,

Mattes (2020) traces the long cultural history of caving and speleology in Austria and the Austro-Hungarian Empire from the Age of Enlightenment to the 1920s by means of historical discourse analysis. To summarise his work in a very tight nutshell, what Mattes searches for are interconnected links, relationships and influences science, theology, philosophy and the arts have had on cave exploration.

Also worth mentioning here are the group of studies that explore how subterranean spaces such as caves are not only integral to geopolitical strategies of control, enclosure and exclusion but nation-building as well. As Rachael Squire and Klaus Dodds (2019) point out, manipulation and handling of natural underground space all too often occur for political and economic reasons, with nation-states and influential corporations in particular findings ways of appropriating and exploiting certain spaces for urban development, mineral extraction, oil and gas production, or special military purposes. What this indicates, as Anthony Bebbington (2012) argues, is that domination over the subterranean has long been instrumental in the accrual of power and control for certain governments, political figures and tycoons, especially when that power and control links to or has an impact on surface territories. This is something María Pérez and María Zurita (2020) address, that both surface and subsurface spaces and territories are often inextricably linked and intertwined.

Another interesting way the natural underground has been interpreted is through the sensorial adventures of a first-time caver. In their paper 'One foot in the cave', Chris Hughes and Clive Palmer (2020) approach the topic of caving in a way that allows them to consider how bodily senses are evoked, felt and understood. What is attention-grabbing about Hughes and Palmer's (2020) contribution is that they approach the natural underground from an amateur's perspective and, therefore, with unfamiliarity in mind. This is a refreshing tactic since this is not the usual way of doing things in the world of caving. Steering themselves away from the wider body of literature associated with the field, the pair use caving as a means of investigating whether new methodologies can be developed, methodologies that enable researchers to further representation of sensory data. A critical observation, however, is that Hughes and Palmer (2020) make the mistake of seeking to create a rigorous and structured means of interpreting sensory experiences. In other words, they are at risk of mirroring the direction of those scientific modes of inquiry discussed earlier in this chapter.

Also acknowledging the significance of sensorial experience in the natural underground is a small body of work that attempts to unpack enlightenment and even altered states of consciousness. There is the work of Veronica della Dora (2011) for example that describes caves as metaphorical spaces charged with biblical and miraculous narratives. Referring to early Christian pilgrims who sought spaces of silence for meditation and prayer, she explores the idea that holy men have long relied on the natural underground because empty voids have allowed them to not only renounce the everyday world but transform their bodies into vessels filled with divine grace.

Following a similar theme to della Dora, there is also the work of Will Hunt and Clayton Eshleman. Reflecting on his time alone in a cave for 24 hours, what Hunt describes are the combined effects of darkness and complete isolation on the human mind and body. What Hunt found is that the environment impacted his senses so poignantly he experienced a '[a] feeling of being peeled open [and] turned inside out' (2019: 217), a feeling he suggests is a completely altered state of consciousness. Eshleman shares the same interest in altered consciousness but does so in a much more florid way. Drawing on his own empirical experience of being plunged into total darkness underground, Eshleman (2003) attempts to explain how he experienced hallucinations and other entopic phenomena. After staring into the dark for ten minutes, he explains that pinpricks of light started to appear like fine snowfall. He goes on to suggest that he later witnessed the snowfall transform into light, light that continued to grow until it became so brilliant and dazzling he felt he had entered the kaleidoscopic realm of a psychedelic trip. Before I continue, I should point out that I am sceptical about Eshleman's claim. While I admire the poetic nature of his work, I have difficulty believing such a state can be reached and wonder whether his description is not a product of wishful thinking rather than anything more tangibly rooted in reality.

Setting all criticism aside, what the literature discussed in this section reveals is that there is much more to natural underground exploration than speleology and traditional science. In other words, the literature identified here serves to remind us of the heterogeneity of subterranean worlds. Keeping this in mind, I want to encourage any readers, especially those who are scientifically minded, to think from this point onwards about human entanglements with underground spaces with a different mindset. Doing so will allow us to move away from the lens of technical regimen, regulation and calculation towards new and original projects. Although the lens of scientific enquiry is highly valued and extremely popular among many cavers, it is important to remind ourselves that the underground has long played a crucial role in stimulating human imaginations, senses and emotions. This is the direction this book takes, the awkward and much less used passage on our left that far fewer people have thought to explore. Drawing inspiration from the examples outlined above, then, and my conviction that there is much more to be said from a sociological standpoint about the exploration of the natural underground, my aim in the remainder of this book is to provide a comprehensive investigation of the societal context in which caving is done and some of the subsequent ways in which caving stimulates imaginations, senses and emotions. My mission, therefore, is to shape the old language of caving into new ideas that will ultimately broaden the possibilities of the sociology of caving.

Before this can be done, however, what will first be useful is if we turn our attention in the next section to issues of control and authority. Doing so will help me further unpack some of the challenges caused by expert beliefs and the prevailing dominance of the scientific approach, both of which continue to cast a shadow over the world of caving. It will also help me address a second problem concerning my own position and standing as a caver. This is important since the book has been written from the perspective of someone who is clearly less interested in the science of caving, or indeed stagnant traditions, who embarked on this investigation without a typical caving background.

Control and Authority over the Natural Underground

As some of the studies mentioned so far attest, there is evidence that attitudes around the 'right' type of caving have started to change in the twenty-first century. Nevertheless, there is still, in general, a particular way of viewing caving from inside the broader 'community'. In fact, caving could well be regarded as a surviving form of 'rational recreation', a type of recreation that follows traditional Victorian ideals (i.e. order and control) to ensure the instilment of moral principles and good values (Cunningham, 2014). After all, certain rules and manners must be followed if the status of 'caver' but more especially 'speleologist' is to be bestowed upon a person. What this means is that across the complex scene of natural underground exploration certain organisations, associations and key figures have typically projected their own sense of order and control over what it means to be an 'authentic' cave person. In his comprehensive analysis of landscape and Englishness, David Matless (2016) has made similar observations. What he argues is that certain 'manners' have traditionally been upheld in the English countryside as the means to the right way of seeing and behaving. Any departures from those dominant 'manners' were (and still are in the eyes of some) deemed to be acts of trespass, acts counterpointed by visions of so-called 'anti-citizens' who were thought to belong to a vulgar, uncontrollable working class (Matless, 2016: 101).

Thinking back to caving, in the twenty-first century where the boundaries of social class have started to dissolve to some degree and people have become consumers who have a high proclivity to consume yet limited ability to understand or know why (Bauman, 2013), it might be argued that so-called 'anti-citizens' are still a problem. Yet, rather than being identified as the vulgar working class, they are more likely to be viewed as superficial and unrealistic individuals, individuals who seem to carry on living their lives without any real knowledge of authenticity and freedom (Blackshaw, 2017). What I am arguing, in other words, is that Matless's original observation is just as applicable today in the world of caving because there are many regulators of the natural underground who view the ideas, behaviours and attitudes of simple consumer sorts as being at loggerheads with their own way of doing things and harmful to the overall integrity of underground exploration (Taylor, 2020).

Interestingly, the issue of social exclusion among cavers is generally quite subtle, often more overt and noticeable in the real world rather than in literature. Furthermore, Taylor (2020) makes the point that it is generally only a problem among cavers and caving intellectuals who would describe themselves first and foremost as speleologists, preservationists or even just as 'experienced'. It is to these individuals that a social and anti-social geography comes into play, along with the assumption that bad conduct emanates from untrained, uneducated consumer sorts who tire quickly, are likely to make mistakes and feel anxious to resurface (Taylor, 2020).

Whether they choose to be subtle about it or not, to a speleologist, preservationist or even just an experienced caver, an 'anti-citizen' might be labelled a 'spelunker', 'tourist', 'cave-buffoon' or even a 'cardboard caver' (Wilson, 2019; Moss et al., 1995). These are derogatory terms used to imply that someone is an untrained and inexperienced caver who views the activity as a whimsical or casual form of leisure or a hobby rather than anything more serious. As Wilson (2019) points out, there are certain individuals, especially those who bring with them balls of string to mark their route, car tow ropes for making descents, alcohol or drugs, spray paints and tools for gathering interesting mineral formations, who act without moral obligation. To borrow Matless's (2016) way of putting it, these individuals are thought to act as a 'cultural grotesque' as they have a complete disregard for important cultural norms. In many ways, then, the individuals described by Moss et al. (1995) and of course Wilson (2019) are no different to the so-called 'Cockneys' Matless (2016) refers to who were said to have invaded the English countryside with litter, noise and disobedient behaviour such as bathing and flower-picking. According to Wilson (2019), inexperienced novices and spelunkers represent a similar lack of order and skilled cavers and speleologists should take action when any sign of inappropriateness is witnessed. For instance, they might recommend that certain items should be left on the surface, or even go so far as to escort inexperienced people back to safety.

I should say, in fairness, that there are many good reasons why divisions exist between 'authentic' (experienced) cavers and speleologists and other 'anti-citizens'. As Taylor (2020) points out, those who possess the appropriate knowledge and skills have developed them over substantial periods of time and they are mindful of how many incidents there have been where people have injured or killed themselves in the natural underground. They also acknowledge that many caves are located on private land and that access rights depend on the maintenance of good relationships with landowners (Taylor, 2020; Gillett, 2007). Furthermore, 'authentic' cavers and speleologists are conscious of excrement and the impact pollution can have on delicate cave environments and ecosystems. Certainly, many popular and well-known caves, particularly their entranceways, have been vandalised with spray paint or by people carving their names into the rock. Many more have been used as dumping grounds for human waste (Henry and Suk, 2017; Taylor, 1996). It is therefore not surprising why good etiquette and strict caving procedures are enforced. As Steven Boga (1997) puts it, cavers are capable of healing when they have broken bones or strained ligaments, but caves are scarred forever when damaged and millions of years of geological history can easily be erased by single acts of vandalism.

The problem, however, good intentions notwithstanding, is that the strict rules and regulations laid out by any self-established 'elite' inevitably cause the exclusion of all 'Others' and their ways of thinking. Naturally, excluding 'Others' is helpful because it isolates and protects a social space against the threat of outside influences (Bauman, 1993). By preserving one specific, dominant ontological stance over others, the fundamental rules, routines and rituals of a collective can be carefully safeguarded. As Paul Ricœur (1992) points out, a sense of 'mythic stability' is created between members of a collective and this helps assert power and control over outsiders. For experienced cavers and speleologists seeking to protect the natural underground, this is very useful, but what it means is that those who are involved must entertain certain 'credentials' and be permitted to join the 'community'; otherwise they are destined to be one of the essential 'Others' who exist on the other side of the imaginary divide that has been carefully assembled. To borrow John Austin's (1975) notion of *felicity conditions*, it can be suggested that unless the 'Other' gains official authorisation to enter the caving 'community', that they believe sincerely they have become part of the collective, and that they are authentic members who treat caving as an essential part of their life, they are forced to remain as 'Others' in amongst a vast sea of strangers. In other words, anyone and everyone who is unable to meet the conditions should expect to be met with deep-seated suspicion and apprehension.

There is a useful label for architects of the 'Other'. They can be described as *legislators*. As Zygmunt Bauman (1987) explains, legislators are the social 'elite'. They make authoritative ideological assertions about how things in the world should work, and they have the power to create 'procedural rules which assure the attainment of truth, the arrival of moral judgement, and the selection of proper artistic taste' (ibid: 4–5). What is special about these rules is that they gradually acquire universal validity. To better contextualise these ideas vis-à-vis the world of caving, it might be argued that one by one caving 'communities', organisations and associations align themselves with the traditions of legislators and in doing so cannot help but become products of legislating perfection. There is, therefore, something decidedly modern about legislative reason in that it particularises truth about natural underground exploration (or indeed any sport or form of leisure) and objectifies things rationally, ontologically and ethically.

Regardless of modern legislating dynamics that have come to restrict the ways in which caves are valued and experienced, and who can visit them, it is important to take stock that modernity, together with its legislative strategies, has begun to transform. This transformation was noted earlier on in the chapter and what this means, as Michel Foucault (1980) argues, is that specific intellectuals as opposed to universal intellectuals are now the product of present modernity. It is Bauman (1987) who goes on to explain this point further using his metaphor of the *interpreter*, a substitute for the legislator mentioned above. Contrary to the legislator's perspective, the interpreter recognises that nothing is simply an object of truth. As Bauman (1987) points out, interpretive work is all about being seduced by the look of an object, by the way it suggests it might be interesting, if someone is prepared to acquire a deeper and more profound understanding of its unique ontological power. In a nutshell, being an interpreter is about acquiring a fuller understanding.

What is especially important about the interpreter's standpoint, as Richard Rorty (1979) argues, is that it can be used to deconstruct the privileged perceptions of legislator figures. To paraphrase Blackshaw (2002), interpretive reason relies on an alternative vocabulary, an 'abnormal' discourse to give it a label, rather than the 'normal' discourse of legislative reason and this allows people to realign their ways of thinking. Nevertheless, it needs to be made clear that if an interpreter is to fulfil their role of supporting difference and encouraging it to grow, if they are to maintain a balance between conversing traditions, they must improve communication between independent 'communities' (Bauman, 1987). They must also ensure that their interpretive work goes beyond translating ideas between self-determining 'communities'; they must strive to make meaning. Once these things have been accomplished, the divide between 'Us' and 'Them' can gradually be undone.

To be clear, just as Bauman (1987) reminds us, there is nothing about the work of the interpreter that can be justified in a rationalist sense using a framework or criteria because interpretive reason succeeds entirely on the basis of its own merit. What this means, as Blackshaw (2002) points out, is that interpretive reason cannot help but work in different ways for different people. This is not to suggest that 'anything goes' for interpreters, or that they cannot tell the difference between good and bad quality intellectual inquiry, it is to point out that their gaze works because it offers what we might call a 'post-scientific' way of understanding things in the world (Blackshaw, 2002). Another way of explaining interpretive reason might be to suggest it is a way of understanding that is not only utterly self-absorbed but also allows the autobiography of an interpreter to intervene. To quote Blackshaw, he refers to this as a 'hermeneutics of cultural orientation' (2005: 71) which, in 'liquid' modern times, frequently reveals its dominance over legislative reason.

In a bid to understand caving less as a scientific activity and something that must be controlled by a legislating culture, then, this sociology of caving endeavours to approach the topic using an interpretive way of thinking. In other words, in line with Bauman's (1987) *interpreter* role, I follow the tacit assumption that there is no single understanding of caving and that all observations cannot help but be discursively positioned. Accordingly, the approach I am taking invites us to acknowledge, examine and question different ontological positions by being mindful of the discourses that produce them. What I am conscious of, however, is that interpreters have far less power and authority compared to legislators, especially when they attempt to intrude on another 'community's' interpretation. This of course can be frustrating since the intellectual acumen of interpreters is frequently blunted for no other reason than spiteful posturing, obstinateness and self-indulgence. With these ideas in mind, what I am asking the reader to do for the time being is suspend their own ontological assumptions while my discursive position is unpacked. If the reader obliges, regardless of whether or not my ideas are accepted by the end, we would have succeeded in some measure in breaking down the one-dimensional reign of legislative reason in the world of caving.

An Outline of the Book's Content

Now I have provided a thumbnail sketch of the focus of my investigation, I find myself in a position to give a chapter-by-chapter breakdown of the rest of the book's central arguments and its thesis.

The next chapter is concerned with the methodological dimensions of the study. The point of this chapter is to make it clear how I broke with more conventional ways of conducting ethnography, opting instead to conduct my research through the joint lens of hermeneutic sociology and sociological hermeneutics. The discussion goes on to explain how I aimed to become a twenty-first-century version of Charles Dickens' 'uncommercial traveller' to help transport my readers directly into the natural underground.

In Chapter 3, I provide a detailed discussion about some of the consequences of present modernity and consumer capitalism. This chapter sets the scene for the remainder of the book as it allows me to unpack how the noise of permanent connectivity and distractions of hyper-mediatisation cause us to forget about things that have been silenced or removed in our everyday lives. As the reader will see, my critical response to this suggestion is that there are various spaces that allow explorers to leave the everyday world behind and embrace different thoughts, feelings and emotions. As I argue, the natural underground is such a space since it enables people to immerse themselves in new existential experiences that penetrate not just the body but both the conscious and subconscious mind as well.

Chapter 4 begins with the rather obvious suggestion that intimacy is something that can be found in underground space. In a nutshell, I use the work of Gaston Bachelard initially to argue that underground spaces can, slowly but surely, be used as a means of escaping everyday worries and problems. This happens when an individual starts to explore the hallways of their own minds in the silence they encounter and, simultaneously, notice and appreciate the intricate details and features of the natural underground. They do this to such an extent that the space not only encourages people to become contemplative but also begins to feel warm, familiar and comfortable. Later in the chapter, I develop this argument to show that there is a great deal more to be said about intimacy. What I put forward is that the natural underground is also about experiencing a lack of visual stimuli which helps people enter what I have termed 'scotopia'. As I suggest, this is an intimate state of being-in-the-world that involves the spectacular eruption of bodily sensation, a sensation that is all too often blunted in our normal day-to-day lives.

In Chapter 5, I address the issue that fear is something many people seem to mask or avoid in the twenty-first century. My suggestion, therefore, is that certain people use the natural underground as a means of disrupting the silencing of fear. To begin with, I consider the relevance of Stephen Lyng's concept of edgework in the natural underground, but after outlining several problems with this idea my attention turns to Michel Foucault's similarly aligned but fundamentally different notion of limit experience. My central argument is that limit experiences are an integral part of caving and that such experiences provide twenty-first-century individuals with a means of liberating themselves from some of the constraints imposed by consumer capitalism.

The tone of the book appears to change in Chapter 6 as I commence with a discussion about death. My argument begins with the suggestion that mortality is something human beings typically fear, so much so that we employ various strategies in our day-to-day lives to help us cope until the moment arrives. Consumer capitalism is, for the most part, a relatively successful and subtle supplier of these strategies and, therefore, does well to render silent thoughts and fears of death. It can, for instance, help us feel more youthful or hyper-athletic, and even transform ideas around death into forms of thanatological-themed pleasure. Nevertheless, the same strategies that work in the surface world become useless in the natural underground because it is much more difficult to commodify. Mindful of this, I argue that people must form their own strategies of survival when they venture inside the natural underground. Bearing the promise of immortality, these are strategies born in and of the kingdom of darkness and they help certain individuals diffuse the awfulness and sheer horror of death. They are, ultimately, a means of knowing who survivors are and, by equal measure, discerning who are not.

It is Jean-François Lyotard's interrelated concepts of the differend and the sublime that set the focus of Chapter 7. The strength of the analysis in this chapter lies in its ability to elucidate the point that different ways of exploring and understanding the natural underground, specifically those I have identified in this book which include intimacy, scotopia, fear and death, all involve the art of seeking sublimation. What the chapter reveals is that the natural underground is in the end all about the delicate art of finding opportunities to witness just the right amount of pain and pleasure in the differend. Whenever such a balance is found, a sublime feeling develops and for a short while life feels as though it is being lived beyond the limitations and restrictions of present modernity.

The final chapter draws the book to a close. It does this by outlining the main conclusions and by ending with one last narrative episode. The episode takes place in the hypogenic maze cave known as Knock Fell Caverns. This is a system renowned for its navigational challenges, muddy crawls, boulder chokes and panic-inducing squeezes but also its generously sized chambers, leisurely walking passages and beautiful formations. In other words, it is by exploiting the power of storytelling that the book closes with one final taste of sublimation.

Notes

1 Among urban explorers, the term 'derp' is used to refer to any generic-looking and heavily visited abandoned building such as an old factory or an empty mansion.
2 Sociedad Venezolana de Espeleología.

References

Austin, J. (1975). *How to Do Things with Words*. Oxford: Oxford University Press.

Bauman, Z. (1987). *Legislators and Interpreters: On Modernity, Post-Modernity and Intellectuals*. Cambridge: Polity.

Bauman, Z. (1993). *Postmodern Ethics*. Cambridge: Polity.

Bauman, Z. (2000). *Liquid Modernity*. Cambridge: Polity.

Bauman, Z. (2013). *Consuming Life*. Cambridge: Polity.

Bebbington, A. (2012). *Social Conflict, Economic Development and Extractive Industry: Evidence from South America*. Oxon: Routledge.

Bedford, B. (1985). *Underground Britain: A Guide to the Wild Caves and Show Caves of England, Scotland and Wales*. London: Willow Books.

Beynon, H. and Hudson, R. (2021). *The Shadow of the Mine: Coal and the End of Industrial Britain*. London: Verso.

Bingham, K. (2020). *An Ethnography of Urban Exploration: Unpacking Heterotopic Social Space*. Cham: Palgrave.

Blackshaw, T. (2002). The Sociology of Sport Reassessed in Light of the Phenomenon of Zygmunt Bauman. *International Review for the Sociology of Sport*. 37(2): 199–217.

Blackshaw, T. (2005). *Zygmunt Bauman*. Oxon: Routledge.

Blackshaw, T. (2017). *Re-Imagining Leisure Studies*. Oxon: Routledge.

Boga, S. (1997). *Caving*. Mechanicsburg, PA: Stackpole Books.

British Cave Research Association (BCRA). (2005). The Formation of BCRA. [Online]. Retrieved from: https://bcra.org.uk/detail/origins.html

Butler, O. (2012). *Parable of the Talents*. London: Headline.

Cant, S. (2006). British Speleologies: Geographies of Science, Personality and Practice, 1935–1953. *Journal of Historical Geography*. 32: 775–795.

Crane, R. and Fletcher, L. (2015). *Cave: Nature and Culture*. London: Reaktion Books.

Creaney, S. (2020). *Newton Aycliffe: A Long History of a New Town*. Newton Aycliffe: Newton Press.

Cunningham, H. (2014). *Time, Work and Leisure: Life Changes in England Since 1700*. Manchester: Manchester University Press.

della Dora. (2011). Anti-Landscapes: Caves and Apophasis in the Christian East. *Environment and Planning D: Society and Space*. 29(5): 761–779.

Eshleman, C. (2003). *Juniper Fuse: Upper Paleolithic Imagination & the Construction of the Underworld*. Middletown: Wesleyan University Press.

Foucault, M. (1980). Truth and Power. In: C. Gordon (Ed), *Michel Foucault: Power/Knowledge*. Hemel Hempstead: Harvester.

Foucault, M. (1984). Of Other Spaces. Trans. J. Miskowiec. *Diacritics*. 16(1): 22–27.

Gemmell, A. and Myers, J. (1952). *Underground Adventure*. London: Blandford Press.

Gillett, J. (2007). *Of Caves and Caving: A Way and a Life*. New York: Writers Club Press.

Gunn, J. (2004). *Encyclopedia of Caves and Karst Science*. London: Fitzroy Dearborn.

Haigh, D. and Cordingley, J. (2017). *Adventures Underground: Tales of cave exploration in the Yorkshire Dales*. Abergavenny: Wild Places Publishing.

Heap, D. (1964). *Potholing: Beneath the Northern Pennines*. London: Routledge and Kegan Paul.

Henry, H. and Suk, W. (2017). Public Health and Karst Groundwater Contamination: From Multidisciplinary Research to Exposure Prevention. In: W. White, J. Herman, E.

Herman and M. Rutigliano (Eds), *Karst Groundwater Contamination and Public Health: Beyond Case Studies*. Cham: Springer.

Hevly, B. (1996). The Heroic Science of Glacier Motion. *Osiris*. 11: 66–86.

Hughes, C. and Palmer, C. (2020). One Foot in the Cave: A Sensorial Adventure of a First-time Caver. *Journal of Qualitative Research in Sport Studies*. 14(1): 335–354.

Hunt, W. (2019). *Underground: A Human History of the Worlds Beneath Our Feet*. London: Simon & Schuster.

Hurd, B. (2003). *Entering the Stone: On Caves and Feeling Through the Dark*. New York: Houghton Mifflin Company.

Lovelock, J. (1969). *Caving*. London: Batsford Limited.

Marshall, D. (2019). *Starless Rivers: Underground Adventures*. Llanrwst: Gwasg Carreg Gwalch.

Mason, E. (1977). *Caves and Caving in Britain*. London: Robert Hale.

Matless, D. (2016). *Landscape and Englishness*. London: Reaktion Books.

Mattes, J. (2020). National Spaces and Deepest Places: Politics and Practices of Verticality in Speleology. *Centaurus*. 62(4): 670–696.

Moss, T., Dilcher, J. and Aughey, P. (1995). Caver's Slang. [Online]. Retrieved from: https://www-sop.inria.fr/agos-sophia/sis/slang.html#:~:text=Buffoon%20%2D%20The%20most%20widely%20used,friendly%20jest%20or%20an%20insult.&text=electric%20cavers)%20in%20a%20crawl,inner%2Dtube%20%2D%20often%20pink.

Palmer, L. (1937). British Speleological Association (BSA). *Caves and Caving*. 1(1): 7–9.

Pérez, M. A. (2015). Exploring the Vertical: Science and Sociality in the Field Among Cavers in Venezuela. *Social & Cultural Geography*. 16(2): 226–247.

Pérez, M. A. (2021). Volumes, Caves, Bodies, Relatedness: The Case of Cuban Speleology and National Defense. *Geoforum*. 127: 412–423.

Pérez, M. A. and Zurita, M. (2020). Underground Exploration Beyond State Reach: Alternative Volumetric Territorial Projects in Venezuela, Cuba and Mexico. *Political Geography*. 79: 102144.

Proudlove, G. (2021). *A Series of Short Passages: Reminiscences, Reflections and Ruminations from a Caving Life*. Graham S. Proudlove.

Ricœur, P. (1992). *Oneself as Another*. Chicago: Chicago University Press.

Rorty, R. (1979). *Philosophy and the Mirror of Nature*. Princeton: Princeton University Press.

Schut, Pierre-Olaf. (2006). E. A. Martel, The Traveller Who Almost Become an Academian. *Acta Carsologica*. 35(1): 1–10.

Shaw, T. (2004). Speleologists. In: J. Gunn's (Ed), *Encyclopedia of Caves and Karst Science*. London: Fitzroy Dearborn, 1466–1473.

Sociedad Venezolana de Espeleología. (2006). Boletín de la Sociedad Venezolana de Espeleología [Bulletin of the Venezuelan Society of Speleology]. [Online]. Retrieved from: https://archive.org/details/boletindelasociedadvenezolanadeespeleologia20060040/page/n1/mode/2up

Squire, R. and Dodds, K. (2019). Introduction to the Special Issue: Subterranean Geopolitics. *Geopolitics*. 25(1): 4–16.

Taylor, M. (1996). *Cave Passages: Roaming the Underground Wilderness*. New York: Scribner.

Taylor, M. (2020). *Hidden Nature: Wild Southern Caves*. Nashville: Vanderbilt University Press.

White, S. (2000). *Sustaining Affirmation: The Strengths of Weak Ontology In Political Theory*. Princeton: Princeton University Press.

White, W. and Culver, D. (2019). Cave, Definition of. In: W. White, D. Culver and T. Pipan (Eds), *Encyclopedia of Caves*. London: Academic Press, 255–259.

Wilson, J. (2019). Recreational Caving. In: W. White, D. Culver and T. Pipan (Eds), *Encyclopedia of Caves*. London: Academic Press, 861–870.

Winkler, L. (2016). *Fire Beyond the Darkness*. Victoria: First Choice Books.

Chapter 2

Descenders, Static Line and Some Methodological Considerations
Choosing 'Tackle' for the Job

An Introductory Interlude

A few weeks after our discovery of the cave inside the culvert, I was eager to experience the natural underground again along with two of the other urban explorers who had shared in the discovery. Together, Ford Mayhem, Rizla Rider and I had tasted the magic of caving and now we had an urge to see more. Our attention, therefore, turned to Sleets Gill Cave, mainly because it doesn't require any 'tackle' but also because it's 2,407 metres long and so offers a lengthy adventure. We were very conscious, however, of this cave's ominous reputation and the high-profile rescue of Les Hewitt and Roy Deane in 1992 when rising water inside Sleets Gill trapped the pair and resulted in them having to be dived out through 250 metres of flooded passage. Having researched the cave before our visit, we knew all about the unusual way in which the cave floods. In normal conditions, with the exception of a few standing pools of water, the main passageway remains dry. The active streamway actually runs underneath in smaller passages which have been suitably named the Hydrophobia Series. It is during periods of heavy flood that Hydrophobia is unable to contain the growing volume of water and so it quickly backs up into the main passageway above. Obviously, the thought of dying inside the cave terrified us, but it was a hot day in August and it hadn't rained for weeks so we felt reasonably confident we wouldn't become trapped and drown.

Parked only five minutes from the entrance in Mayhem's ex-British Gas van, the three of us changed into grubby waterproof clothing and wellies. Just ahead we could see a bone-dry ghyll sloping down from the hillside. This was something we took to be a good sign since this is what we would soon be ascending. Ten minutes later, ignoring a growing sense of trepidation, we clumped our way up to the entrance which appeared at first to be a traditional cave entrance in the side of a limestone cliff, the sort that would typically lead an unsuspecting person into a bear's den or a dragon's lair in a novel. We quickly discovered that the entrance was in fact quite different.

Once inside, a long ramp of gravel and rocks allowed us to descend at a steep angle by about 60 metres until we reached a short crawl (Figure 2.1) and

DOI: 10.4324/9781003301752-2

Figure 2.1 The rocky crawl.

a left-hand turn leading into the main passageway. During the descent, the scree moved beneath our feet. Trembling under our weight, it threatened to give at any moment and send us tumbling to the bottom. When we finally made it, we joked to ease the tension. Conscious at this point that we were well under what could potentially be the waterline, we made light of the fact that we'd be 'fucked' if it were to suddenly flood. Mayhem and Rizla joked anyway. Truthfully, I was feeling extremely uneasy about the possible drowning issue.

Soon after the crawl, we emerged in a passage the size of a railway tunnel which made us forget about flood waters for a moment. Awestruck by the sheer scale of the main gallery, we followed it for a while, until we reached a spectacular series of sand dunes (Figure 2.2). This was only our second time in the natural underground and the only other place we'd ever seen dunes was the seaside, so

Figure 2.2 First glimpses of the dunes.

once again we were momentarily captivated. Of course, these weren't anything like the 15 steep sand hills of the Camel Raceway Michael Taylor (2020) talks about, but for three individuals new to the wonders of the natural underground they were still remarkable. We sat down in the sand for a while, taking some time to enjoy our surroundings before we decided we should look for the famous section known as Hydrophobia which is said to lead to a second ramp and an interesting gallery of stalactites known as 'straws'. The name of this new passage didn't do much for our confidence, nor did our poor map reading skills. The map of the system only made partial sense to us. It was starkly different to the Ordnance Survey style of map we were more familiar with. We found the cave itself hard to navigate as well. Unlike an abandoned mine or military bunker, it had no logical structure or pathway. Consequently, it took us a long time to find the small entrance to Hydrophobia, down on the left some 20 metres before the end of the main passage.

Sadly, we never did make it into the Hydrophobia Series. Although we eventually found it, the tiny passage didn't look inviting in the slightest, nor did the ice-cold stream running through it. Mayhem and Rizla were already feeling cold, and I was worried about becoming trapped in a tight, watery squeeze. We didn't admit this to one another, not immediately anyway for fear of losing face, but each of us must have sensed we were ready to return to the surface by this point. Although we'd remained completely silent about it, in the hour or so we'd spent inside Sleets Gill a mounting sense of anxiety had grown in each of us. This feeling increased to such a point that we started to repeatedly question, as casually as possible of course, whether the water level had risen. Our minds would occasionally wander as well, drifting into an imaginative state predicting what it might feel like to be trapped or even drown. As we confessed on our journey home, none of us had wanted to be the first to admit feeling uneasy. Nevertheless, we had all felt it and we were relieved beyond doubt when we made the mutual decision to revisit when we'd acquired some better gear. In the moment, we convinced ourselves that we needed descenders, some static line, and possibly even better wellies before we revisited. Really, we didn't need any of this gear for this cave. What we needed was more experience in the natural underground, something we would inevitably gain in time.

The return climb to the surface was hard going. Jagged rocks felt like they were puncturing our kneecaps as we crawled back towards the ramp. All three of us swore loudly and we each vowed we wouldn't cave again until we'd also sourced some knee pads. Past the crawl, we began our slow ascent to freedom. The rocks snagged our clothing and would occasionally move awkwardly beneath our feet, but we managed to make gradual progress upwards. When we finally emerged on the surface we were bruised and battered. Our bodies never felt this way after an urbex, regardless of whether we'd ascended a crane in the early hours, stooped through a storm drain network or walked for miles around an abandoned factory. Our clothes and equipment hadn't fared much better either. Mayhem's waterproof trousers had a large tear down his right leg and his tripod no longer stood straight. As for Rizla, his headtorch no longer worked. And me, my jacket was pitted with small holes, and my camera, having been accidentally smashed against the ceiling of the ramp, was stuck midway through taking a photograph.

It was precisely at this moment we realised that we would have to think about discarding our old urban explorer identities and equipment if we wanted to enter the natural underground again. They were incompatible with this new world and so we knew it was time to adopt new ways of *being* that might instead be packed into brightly coloured oversuits. Naturally, we weren't quite sure what these identities would look like at this point, but we knew they would have to be much more durable and resilient than our former urbexer selves. In other words, we not only needed to rethink our 'tackle' for the job but crucially how we were going to reinvent ourselves.

Introduction

As caving is for the most part still a form of rational recreation, a specialist functionalist attitude cannot help but remain integral to the structure and subsequent orientation of many caving groups and organisations. It is this attitude that supports the positive 'functions' performed by cavers and speleologists and it encourages them to replicate their own special kind of social order and control. As I suggested in the previous chapter, this mindset is one that views caving as something that should be methodically driven by disciplined researchers and experts and their application of scientific method. What is argued in this chapter, therefore, given that important social and cultural changes have occurred in present modernity, is that there is a need to revolutionise understanding of caving. In other words, in this chapter, it is argued that in order to open up a critical conversation about 'Other' cavers without distorting their leisure lives, it is imperative that the dominant order of things, together with its intellectual claims, is appropriately challenged.

To remind the reader, it was Zygmunt Bauman (1987) who in his persuasive analysis of modern intellectual work explained that *legislators* represent a collection of people who have attained power, people who make authoritative statements and rules which enable them to secure absolute control over certain 'truths'. Not only this, but they also regulate artistic taste and judgement over moral ruling. Drawing on this idea, it is my view that the authority of legislators has lessened in the twenty-first century which means it is vital we think critically about surviving mechanisms of legislative truth and that we risk challenging them when we believe it is necessary. The key advantage of doing this, if we turn our attention back to the natural underground, is that dominant ways of practising caving can be undermined by an alternative *interpretive* outlook (Bauman, 1987). This is a different way of thinking about caving that might be described as more democratic, a way of thinking centred around the special and sometimes unique ways in which 'ordinary' people construct and understand their own leisure worlds. With this in mind, the thesis underpinning this book invites readers to embrace the pluralism of leisure to ensure activities such as caving are not limited by a certain style or way of looking. Any understanding of caving must therefore be extended to include practices that are not only more 'leisurely' in nature but also elude the prevailing functionalist epistemic.

Before I continue any further, it is important to reiterate that I do not mean to suggest that those interested in the scientific investigation of the natural underground do not themselves ever appreciate the more leisurely side of caving. In reality, many do just as much as the next person. As Taylor (2020, 1996) points out, organised conventions and caving festivals have long been a part of the culture and they include things like pavilions for rock bands and beer drinking, nude hot tub parties and annual events such as the Speleolympics. Nevertheless, when faced with the physical immediacy of the natural underground, a particular kind of reality tends to come to life for many cavers, an austere reality serving functionalist behaviours and assumptions.

With the above ideas in mind, the remainder of this chapter is used to map out an alternative means of understanding the natural underground from the perspective of individuals who view it as a site of leisure and a primary sphere of *anthropoetechnics* (a term coined by Peter Sloterdijk (2013) to refer to the process of self-creation). Viewing caving in this way transforms it into a different kind of life practice that not only alters people's interpretations and understandings of themselves and the wider world but also makes them appreciate and value what Sloterdijk (2013) refers to as the *art of living*. As the reader will see, with some new 'rules' of method, which should not be taken literally as being a new set of rules replacing the old, I explore in detail a different story of the natural underground, a story told by people who cave to find the innumerable pains and pleasures of a strange new world. Only by doing things in this way has it been possible to unpack what the natural underground brings to my life, and to the lives of those 'Others' who were there with me.

Auto-ethnography vs Auto-hermeneutics

Analogous to Arthur Gemmell and Jack Myers' (1952) book *Underground Adventure*, David Heap's (1964) classic Yorkshire Dales caving guide *Potholing: Beneath the Northern Pennines* and Michael Ray Taylor's (2020) much more recent contribution *Hidden Nature*, the proposed monograph is concerned with bringing the underground world to life in a way that appeals to the imagination of a reader. Using a similar style of writing, I have sought to produce an immersive first-hand account detailing what it means to explore the natural underground. With that being said, it might be assumed that my methodological approach followed a typical auto-ethnographic research design or perhaps a design underpinned by auto-hermeneutics. In actual fact, neither were selected since I opted to follow a reciprocal process laid out by Tony Blackshaw (2017) that exploits the combined methods of hermeneutic sociology and sociological hermeneutics. More on this will be discussed later in the chapter, but first it is necessary to explain why I made a departure from traditional methodological approaches.

It has been argued that auto-methodologies allow researchers to conduct investigations that would otherwise be very difficult to conduct (Gorichanaz, 2017). They let researchers access their own thoughts in such a way that the emerging 'data' is potentially richer, more expressive and person-centred (ibid). Moreover, auto-methodologies have been commended for their usefulness in making vital advances in the social sciences as they encourage investigators to embrace subjective biases that would otherwise remain silenced in traditional studies seeking objectivity (Zahavi, 2005). From an ontological standpoint, auto-methodologies are used when a researcher accepts that social research can only ever be a product of diverse 'truths' that sometimes (but not always) happen to interweave (O'Grady, 2014). Auto-ethnography is the better-known auto-methodology, and in recent years, it has become a popular means of investigating sport and leisure (see Stanley, 2022; Larsen and Jensen, 2021; Laviolette, 2016). By contrast, the use of auto-hermeneutics has been less popular, most likely because fewer methodological books and papers advocate its use. This may be due to the extreme degree of bias associated with the approach. The popularity of either methodology notwithstanding, what I want to move on to discuss here is why neither was suitable for this investigation. First, I will turn to auto-ethnography.

According to Arthur Bochner and Carolyn Ellis (2016), auto-ethnography emerged in a time when poststructuralists and postmodernists were carrying out persistent attacks on the authority of traditional scientific method. To paraphrase Richard Rorty (1990) who at the time was contesting the viability of the foundations of social science, what was needed was an 'experimental attitude', a research approach emphasising the utility of vocabularies and narratives instead of objective theories and laws. As a result, some scholars began to view the era in which they were living as a moment of experimentation, one inviting change, innovation and risk (Harré and Secord, 1972; Geertz, 1988; Tedlock, 1991). In response to this shift of thought, what emerged was a call to treat researchers as experimental subjects and their personal experiences as raw 'data'. As Bochner and Ellis (2016) point out, in retrospect this shift was not all that radical. It was about recognising that researchers are part and parcel of the world as well and that they face the same 'problems of being alive and [those] serious existential and moral questions related to mortality, loss, belonging, loneliness, love, adversity, violence, racism, discrimination, and complicated feelings [that can] affect all people' (2016: 50). Still, what emerged was a means of using storytelling to underscore emotionality, subjectivity and self-reflexivity. In other words, from the perspective of the first-person readers were suddenly encouraged to contend with tangible, often intimate and traumatic, circumstances of lived experience.

At the beginning of the narrative turn there was much uncertainty over what to call the new work being conducted, whether it should be referred to as self-ethnography, socio-autobiography, ethnographic autobiography, personal ethnography, confessional storytelling or simply a form of personal essay (Adams, Ellis and Jones, 2015). In the end, scholars drifted towards Karl Heider's (1975) term 'auto-ethnography', and by the 1990s, it became the research design of choice for using personal reflexivity and experience to investigate different social realities (Bochner and Ellis, 2016). At this point, it was generally accepted that auto-ethnography required researchers to work somewhere between ethnography and autobiography to create evocative and clear representations of different cultures and give readers a sense of what it feels like to be positioned in the field of study. In general, then, auto-ethnography is used to examine a cultural field for an extended period of time in a way that allows a researcher to articulate their insider knowledge of a certain type of cultural life (Adams et al., 2015). In other words, auto-ethnographers use personal experiences and understandings which are not always available to researchers to fill in gaps or complement existing research about a culture.

30 Methodological Considerations

For the purposes of this study, the fact auto-ethnography is used to understand life lived inside established cultural contexts posed a problem. The issue I had was that I was not trying to investigate an already existing or acknowledged social context. I was, rather, trying to break away from any sort of caving culture that determines how the natural underground should be experienced and understood. This presented a problem as there are many scholars such as Sarah Wall (2016) who are clear that they expect any auto-ethnographic analysis of an experience to link personal interpretations with wider social environments and concerns because this helps to prevent papers from becoming egocentric and self-indulgent. From this perspective, it is also commonly argued that personal experiences should connect with existing cultures because this ensures knowledge of those cultures will be continually advanced (Andrew, 2017). It was with these points in mind that I decided another methodological approach would be needed. I was also concerned that auto-ethnographers like Wall (2016) often make the crucial mistake of overlooking the underlying significance of micro-spheres of self-creation. To further explain this idea, our attention must turn to the work of Peter Sloterdijk (2016), specifically his metaphor of foam which denotes a structure comprising any number of bubbles or independent spaces.

As Sloterdijk (2016) suggests, foam consists of bubbles which are each separated from one another by a delicate, easily collapsible wall. It can be argued, therefore, that each micro-sphere exists alongside multiple others in a constant state of co-fragility and co-dependence (ibid). At first, not unlike Wall (2016), this might encourage us to think that individual spheres of existence are inherently related to one another meaning they cannot help but be defined by their relations to others and therefore certain cultural contexts. However, thinking about the foam metaphor in this way only takes into consideration the tight proximity of fragile bubbles and their contexts, something comparable to Deleuzian assemblages, and it ignores the idea of the necessary self-enclosure of each foam bubble (Sloterdijk, 2016).

Curiously, self-enclosure can encourage us to think about the intense individualisation and isolation that is part and parcel of our present-day world and how older forms of stability can easily dissipate and be lost since foam structures are unable to coagulate. Furthermore, the idea of self-enclosure can also make us think about how foam is able to grow, expand and redistribute itself since the bursting of older bubbles often produces new ones which are each distinct in their own right. It is knowledge and understanding of this self-enclosure I seek because I am acutely aware that human thoughts and actions can both be *determined* and *limited* by their proximity to other human beings. Indeed, as Bauman (2000) reminds us, what goes hand-in-hand with any kind of excess of opportunity, which is one of the hallmarks of twenty-first-century living, is the task of having to self-identify. Some of the side-effects of self-identification, though, are of course fragmentation, de-structuration and the increase of incompatible driving forces (ibid). What I want to argue is that these side-effects should be just as much of a focus for scholars in present modernity which means it is our task to uncover their impact on forms of leisure in the twenty-first century.

Of course, I do not deny that the interconnectivity of micro-spheres is important, and that there is an inherent relationality in human nature especially in an increasingly 'liquid' modern world. However, I recognise that spatiality, distance and separateness can be other determining ontological characteristics of human beings. What I am suggesting in other words is that sometimes we should look beyond the togetherness of Heidegger's *being-in-the-world* to a new conception of humans sometimes *being-in-spheres*. From this perspective, it is important we occasionally try thinking inside the box, about the building-up (and possibly the inevitable breaking-down) of new or emerging spatial collectivities, before we start thinking about what lies just outside them and how they can be traced into broader contexts.

Alongside auto-ethnography, auto-hermeneutics has emerged as an alternative research approach that allows social investigators to examine their own lived experiences, normally using their own independent writings. As Daniel Dennett (1992) suggests, the approach allows a researcher to think about the significance of their own memories, experiences and pasts, and also rethink and rewrite them. Indeed, it might be argued that traditional hermeneutic investigation naturally caters to auto-subjective styles of self-interpretation anyway, but John Caputo (2018) is right in pointing out that hermeneutics has generally been used to analyse and interpret other people's writings. Where auto-hermeneutics is especially useful is in the way it can be used to understand novel experiences and understandings that have yet to be documented publicly or in wider literature (Gorichanaz, 2017). Furthermore, it has been argued that in its present-day incarnation, the auto-hermeneutic approach has evolved from classical hermeneutics to include interpretations of non-traditional texts as legitimate sources of information (Benjamin, 2014). For example, such texts can be in the form of autobiographical stories or diary entries, providing the person exploiting them has a high degree of mindfulness and self-awareness (ibid).

As indicated above, where auto-hermeneutics differs from auto-ethnography is in the way it is generally used to explore and unpack discrete phenomena through a single person's perspective (Gorichanaz, 2017). Auto-ethnographic research on the other hand endeavours to outline someone's amalgamated experience of living within a particular culture (Adams et al., 2015). The idea that there is a definitive boundary between the two research approaches, however, has been queried by Gorichanaz (2017) who suggests that culture and lived experience are often intertwined and therefore cannot help but be inseparable. This is an important point, one that serves to remind us that auto-hermeneutic accounts can easily stray into those cultural aspects that help to characterise auto-ethnography. When planning this research project, this was something I was especially wary of since it was my intention to distance myself as far away as possible from the dominant caving culture that seems to direct interpretations of the natural underground. Conscious of how easily auto-hermeneutic analysis

32 Methodological Considerations

can slide into pre-existing cultural standards of practice, then, I decided another methodological approach would perhaps be more suited to my project. More on this will be discussed in the next section of this chapter.

Before moving on, another key criticism of the auto-hermeneutic approach that should be noted is the suggestion that it requires an explicit focus on 'the self' (Arslanbek, 2021). This is something I grew increasingly concerned about, knowing I would inevitably need to merge my own self-awareness of the natural underground with that of the others I was caving with. While any good empirical auto-methodology should be conducted using an intuitive and empathetic body-in-action, I realise it should also acknowledge the presence of additional living bodies that are encountered over the course of the research journey. For this reason, I decided to rely on a different kind of hermeneutics that gives a researcher greater freedom and flexibility since it can be used in a self-reflective way that takes into account the thoughts, opinions and ideas of other human beings (see Blackshaw, 2017 and Bingham, 2020).

As I will argue, with hermeneutic sociology and sociological hermeneutics at its heart, this study manages to retain the depth, vividness and intensity of the world being investigated, the same depth, vividness and intensity expected in any auto-methodology. At the same time, however, the study demonstrates the importance of leisure and how it brings people and their ideas together. In other words, this investigation makes a broader commitment to reflexivity – something that is characterised by intersubjectivity – by taking into account other people's experiences while maintaining an acute awareness of my own self in relation to those others and my surroundings (Klesse, 2012).

Research Design: Hermeneutic Sociology and Sociological Hermeneutics

To start unpacking my research approach, this section of the chapter informs the reader about the methodology I decided to follow. From the very beginning, I was mindful of Blackshaw's (2017) suggestion that any good sociological investigation must involve a two-way process that turns everyday experiences into sociology but also turns sociology into everyday experience. This suggestion follows Anthony Giddens' (1984) thoughts on understanding the relationship between sociology and its subject matter as a 'double hermeneutic' and encourages us to think about the importance of collapsing the dichotomy between what is really going on in the world from the perspective of 'lay people' and what the social sciences argue is happening. With this in mind, I set out to volunteer myself as an intermediary to demonstrate that a leisure world is better uncovered by getting involved directly rather than through abstract ideas and theory alone.

Anticipating there may be critics of my approach, I want to be clear that my research design also follows Robin Collingwood's (1946/1994) proposition that knowledge of and about an event can only be relived in a person's mind through the re-enactment of past thoughts. As Collingwood (1946/1994) argues, it is only by rethinking past events within the context of an individual's own experience that a person can produce knowledge of and about different kinds of people and their subsequent cultures and social spaces. What this means is that an investigator's mind and the pasts which they come to know through rethinking and re-enactment cannot help but be intertwined, but it also means researchers have the potential to become microcosms of self-knowledge which is at the same time their knowledge of the wider world and other people's thoughts or affairs. This is my justification for becoming the intermediary between the surface world and the natural underground, and it reinforces why experiences must be lived through rather than analysed from a comfortable distance. Like Collingwood (1946/1994), though, I am acutely aware that the work of a sociologist is very different to that of a novelist or poet in that it must remain faithful to the evidence. In other words, unlike a novelist, the narrative of a good sociologist must be concentrated on a time and space that has truly existed, and it must be rooted in evidence that has been gathered from dependable sources (Collingwood, 1994). I can confirm that the narrative informing the contents of this book is both.

Of course, it was not enough to simply state that my plan was to become an intermediary who would somehow be capable of jumping between the intellectual world of sociology and the very real world of the natural underground. More explanation and unpacking of my thinking around this approach would be required, which is why I turn once more to the important work of Zygmunt Bauman. What Bauman (1992) argues is that there are two kinds of hermeneutics that are available to researchers with sociological interest, two kinds of hermeneutics that would effectively solve my problem of applying Giddens' (1984) idea of the 'double hermeneutic' which, as I mentioned earlier, is used to illustrate how sociology and social life continually inform one another. The two kinds of hermeneutics I found would be useful to me, therefore, are *hermeneutic sociology* and *sociological hermeneutics*.

It is well known that Bauman's own work is largely rooted in sociological hermeneutics, and that he not only uses it to defamiliarise the social world around us but also concepts that all-too-often outlive their usefulness and relevance to everyday lives. It has been argued that his emphasis on defamiliarisation is tied with his intention that more awareness and more comprehension of our surroundings can improve our world (Jacobsen and Poder, 2016). What this means nonetheless is that Bauman, as a sociologist, is less interested in becoming a man out in the field. His main concern centres around how profound insights of and about people's lives can be translated into something that is emphatically political. This is not to suggest that Bauman overlooks the significance of real people who are shaped by social developments and other key transformations because he is clear that sociology must never stop short of being a collaborative and ongoing interpretation of the human world (Jacobsen and Poder, 2016). It might be argued, however, as Blackshaw (2017) points out, that Bauman's central concern is about pulling his readers away from glimpsed ethnographies into rich, critical accounts of the bigger factors that bear down on our lives.

34 Methodological Considerations

Having drawn inspiration from Bauman (1992), I want to be clear that my experiences of the natural underground discussed in this book are similarly shaped by sociological hermeneutics. My reason for doing this is simple; I knew it would be important to carefully analyse my experiences inside caves while being cognisant of 'surface' phenomena that is generally part and parcel of both our leisure worlds and the societies in which we reside. Few things in the twenty-first century are independent of the consumerist world in which we live, yet I would argue that the natural underground is an example of something that still manages to resist and withstand many of its influences. It is this observation that has influenced my interpretation of the natural underground. As the reader will see in the next chapter, I have viewed everything important in the natural underground as being important precisely because our everyday lives are driven by consumer capitalism.

A key critique of Bauman of course, as it was intimated above, is that he rarely reports on what it feels like to experience things in present modernity, things such as leisure. Nevertheless, it is clear he still has much admiration for scholars such as Henning Bech (1997) who practise hermeneutic sociology because they find ways of informing us about what is actually going on in the real world (how it is experienced and viewed), but more crucially ways of informing that reflect the language and intimacy of the inhabitants of the world under investigation. In other words, Bauman (1992) recognises that hermeneutic sociology is a special craft, one that not only requires scholars to speak differently using a style of language that might be described as poetic but also to have a post-scientific 'sociological imagination'. Aware of the significance of hermeneutic sociology as a method of immersion, then, I decided it would be essential in shaping some of the contents of this book.

To borrow Henning Bech's way of putting it, this kind of hermeneutic approach is extremely valuable because it is a way of 'snuggle[ing] up to [the] quotidian and recognisable, even trivial' (1997: 6). In other words, as I have written elsewhere (Bingham, 2020), this approach to research involves being a little like Lewis Carroll's Alice who after tumbling down the rabbit hole discovers she has entered a completely different world, a world of curious things and unexpected surprises. This is the kind of experience I wanted to offer readers of this book, a 'mimetic representation' that succeeds in being vivid and intense enough to make an outsider feel more like an insider (Bauman, 1992: 42). After all, as Bauman (1992) reminds us, it is this style of writing that exposes the pure magic and intimacy of existence.

On Being an 'Uncommercial Traveller'

When I started thinking seriously about writing a book around the topic of the natural underground and was settled on the idea of using two kinds of hermeneutics, I began to wonder whether Charles Baudelaire's (1863/1995) figure of the *flâneur*, or something to this effect, might be a useful way of anthropomorphising and humanising an interesting and unfamiliar leisure world. I was after all accustomed to wandering around abandoned spaces for the sake of leisure as an urban explorer. The immediate problem I had with this idea, however, is the fact that Baudelaire (1863/1995) describes the flâneur as a gentleman stroller of the city streets and the idea of a gentleman stroller of the natural underground not only seemed incredibly pretentious but also unrealistic.

Faced with this concern, I shifted my attention to Walter Benjamin's (1999) idea of the flâneur since he views the figure not only as the quintessential man of leisure but also as an amateur journalistic character astutely aware of the subjectivity of the world. By drifting through places as an invisible observer, this figure was said to be capable of imaginatively reworking the places he visits and, most importantly, making sense of unexpected sights and juxtapositions. Of course, what Benjamin (1999) had in mind when he wrote about the flâneur was still an urban wanderer, an individual who might saunter through nineteenth-century Parisian arcades in search of enchantment through memories or anything uniquely exotic and picturesque. The crucial difference between this interpretation and the former, however, which I found especially useful is the metamorphosis the flâneur undergoes. As Buck-Morss (1991) points out, the original intellectual flâneur goes from being a stroller to something more akin to a photojournalist or reporter who observes the effects (which are often perceived to be damaging) modernity and capitalism have on the world around us.

Nevertheless, the concept of the flâneur still raised concerns and I started to wonder whether there might be another metaphor that could help me better explore and understand the natural underground. In addition to the drawbacks of the bourgeois aesthetic and the emphasis on moving through urban space, a major issue I had with Benjamin's (1999) interpretation is the dependence on interpretation from the perspective of a detached spectator. In short, I wanted to do more than observe from a distance, I wanted to be involved in the action. In my mind, getting involved in research is about experimentation and bringing the imagination to life, and about becoming a person who, in being a part of the world under investigation, is just as much a watchable feature of it.

In addition to the problem of distance, I found there were further complications with the concept of the flâneur. Not unlike microcracks in rock which gradually interact with one another and grow, these problems weighed on my mind and in the end convinced me to reach for a different concept. For example, the question of whether becoming a flâneur is little more than a defiant response to the burden of fierce loneliness human beings feel over the course of their lives troubled me. As Benjamin (1999) suggests, in capitalist modernity loneliness becomes a compelling state of mind for the flâneur, but it is one that can be used for purposes of enhancement if that flâneur exploits their own critical faculties of imagination. In other words, the flâneur is said to depend on states of melancholy because it is within melancholy that a person can search for their own markers of life and points of orientation (Gleber, 1999). The obvious problem with this idea is that the flâneur must unwittingly assume the world is not only isolating and perpetually tedious, but a place that constantly incites powerful feelings of sadness, incapacity and hopelessness. While I agree the world can be exactly like this at times, filled with the gloom and isolation of global pandemics, war and rising costs of living, I would also argue that enchantment is just as much a real part of our world which means it is created in more ways than just through the imaginations of observing flâneurs.

Another problem with the concept of the flâneur surrounds their typical 'playing' grounds. Once again this takes us back to the issue of urbanity and the idea that for both Benjamin and Baudelaire only a particular type of space can be used to encounter flânerie. In a nutshell, this space tended to comprise brilliant Parisian boulevards or arcades, each lined with the tasteful façades of luxury shops and pleasant cafés. Even if scholars such as Petra Kuppers (1999) have argued that human beings rather than bricks, concrete and glass create space, it is still presumed that activities of the flâneur involve being-in-the-street. In reality, though, as Bauman (2000) argues, the grazing grounds of twenty-first-century individuals have changed. In fact, as Blackshaw (2017) points out, the very idea of leisure has changed. What this means is that in present modernity places and spaces of imaginative stimulation and action can be found anywhere. This of course has long been a criticism of flânerie. The fact flâneurs never ventured into areas beyond paved boulevards and arcades, areas that were perhaps still narrow, filthy and came with the risk of being splashed by sewage or mud, means that a strong sense of dislocation between a small bourgeois class and the rest of society materialised (Scobie, 2010). Consequently, the flâneur has become better known as a figure of urban alienation and insufferable idleness, a pompous figure bearing characteristics that actually undermine the creativity and imagination that should be integral to flânerie (Wrigley, 2014). It is precisely with these ideas in mind that I decided a different kind of figure would be essential in my methodological and theoretical framework.

To distance myself from some of the common criticisms and limitations of flânerie, the idea of becoming an *uncommercial traveller* appealed to me. This is an approach inspired by Charles Dickens' series of episodic semi-autobiographical essays titled *The Uncommercial Traveller*. In other words, I endeavoured to become a twenty-first-century version of Dickens' (1895) uncommercial traveller who in focusing on events that might seem minor or trivial to an outsider would be able to transport readers into the sensuousness of the natural underground. I was acutely aware, of course, that Dickens has been accused of being a flâneur for he did indeed adopt the spirit of an urban wanderer in several of his books, and that by using his work to inform my framework I would likely open myself to attack from critics. Hence, using the remainder of this section of the chapter, I want to highlight the strengths of this approach and make it clear how my uncommercial travelling, not unlike Dickens, is less in the mould of the typical flâneur and more about being an individual who does not conform or see things according to expectation.

As I noted above, the idea of becoming an uncommercial traveller is drawn from a collection of short essays written by Dickens in the 1860s. The essays are a collection of memories and notes of personal travel intertwined with literary purpose which means they are intended to detail slices of the real world but also entertain readers and give the writing greater aesthetic pleasure (Smith, 2005). Under the guise of the uncommercial traveller, Dickens produced 28 unrelated and sporadic episodes that might be described as simple observations of contemporary life. This is one way of looking at this work. Another way of looking at it is to appreciate it for its rawness and heavy depth. Unlike his famous novels, this collection documents the dryness of everyday experience, the bleakness and events that are highly personal.

For some readers this journalistic approach is not to their taste, and it has been argued, as John Drew (1996) points out, that *The Uncommercial Traveller* is mixed in quality compared to Dickens' novels. Some of the very same critics, however, have noted that the book still captures some of the author's best writing and that this dichotomy reflects the beauty of the text (Drew, 1996). Somewhere between being tedious and attention-grabbing, Dickens manages to unveil a combination of hard-hitting journalism, artistic method and humour, and in brief snapshots succeeds in sketching the suffering of an underclass, the whimsical and digressive ramblings of an observer, and a realistic depiction of people and places that have been visited (Smith, 2005). This, I decided, is just the style of writing I needed to document my experiences of the natural underground.

Of course, it cannot be overlooked that Dickens might still be personified as a typical flâneur figure. This is certainly how some scholars describe him (see Benjamin, 1999). My response, however, is that this description is not entirely accurate. As Rüdiger Görner (2015) points out, Dickens was far from being an idle wanderer for this is a pace unfamiliar to a man who was always in a hurry. Born into poor conditions, Dickens had no time for strolling the streets in search of imagined spaces of the mind (Görner, 2015). What is more, as Bruce Mazlish (2015) reminds us, a flâneur is typically viewed as a figure of leisure and a strolling opportunist, a fanciful observer and imaginer of the crowd who 'aspires to insensitivity' and to be blasé. By contrast, Dickens is a man who often appears robbed of his leisure as he observes the world around him, which means he understands more than the subjective pleasures and opportunities of the world. He also approaches other people with genuine feelings of empathy and a strong sense of intuitive awareness. It might be argued, therefore, that he understands the world's dark secrets as well, its demons and irrational forces. For all of the reasons discussed here, the true parallel between the uncommercial traveller and the flâneur does not exist, hence why Dickens' version of wandering interested me.

One additional criticism I anticipate I might face for choosing to become an uncommercial traveller is that Dickens was, like the traditional flâneur, still a city wanderer. In other words, readers might question whether an approach created within the realm of urbanity is the most suitable for understanding the natural underground. In response, I would remind critics that I myself began as an urban explorer who was more familiar with a cityscape than a cave which means I share similar beginnings. Yet, my background does not prevent me from entering the kingdom of the dark. Instead, what it demonstrates, as it did with Dickens, is my willingness to enter those inhospitable, grubby spaces that do not fit well with the glittering promises of the consumer world, a willingness that was developed precisely because of my experiences in the city. That is to say, like Dickens I would argue that I have not been entirely duped by the spectacle and its commodity forms. I do not always submit to the allure of the market world, nor do I depend on it to be an explorer since I can find mystery and satisfaction in the most banal of places – in places that are easily forgotten and appear to have lost their essential purpose or function.

What this makes me in no uncertain terms is an *uncommercial traveller*, an individual who does not always conform or see things according to expectation and who is willing to shun dependence on the market for the cold mud and damp of a cave. In other words, by assuming the role of twenty-first-century version of the uncommercial traveller, I am able to focus on events that might seem minor or trivial to an outsider. In this role, it becomes possible to transport readers directly into the reality of the natural underground.

Some Additional Notes on Travelling Underground

As the reader discovered in Chapter 1, my introduction to caving began in a previous leisure life. Although I did not realise it at the time, our exploration of the Victorian culvert marked the beginning of the end for the group I regularly 'urbexed' with. Shortly afterwards, the remaining members grew progressively more distant from one another, and our involvement together in urban exploration became much less frequent. In fact, since the beginning of 2020, only a handful of us have managed to remain in regular contact. It was around this time, however, that a handful of us decided to try our hand at caving. What follows in the remainder of this book is an in-depth account of our subsequent transition into the unknownness of the natural underground, along with a detailed narration of the things that continue to lure us inside.

Just as I tried in my previous book, I have throughout the research process endeavoured to follow Henning Bech's notion of 'sticking to the phenomena in question' (1997: 5) by getting involved and taking part in everything the others around me have done. My aim was to keep treating my trips underground as adventures rather than research being conducted in the 'field'. Hence, other than subtly documenting brief ideas and quotes on my phone and capturing photographs[1] or snippets of videoed conversation on camera (on those rare occasions when I was actually able to), I did not write anything down or record anything while I was underground. After every trip I would instead produce a set of notes describing what happened in as much detail as I was able to recall. When chronicling key events, I was careful to adhere to Clifford Geertz's (1973) practice of 'thick description' so that the world I was experiencing might be brought to life. Using this approach means my findings cannot be codified or made generalisable, but this does not matter since the point of this research is that it serves the *verisimilitude* – the feel of the experience. This is not to suggest that the research is fictitious in any way, or based on guesswork, only that it deals with the fiction human beings create for themselves (Collingwood, 1994).

Before I continue, it is worth reiterating that none of the people involved in this investigation had any 'proper' knowledge of caving before we began venturing underground. While we were all proficient climbers, educated in climbing safety and technique, none of us had received any formal training in how to be a caver. Of course, we could have joined a caving club and used this as a way of easing ourselves into the world of caving, but we chose not to do this. This is not to say we did not consider it. We very nearly attended a couple of caving club meets, but quickly bailed when we discovered they involved their own rules and were held in Conservative Clubs or student unions attached to prestigious universities. There were of course other clubs we researched, but these also seemed uncomfortably different to what we were familiar with. We were especially worried about being forced to adopt the rules, behaviours and idiosyncrasies of complete strangers, strangers we might not get along with. We were worried they might try to turn us into speleologists. Simply put, the 'official' club scene was not for us so we decided very early on in our caving journey that we would go it alone. This does not mean we did not encounter 'Others' along the way. As the reader will see, we joined with several 'Others' on our caving journey whose circumstances and mindsets were similar to our own. What follows now is *our* understanding of the natural underground.

Note

1 The reader will have noticed that I have included a selection of photographs in the book. Doing so may be viewed by some as contradicting my critique in Chapter 4 where I have raised concerns about the visual sensory system unfairly dominating twenty-first-century life. I feel, however, that their inclusion compliments the monograph in a very subtle manner because the images do not detract from the central focus of the text. Rather than convey a specific point or idea, each photograph serves the sole purpose at strategic intervals of enabling the reader to see precisely what I could see. In turn, this helps ensure that the focus of the book remains targeted towards the imaginations, senses and emotions of myself and the people with me which is after all what this book is about.

References

Adams, T., Ellis, C. and Jones, S. (2015). *Autoethnography*. Oxford: Oxford University Press.

Andrew, S. (2017). *Searching for an Autoethnographic Ethic*. Oxon: Routledge.

Arslanbek, A. (2021). Exploring the Adolescent-self Through Written and Visual Diaries. *The Arts in Psychotherapy*. 75: 101825.

Baudelaire, C. (1863/1995). *The Painters of Modern Life*. Trans. J. Mayne. New York: Phaidon Press.

40 Methodological Considerations

Bauman, Z. (1987). *Legislators and Interpreters: On Modernity, Postmodernity and Intellectuals.* Cambridge: Polity.

Bauman, Z. (1992). *Intimations of Postmodernity.* London: Routledge.

Bauman, Z. (2000). *Liquid Modernity.* Cambridge: Polity.

Bech, H. (1997). *When Men Meet: Homosexuality and Modernity.* London: Routledge.

Benjamin, E. (2014). *Life after Death: An Experiential Exploration with Mediums by an Agnostic Investigator.* Morrisville: Lulu Publishing Services.

Benjamin, W. (1999). *The Arcades Project.* Trans. H. J. Eiland and K. McLaughlin. Cambridge, MA: The Belknap Press of Harvard University Press.

Bingham, K. (2020). *An Ethnography of Urban Exploration: Unpacking Heterotopic Social Space.* Cham: Palgrave.

Blackshaw, T. (2017). *Re-Imagining Leisure Studies.* Oxon: Routledge.

Bochner, A. and Ellis, C. (2016). *Evocative Autoethnography: Writing Lives and Telling Stories.* Oxon: Routledge.

Buck-Morss, S. (1991). *The Dialectics of Seeing: Walter Benjamin and the Arcades Project.* Cambridge, MA: MIT Press.

Caputo, J. (2018). *Hermeneutics: Facts and Interpretation in the Age of Information.* London: Pelican Books.

Collingwood, R. (1946/1994). *The Idea of History: Revised Edition with Lectures 1926–1928.* Ed. J. van Der Dussen. Oxford: Clarendon Press.

Dennett, D. (1992). The Self as a Center of Narrative Gravity. In: F. Kessel, P. Cole and D. Johnson (Eds), *Self and Consciousness: Multiple Perspectives.* Hillsdale, NJ: Erlbaum, 103–115.

Dickens, C. (1895). *The Uncommercial Traveller.* London: Chapman & Hall.

Drew, J. (1996). Voyages Extraordinaires: Dickens's Travelling Essays and The Uncommercial Traveller. *Dickens Quarterly.* 13(3): 127–150.

Geertz, C. (1973). *Toward an Interpretive Theory of Culture.* New York: Basic Books.

Geertz, C. (1988). *Works and Lives: The Anthropologist as Author.* Stanford: Stanford University Press.

Gemmell, A. and Myers, J. (1952). *Underground Adventure.* London: Blandford Press.

Giddens, A. (1984). *The Constitution of Society: Outline of the Theory of Structuration.* Cambridge: Polity.

Gleber, A. (1999). *The Art of Taking a Walk: Flanerie, Literature, and Film in Weimar Culture.* Princeton: Princeton University Press.

Gorichanaz, T. (2017). Auto-hermeneutics: A phenomenological approach to information experience. *Library & Information Science Research.* 39(1): 1–7.

Görner, R. (2015). *London Fragments: A Literary Expedition.* London: Haus Publishing.

Harré, R. and Secord, P. (1972). *The Explanation of Social Behavior.* Oxford: Blackwell.

Heap, D. (1964). *Potholing: Beneath the Northern Pennines.* London: Routledge and Kegan Paul.

Heider, K. (1975). What Do People Do? Dani Auto-Ethnography. *Journal of Anthropological Research.* 31(1): 3–17.

Jacobsen, M. and Poder, P. (2016). *The Sociology of Zygmunt Bauman: Challenges and Critique.* Oxon: Routledge.

Klesse, C. (2012). Telling Personal Stories in Academic Research Publications: Reflexivity, Intersubjectivity and Contextual Positionalities. In: S. Hines and Y. Taylor (Eds), *Sexualities: Past Reflections, Future Directions.* London: Palgrave, 68–90.

Kuppers, P. (1999). Moving in the Cityscape: Performance and the Embodied Experience of the *Flâneur*. *New Theatre Quarterly*. 15(4): 308–317.

Larsden, J. and Jensen, O. (2021). Running with the Weather: The Case of Marathon. In: K. Barry, M. Borovnik and T. Edensor (Eds), *Weather: Spaces, Mobilities and Affects*. Oxon: Routledge, 67–80.

Laviolette, P. (2016). *Extreme Landscapes of Leisure: Not a Hap-Hazardous Sport*. Oxon: Routledge.

Mazlish, B. (2015). The *Flâneur*: From Spectator to Representation. In: K. Tester (Ed), *The Flâneur*. Oxon: Routledge, 43–60.

O'Grady, P. (2014). *Relativism*. Oxon: Routledge.

Rorty, R. (1990). *Objectivity, Relativism, and Truth*. Cambridge: Cambridge University Press.

Scobie, S. (2010). *The Measure of Paris*. Alberta: The University of Alberta Press.

Sloterdijk, P. (2013). *You Must Change Your Life*. Trans. W. Hoban. Cambridge: Polity.

Sloterdijk, P. (2016). *Foams: Spheres III*. Trans. W. Hoban. Cambridge: MIT Press.

Smith, G. (2005). The Travelling Lanternist and The Uncommercial Traveller: An Experiment in Correspondences. In: D. Seed (Ed), *Literature and the Visual Media*. Cambridge: D.S. Brewer, 29–47.

Stanley, P. (2022). *An Autoethnography of Fitting In: On Spinsterhood, Fatness, and Backpacker Tourism*. Oxon: Routledge.

Taylor, M. (1996). *Cave Passages: Roaming the Underground Wilderness*. New York: Scribner.

Taylor, M. (2020). *Hidden Nature: Wild Southern Caves*. Nashville: Vanderbilt University Press.

Tedlock, B. (1991). From Participant Observation to the Observation of Participation: The Emergence of Narrative Ethnography. *Journal of Anthropological Research*. 47: 69–94.

Wall, S. (2016). Toward a Moderate Autoethnography. *International Journal of Qualitative Methods*. December: 15(1): 1–9.

Wrigley, R. (2014). *The Flâneur Abroad: Historical and International Perspectives*. Newcastle upon Tyne: Cambridge Scholars Publishing.

Zahavi, D. (2005). *Subjectivity and Selfhood: Investigating the First-Person Perspective*. Cambridge, MA: MIT Press.

Chapter 3

The Underside of Modernity

Introduction

Before attention can be turned exclusively to the natural underground, it is important that the world in which you, I and everybody else find ourselves is appropriately framed. Hence, this chapter sets the scene for the analysis developed in the remainder of the book by contextualising modernity in the twenty-first century. Following Zygmunt Bauman's (2000) suggestion that western societies are characterised by commodification, precarisation and individualisation, it is argued that consumer capitalism has for some people created a world of disenchantment and disillusionment. For these individuals, everything in the world appears to be a little too prosaic and achieved through consumerist means which leaves little room for imagination. With these thoughts in mind, it is my suggestion that the natural underground is less domesticated and much more resistant to the disenchantment and disillusionment found in the surface world. What caves offer – or so it will be intimated in the remainder of this book – is a world that is difficult to put into words but also a place where emotions, senses and identities can be experienced very differently.

It was a cool July morning in the 'the Peak', just along the Old Mam Tor Road. I killed my car's engine 50 metres or so ahead of a turning circle for buses, the point that marks the road end. Annoyingly, I was the first to arrive. Just as I'd anticipated would happen earlier that morning, the others were running late. I suspected a heavy night out in Manchester was to blame.

Up ahead, I could see the crumbling remains of the old road that was originally used to transport spoil from Odin Mine. Following a series of landslides, the road was closed in 1977 and since then it hasn't undergone any kind of maintenance work, meaning it's become inaccessible to normal road vehicles. To my left I could see the outline of Odin's Cave, a 2-metre-wide entrance that extends about 10 metres underground. Our interest wasn't in the cave though; it was in the mine that lies in a limestone gorge just beyond the cave. History surrounding the mine is imprecise, but the rumour is that it was first opened by the Romans in their search for lead. At its height, sometime around the early 1800s, the mine comprised three main levels and ran into the hillside for roughly 1500 metres.

DOI: 10.4324/9781003301752-3

While it's not strictly a cave, what attracted us is that parts of it are natural. As miners followed rich veins of ore, they cut through into several pipe caverns and other natural passages. As we were transitioning into caving, then, this site seemed perfect.

As interesting as the history of the site was, things quickly became monotonous while I was waiting for the others. My knowledge of the mine and a light morning mist had sustained my interest for a short while, but it wasn't long before I found myself reaching for my phone to pass the time. I could have gotten out of the car to light my camping stove and make a pan of coffee for the others while I waited, or at least started to organise some of the ropes we'd be using, but I did neither of these things. I reasoned that the ropes could wait, and that I'd already bought a large Costa on my way across as I hadn't wanted to waste time making one at home. So, emails drew my attention instead.

It's strange, and certainly frustrating at times, but I often find I have an irresistible urge to check email, even when I know there's nothing new or interesting to read. Immediately after opening and closing my Gmail account and my work email, I decided to do some online browsing for shiny new caving equipment. At this point in my caving journey, I was quite conscious that Mayhem, Rizla and I were still relying on a lot of climbing equipment and bits of kit we'd acquired as urban explorers. I was worried that we might look like amateurs if other cavers caught glimpse of us. The problem was that we *were* amateur cavers. Of course, this was nothing to be embarrassed about really, but that's the rational me thinking. At the time Mayhem, Rizla and I were resolute; we didn't want to give any kind of impression we were ill-prepared or worse still incompetent.

Twenty more minutes passed, and the last of my patience faded. I couldn't help but think about the things I needed to do later in the day. In addition to meeting a friend for a few beers later that evening, I wanted to meet my wife for an afternoon swim at a nearby river as it was forecast to be a sunny day. Because of this, I began plotting how quickly we could teach James Mcnally, a housemate Mayhem was bringing along for the first time, how to descend and then reascend a rope before going underground. To save time, I convinced myself that he would probably get the gist as we went along. What better way to learn, I thought to myself, than just doing it? Just as I'd made up my mind about how things were going to run, I happened to glance up into my rear-view mirror. Mayhem was pulling up behind me in his van. Sat in the passenger seat next to him was Mcnally. Pale and bleary-eyed, it was immediately clear that the pair were 'hungover to fuck'.

Life on the Surface

Life in the twenty-first century, as Bauman (2000) points out, is best described as an age of relentless reinvention. In other words, constant change has become one of the main catchphrases of our era. Certainly, if we glance around we see it everywhere, both in material and spiritual creations, and in the general acceptance that information has become more valuable than knowledge because in a world that never stands still knowledge has become just as impractical as it is unserviceable (Agger, 2013). To borrow some choice words of Bauman, the axiom 'until further notice' (2000: 147) governs most people's lives in present modernity, meaning they must be ready to adapt ideals, replace 'truths' and retrain themselves at short notice. People have little choice as well; they must step up and move with a train of transformation; otherwise they run the risk of being left behind on the platform which is not a place anybody should be left standing.

To fully understand the implications of change in the twenty-first century, it is useful to first think about the process of modernity and how its initial shape aimed to solidify and fix things. At the heart of this kind of modernity was an incessant obsession to modernise, to ensure progress never ground to a halt (Bauman, 2000). What this means is that 'solid' modern thinking frequently involved the search for perfection, a final state requiring no further change or improvement. The idea was that once the archetypal state was achieved, any further change would disrupt the perfect and rational order of things. In more ways than one, as it was revealed in Chapter 1, the development of caving as an organised sporting science or a form of rational recreation adhered to this process of modernisation and the mindset that the world works best when its key components and features (labour, hierarchies, class, social skills, etc.) are organised, stolid and governed by exact rules, regulations and procedures. In other words, 'solid' modernity was all about conformity and people being able to adjust their conduct according to the shape of the world. As Bauman (2000) reminds us, 'solid' modernity was responsible for the 'solid' modern imagination which looked for reason, functionality and justification in everything, and it was this that was the impetus behind the materialisation of science as the dominant discourse of the twentieth century.

The world of course has not quite transformed in the way planners predicted. It never did become as systematic and orderly as they perhaps envisaged. In fact, the world has taken a Borgesian turn as an infinite number of diverging paths have been discovered, paths that encourage us to rethink the rules and structures of 'solid' modernity. What this means is that there cannot be a definite plan for the world or an incontrovertible theory to encapsulate how things work because our era is becoming one of fluidity, mobility and inconstancy. Reinventing his own category of Karl Marx's idea that in modernity 'all that is solid melts into air', Bauman (2000) refers to this accelerated 'melting process' as the arrival of the 'liquid' modern world. In highlighting the differences between 'solid' and 'liquid' modernity, what Bauman (2000) argues is that the striking features of life in the twenty-first century are fragmentation, insecurity, uncertainty, reregulation, speed and lability. He goes on to highlight that the struggles and contradictions emerging from this changed world are reflected in complex ways, ways that require new epistemological frameworks coupled with a sociological imagination to make sense of them.

According to Bauman (2016), there are two ways of viewing the transition from 'solid' to 'liquid' modernity. The first is that freedom is being made available to everyday people for they are suddenly able to choose who they are and how they want to live their lives. Indeed, this is how it is celebrated in most postmodernist literature, where it is suggested that people have gained the ability to reject or refute identities that were historically prescribed or enforced by others and instead become idiosyncratic (Bauman, 2016; Bauman, 1998a). It is this freedom of course that has made it possible for me and a small group of others to enter the natural underground as self-invented cavers. This is freedom in other words that is no longer the sole privilege of a global elite. It is freedom to choose at will what we make of our lives and how much of it we choose to spend being men and women of leisure.

On the other hand, there is the idea that any freedom is illusionary. As Bauman (2000) argues, there is no other way to pursue freedom than to follow its norms, patterns and routines which are all situated under the all-too-comfortable umbrella of consumer capitalism. To borrow Blackshaw's way of putting it, consumerism is 'as loud and shiny as lip gloss' (2005: 113) – it is everywhere which calls to mind Baudrillard's world of images built upon images. Not only does it thrive in popular culture, but it is also part and parcel of the pace of everyday life. It is in the immediacy of fast food, in the waistlines of obese punters, in designer clothing, in handheld electronic devices, and in flash cars, e-scooters and electric bicycles. It is in the music channelled through AirPods; it is the voice of twenty-first-century individuals, and so deeply embedded that it has become the very language of our streets. To borrow Blackshaw's choice words once again, quite simply 'there is (no)thing that is uncommodifiable in liquid modernity' (2005: 113). What this suggests is that twenty-first-century beings are faced with the perpetual agony of living in a world of possession and the possessed. Living their lives through objects of consumption forces individuals to live surface lives which lack important things such as substance, depth and history.

Similar ideas to those of Bauman were of course originally developed by intellectuals belonging to the Frankfurt School. One of the key figures of the school of social theory, Herbert Marcuse (1964), concluded that the immense economic productivity of advanced industrial societies (i.e. consumer capitalism) is in direct opposition to the free development of people's capabilities and needs. What he suggests, in a nutshell, is that people end up surrendering their freedom and individuality to a system that creates values, hopes and aspirations for them. As Marcuse (1964) argues, by satisfying false and superimposed needs, the consumer way of life has transformed people into one-dimensional beings – people who are oblivious to the fact, or indeed simply do not care, that their bodies have developed a one-dimensional consumer duty that denies them of any possibility of being authentic. Sat here now, reflecting on myself as I was waiting outside Odin Mine, I realise this is precisely the sort of individual I have become in everyday surface life, someone who buys coffee on the go instead of making a cup outdoors on a primus stove. I am often more about convenience and buying the things I desire, someone whose life has gradually become more organised around consuming experiences than producing them for myself. In fact, it is glaringly obvious now that I am quick to involve myself in things I sometimes think I despise. I am, perhaps, the classic example of a one-dimensional 'liquid' modern man.

It is axiomatic that there are consequences to living our lives as one-dimensional consumer sorts. It was Erich Fromm (1991), another important figure of the Frankfurt School, who warned us that unrestricted satisfaction of desires does not lead to happiness, security or comfort. This is a point Bauman (2011) has gone on to interrogate further, to the extent that he has questioned whether people are ever able to reach a 'natural' state of happiness or contentment. Drawing on Jean-Jacques Rousseau's work on the origins of human needs what Bauman (2011) concludes is that in a highly changeable consumer-driven world individuals find themselves less able to derive pleasure and satisfaction from modest and unperverted needs, or splendours that are splendorous precisely because they have somehow remained unchanged. This is an important point that will be revisited later in the book.

Before that, another sociologist who has unpacked the consequences of present modernity is Anthony Giddens. As he wrote almost 40 years ago, *ontological security* which involves socialisation and routinisation is vital if people are to maintain a 'true' or 'authentic' sense of self (Giddens, 1984). Simply put, Giddens' understanding of ontological security can be understood as a sense of stability in the world rather than something that is constantly negotiated and dependent upon ever-changing social contexts. The problem, however, is that the controlling effect of consumer-guided lifestyles has not only caused people to lose their ontological confidence but also their sense of existence which empowers them and provides feelings of confidence. The natural outcome of ontological insecurity is self-consciousness because people find themselves unable to enjoy their own worldly existence without feeling anxious about whether their performative bodies are the measure of worth in the eyes of other people (Giddens, 1991). Under these seemingly Orwellian conditions, life becomes more stage-like and carefully coordinated in a choreographic sort of way. If the reader thinks back to the opening episode, I should like to argue that it was this exact sense of ontological insecurity that made me worried about looking inauthentic and too much like a novice.

For Bauman, however, the problem of ontological insecurity is merely one way of thinking about the consequences of 'liquid' modernity. In Bauman's (1998b) mind, there is more too to be said about *existential insecurity*. What Bauman draws our attention to are the day-to-day existential dilemmas people face. For instance, a person brought up in present modernity in a family that has for several generations worked in industrial engineering is likely to be torn between a lifetime of tradition, especially deep-rooted feelings of admiration and respect for their family's commitment to upkeeping certain practices and knowledge, and their ties to the choices of a 'liquid' modern world. Astutely aware of this dilemma many twenty-first-century individuals face, what Bauman (2016) argues is that people are not only forced to contend with volatile, highly changeable identities, they must somehow balance competing and conflicting identities.

An interesting example of existential insecurity can be drawn from my own experience while producing this book. The more I caved and gained experience in the natural underground, the more I felt conflicted about my role and identity as a caver. There were many times when I began to doubt whether I was wrong for criticising the scientific foundations of caving and whether I was in fact losing touch with my older, pre-caving self. This issue escalated so greatly that I began to question whether I was becoming more of a serious caver sort as I began to attend cave rescue open days, adhere to rules such as paying fees to access caves on private farmland, and as I said before even feel the pangs of self-consciousness over whether I looked enough like a 'real' caver. In a sense, I was correct in thinking my identity was changing. It would be false to say otherwise. Yet, at the same time it took me a while to realise that I had not lost my former identity (namely that of an urban explorer as opposed to a caver). It is precisely this dilemma many people face in the twenty-first century because 'liquid' modernity is about going it alone but going it alone while struggling to relate to others, while holding partnerships down, and while breaking free from commitments that become too constraining (Bauman, 2016). What I experienced, then, was quite simply a taste of a world of existential insecurity.

A Short Interposition

Although they looked like they needed a minute or two to sip coffee and catch a little more sleep, Mayhem and Mcnally were surprisingly spritely getting out of the van. As they were due to be out on 'the piss' again later that day, they too were on a tight schedule and so were keen to get cracking. In a way, this pleased me as I was also eager to get finished, but it did make me feel a bit disheartened to think that we were unable to spend a single day caving without other things getting in the way.

Hovering around the back door of the van, we began to gear up. By this point, Mayhem and I had acquired most of the basic gear needed for caving – Warmbac oversuits, Petzl descenders, single rope technique (SRT) equipment, helmets and reliable Fenix headtorches. In our minds, we were beginning to look like the real deal. As for Mcnally, however, this was his first trip underground and despite giving him several warnings that he should invest in some real gear, at the very least a helmet and some overalls, he hadn't gone to the trouble. Too busy was his reason. He pointed out that he'd looked online for some gear, but the delivery time would have taken too long so he'd decided to improvise with things he'd had lying around. As I fastened up my harness, I watched with a sense of disbelief as Mcnally placed a cycling helmet on top of his head and slid a transparent bin bag over the upper part of his body to act as a makeshift waterproof vest.

Shaking my head, I asked Mcnally if he'd ever done any kind of ropework at all. I already knew he hadn't but saying it out loud helped me better comprehend the insane idea that we were about to take this guy underground. He looked up at me, and with a wide grin replied, 'Not so much mate, but I've got that interview for HART[1] next week so I've come to learn how to tie knots and remind myself how to use ropes'. I replied by asking him if he'd done much climbing before. He grinned again and responded with a decisive, 'I'll be honest, not really, dude. But, how hard can it be? I'm a fast learner, I'll pick it all up after today.' Worried for his life, I immediately ditched the plan I'd made sitting in my car. I turned to look at Mayhem. No words were required; it was decided that we needed to get Mcnally some practice in. As we made our way to the top of the gorge, just beyond Odin's Cave, Mayhem announced that Mcnally should have a go at abseiling down a steep bank before he committed himself to the underground. Mcnally agreed, but it was clear he was feeling frustrated we weren't just getting on with some caving (Figure 3.1).

Figure 3.1 An unprepared Mcnally learns to abseil.

Having been forced to adapt to conditions of relentless change, Bauman (2000) describes twenty-first-century individuals as perpetual shapeshifters who have developed the ability to metamorphose depending on the form they must assume at any given moment. The best way to survive in this environment is of course to shun the idea of building a specialised Bourdieuian habitus and instead focus on learning how to move between *habitats* (that other word for social form) (Blackshaw, 2017; Bauman, 1992). Doing so enables individuals to reimagine how the sense of self can be continually recast and expressed in different ways. In other words, identities and social relations must be experienced swiftly and as transiently as possible to ensure the process of dis-embedding and re-embedding continues and does not become stagnant. The downside, of course, is that the sense of self is never stable, entirely comfortable or ever fully convincing.

To expound further on the significance of shapeshifting, it is important to be clear that although Mayhem and I had already ventured into a handful of caves by the time we had come to explore Odin Mine, I would certainly not have described us as real cavers. For obvious reasons, neither would Mcnally. However, this did not stop us from fashioning new awkward-looking caver identities and experimenting with them. Thanks to our experience of living in a world of fluidity, ontological instability and existential insecurity, we have come to realise that surviving in 'liquid' modernity involves becoming responsible for our own choices and judgements, and that a specialised habitat constructed by ourselves is what is necessary if intimations of freedom are to be found. In other words, since there is little guidance in present modernity on how people are destined to live their lives, Mayhem, Mcnally and I have become skilled at being adaptable and used to the 'labour of self-composition' (Bauman, in Bauman and Raud, 2015: 103). Guided by what Scott Lash has described as 'a radical individualism' (1994: 144), then, and the knowledge that 'liquid' moderns must make their own Frankensteinian place in the world, the three of us moulded our identities to what we believed a caver should look like.

As for the downside to dressing in the frenetic attire of states of habitat, it is inevitable that the likes of myself, Mayhem and Mcnally will always be destined to exist on the margins of existing social structures and never truly have a place as 'authentic' cavers (if we ever decided we wanted this). And we were aware of this. We were constantly aware of our outsider status. What this reinforces, therefore, as Bauman (2005) points out, is that being a 'liquid' modern is a precarious way of living, one that inevitably prevents everyday people from ever experiencing authenticity as identities are never given enough time to solidify and produce streams of history.

Another key consequence of living in 'liquid' modernity is the craving for instant gratification it causes. To further explain this idea, it has been argued that while 'solid' modernity was a world that involved suppressing desires and longings, 'liquid' modernity is all about the satisfaction of what Sigmund Freud (1920) referred to as the 'pleasure principle'. What this means is that life in the twenty-first century has become more of a search for instant pleasures than it

50 The Underside of Modernity

has patience and stamina. To borrow Fredric Jameson's (1991) way of putting it, a new cultural logic has become dominant as we slip deeper into a world of electronic communication and transient living. Twenty-first-century individuals are in other words witnesses to the dawning of an era of instantaneity which has not only transformed human beings' relations with the world but also with other people and with their own bodies. For consumer culture, this is one of its greatest achievements. It takes waiting out of wanting and makes us willingly engage only with those things that are readily available and easy to dispense with (Bauman, 2005). When things do not go to plan, when we are left wanting, dissatisfaction quickly follows, along with frustration, irritation and in some instances even bursts of rage (Bingham, 2021).

It is possible to evidence the point about instantaneity by once again reflecting on the episode provided at the beginning of the chapter. Although I was out to cave and had set aside the day specifically to go caving, I found myself consumed with frustration over wasting time. In fact, while I was waiting for the others to arrive, I found it impossible to embrace any sort of feeling of excitement, or really think about Odin Mine at all for that matter, because my mind was entirely focused on the other things I had planned later that day. Consequently, rather than wait patiently and accept that some time would inevitably be lost and that I had perhaps tried to squeeze too much into my day, I found myself desperate to devise ways of speeding things up and clawing back lost time. Guided entirely by Freud's 'pleasure principle' and (ironically) my desire for enjoyment, my solution, as I noted earlier, was to cut corners and risk taking a completely inexperienced person caving. As reprehensible and irresponsible as it seems now, at the time I was convinced that by showing Mcnally on the move how caving equipment works and how ropes are correctly used, we would all save some time and be a lot better off for it.

The discussion so far notwithstanding, what comes next is a change in focus. These foregoing insights merely serve as the basis of my own sociological investigation. The aim now, in the remainder of this chapter, is to encourage the reader to think more about the magic and enchantment of an alternative underground reality where things work differently. What is being proposed is the idea that the natural underground is a space of escape, a place of perceived ontological security in an otherwise insecure world. To remind the reader, this book is less about viewing the natural underground through the lens of tradition or as a site of science because I am more concerned with the idea that caves help us reinvigorate how imagination, freedom and sources of pleasure can be experimented with in the twenty-first century.

The Call of the Caves

One of the main things that sets the natural underground apart from the surface world is that it has not yet been fully dominated or tamed by human beings (Macfarlane, 2020). On this point, there are three things of importance to note.

First, the natural underground seems to evade most of the influences of 'liquid' modernity because consumer capitalism has not yet managed to find a secure enough foothold in the subterranean world. Of course, plenty of show caves exist from Ingleborough Cave in the Yorkshire Dales to Kartchner Caverns in Arizona, but these spaces are different to the real natural underground. A show cave has been made accessible to the general public and usually features artificial walkways and equipment to illuminate the space with lights and sounds. Caving experience days exist as well, with groups being safely guided through well-known passageways and caverns under the constant supervision of trained instructors. These are examples of consumer capitalism digging its twisted fingers into things that were previously thought to have been uncommodifiable. For the most part, though, the natural underground would appear to be more resistant to most of the 'liquid' influences found on the surface. As Jeanne Hanson (2007) points out, most caves on our planet have in fact not yet even been discovered with geologists estimating there are millions worldwide still waiting to be found and explored. More recently, Maya Wei-Haas (2022) has described caves as the 'last frontier of exploration'.

The second important thing to note is that caves are generally more difficult to commodify than surface spaces because of the powerful association they have with horror, rebellion and death. According to Crane and Fletcher (2015), caves are places of extreme imagination that tend to stimulate primal fears, such as being trapped alone or buried in the dark. They can also cause people to develop thoughts and ideas that would normally remain hidden in the deep subconscious recesses of the mind (Hurd, 2003). Certainly, philosophers such as Sigmund Freud and Plato used caves for this exact purpose, as analogues for systems of ignorance and unreality, or vessels for hidden secrets and lost dreams. Following a similar theme, Marion Dowd (2015) has gone on to draw attention to the idea that the isolated nature of caves and their noiseless interiors mean they have repeatedly been used as metaphors for loneliness, grief and depression. For others, as Dowd (2015) suggests, caves also represent spaces of counterculture and anti-establishment movements, spaces that play home to dangerous individuals who are set on destroying the world as we know it.

As the above examples reveal, the powerful association of darkness coupled with terror and fear of the unknown has greatly influenced how caves are perceived and understood by most everyday people. It is not difficult to comprehend why, nor why a great effort has been undertaken to create immersive publicly accessible caves or 'authentic' duplications that are completely safe, for entering any natural cave is to move towards absolute darkness and ambiguity (Hurd, 2003). This is a point James Lovelock (1963) emphasises in his suggestion that real caves cannot help but function as indeterminate gateways between the laws and rules of the world above ground and the uncontrollable one below. What this means, crucially, is that most of us can think of a myriad of reasons why we should not pass through the twilight zone – that initial liminal space that is neither dark nor light but leads directly into the underground – and considerably fewer reasons as to why we should. Nevertheless, there are still a minority who feel the lure of the world of subterranean darkness. As John Gillett (2002) points out, for these individuals an uncommodifiable natural underground might be dangerous, but at the same time it is exhilarating. It might be more physically demanding than most forms of sport and leisure too, but it is a source of intense pleasure and involves a high degree of imagination; and while it might very well be the home of darkness, it is often found to be inexplicably illuminating (Gillett, 2002).

The third thing that limits the domination of the natural underground is the general inaccessibility of most subterranean spaces. Indeed, James Tabor's (2011) description of caves being analogous to living organisms is not inaccurate. As he suggests, like human beings they have respiratory systems and bloodstreams, and are just as susceptible to infection or infestation. What this means is that they can be highly unpredictable and therefore extremely difficult to control or tame. The infamous Tham Luang cave rescue attests to this last point. Although 12 young footballers and their coach managed to reach an approximate distance of 4 kilometres inside Tham Luang, sudden and continuous rainfall rapidly flooded part of the cave leaving some of them stranded for 18 days (Massola, 2019). While entering the cave had been relatively straightforward, returning to the surface again was a different story. Many of the passageways and chambers the team had passed through on their way to the Nern Nom Sao Slope flooded completely. Issues with powerful currents and zero visibility further complicated matters, along with falling oxygen levels (Massola, 2019). In the end, as Massola points out, thousands of people were recruited to conduct a rescue mission, an effort involving over 100 divers, 2,000 volunteers, more than 700 dive tanks, and sadly the deaths of two rescuers, one by drowning and the other due to a blood infection.

Having considered the three points above, hopefully the reader will agree that contemplating how and why the natural underground is less susceptible to commodification is a useful place to start when thinking about the special lure of caves. Of course, my discussion of caves being uncommodifiable is likely to raise a few eyebrows since I have not made the idea of exploring the natural underground seem particularly appealing so far. In fact, readers who are yet to experience the kingdom of the dark for themselves may well be wondering why on earth anybody would choose to visit such an inhospitable world in the first place. Nevertheless, I want to reiterate an earlier point which is that consumer capitalism has for some people created a world of disillusionment and disenchantment. From this perspective, the surface world is lacking in imagination and certain other things such as security and community which appear to have diminished in value in the twenty-first century (Bauman, 2000). What caves provide for some individuals, then, is an environment that is perhaps less repressed, a place of retreat where it is possible to resist the disenchantment of 'liquid' modernity and appreciate the value of other things that might seem otherwise unimportant or unattainable in everyday life.

Indeed, David Heap made the point decades ago that there should be no denying of the 'comprehensive, poetic-sensuous appeal of caves' (1964: 7). This is a point I will inevitably return to later in the book as it requires further critical discussion. For now, though, it is enough to note that while many people might view the natural underground as abiotic and empty, as frightening, or as containing darkness so great human eyes cannot properly acclimate, there are some individuals who have come to discover how their minds and senses are capable of adapting and injecting this mysterious world with life. From this perspective, as the Georgian poet John Freeman uncovers in his poem *The Caves*, the natural underground can be thought of as containing 'lightless labyrinths of thought' which are filled with 'eternal motion grave and deep' (1920: 30). As my discussion in Chapter 1 already revealed, I have adopted a similar way of thinking to the likes of Heap and Freeman. In doing so, my intention is that I have in the remainder of the book been able to unpack some of the ways in which the natural underground stimulates different imaginations, senses and emotions.

Foggy Lenses and Broken Screens

Before I continue to unpack imagination, sense and emotion in the natural underground, it is worth pausing first – just briefly – to think about digital technology. So far it has not been addressed in this chapter, yet I recognise how much of an important role it plays in preserving the mystery and enchantment of caves.

It is an obvious point, but an important one nonetheless, to suggest that digital technology has become an integral part of everyday life in present modernity. It was only a few years ago for example that young people were estimated to spend over a third of their leisure time using electronic devices such as smartphones, laptops and tablets (Office for National Statistics, 2017). It was further estimated that people who use such devices are more likely to be heavy users of social media, mass media and computer games (ibid). As for internet access, it was recently estimated that 96% of households in the United Kingdom are connected and that 87% of adults now use it for everyday activities such as shopping (Office for National Statistics, 2020). While on the one level it might be argued that using digital technology in this way provides greater convenience and allows for enhanced connectedness with people and information than we have ever experienced before (Cin, Mustafaj and Nielsen, 2021), others have argued that it is having a profound effect on culture, the things people value and how we engage in leisure.

There are certainly countless positives when we think about the implications of the present technological revolution. As Karl Spracklen (2015) argues, thinking about the topic from a leisure perspective, forms of digital leisure not only have the appearance of novelty, but they also provide public spaces for new cultures, especially cultures of counter-hegemonic resistance and communicative action. Others such as Carnicelli et al. (2018) have gone on to point out how the digital turn has also transformed the very idea of leisure and how people can play, learn and seek sources of entertainment. What they also argue is that increased use of digital technology means leisure is no longer constrained by

54 The Underside of Modernity

geographical boundaries. Despite the perceived benefits, though, it has been noted that the same technologies can take just as much away, especially in the way they change how people engage with quotidian tasks. As Judy Wajcman (2015) and Sherry Turkle (2017) point out, the vast majority of us frequently complain about being *tethered* to electronic devices in present modernity and how addiction has contributed to the accelerated pace life that has become a normal feature of modern-day living. With this development comes increased anxiety and anti-social tendencies, and a range of other problems from the idea that nobody appreciates depth anymore (of literature and ideas for example) to the argument that fewer people are critical thinkers.

The above points about anxiety and introversion notwithstanding, the main issue underpinning all of these problems is that we have moved into a world where 'nothing is ever fundamentally *off* and there is never an actual state of rest' (Carnicelli et al., 2018: 4). In other words, we return to that fundamental term 'tethering' and the idea that there is an expectation in present modernity that electronic devices, regardless of the setting or situation, must be used and be permanently connected. Failure to do so might result in missing out on the myriad experiences that are available in a consumer-driven world. As Carnicelli et al. (2018) argue, if they have not fully disappeared already those aspects of life that were once protected and considered to be sacred have been severely weakened in the digital age. They have weakened because it has become the expectation that emails should be responded to immediately, that files and information should be retrievable almost instantaneously, and that access to a network should be achievable anywhere (ibid). For scholars such as Turkle (2017), tethering effectively becomes a 'second life' that runs parallel to the non-virtual everyday world. It is Bauman (in Bauman and Lyon, 2013), however, who views the world for what it is. He argues that the 'real' world and the digital one regularly interpenetrate so they can no longer be described as dichotomous.

There are, however, places where a dichotomous split can be perhaps resurrected to some extent, and I would argue that the natural underground is one of those places. With the exception of caving equipment which has undergone various technical and mechanical improvements in the last few decades, it can be argued that day-to-day technology, especially the sort that is digital and likely to cause tethering, does not enhance experiences of the natural underground or even come in particularly useful if it is used. In fact, it becomes more of a hindrance than something that might aid or benefit the experience. What this reinforces is that caves can be taken collectively to be a place yet to be tamed by human beings. In fact, the lack of influence of technology, or so it will be argued shortly, helps to preserve the mystery and enchantment of the natural underground.

Another Interposition

After rigging a fixed abseil to a large tree, Mayhem descended first into the limestone gorge. While he went to scout out the entrance to Odin Mine and rig the first pitch, I stayed up top to make sure Mcnally didn't kill himself with my descender. I watched carefully as he set it up. As expected, he tried setting it up the wrong way around to begin with, but after pointing out his error he turned it the right way up. When he was finally ready, after much fumbling and second-guessing, I attached him onto a safety line just to be on the safe side. The drop wasn't enormous, but it was certainly enough to break his legs if he messed up.

Mcnally descended with relative ease and once he reached a boulder platform I followed. From the platform, we followed Mayhem's voice to the right where there were three entrances. Mayhem had chosen the left one, an unbolted 10-metre pitch and warned us it was unpleasant. He recommended taking the lower right entrance. Following his advice, we dropped a short line down the lower right-hand passage and then made our way into the hillside. We used the rope to make a short 4-metre descent through an awkwardly shaped fissure in the rock, until we finally dropped down into a muddy rift that was partly filled with dead leaves. This is where we found Mayhem; his head was poking out of a small passage on our left. He looked a little solemn. Puzzled as to why, Mcnally and I checked to see if he was okay. In silence, he held up his phone to reveal its screen was cracked and bleeding pixelated ink spots. He allowed us a moment to comprehend the scale of the damage before he explained what had happened: 'It was in me front pocket wasn't it. I forgot when I was squeezing through this tight cunt. I must have squashed it. Bastard' (Figure 3.2).

Reunited inside the main vein, we continued until we reached a large opening in the floor that spanned the entire width of the passage. A quick glance down confirmed it was deep. To bypass it, we used another rope to rig a safe traverse. As I set up the roped crossing, Mcnally attempted to do some filming on his phone. The problem he found, however, was that everything was caked in sticky mud. He tried wiping the camera lens and main screen on his uncovered fleece sleeves, but this did little more than smudge the dirt around a bit. Clearly frustrated as he wanted video footage for Facebook and some images for Instagram, he spent just as long trying to clean the phone as it took me to set up the traverse.

Once we were all safely across the precarious-looking hole, we reached a second pitch that required us to ascend a slippery slope that rose at a very sharp angle and then squeeze through a narrow vertical section to reach an open shaft above us. Again, Mayhem went first and Mcnally and I waited as he struggled to gain purchase on the slippery mud. Knowing I had a few minutes before it was my turn as Mcnally was next up, I decided to check the map on my own phone to see how much progress we'd made. Like the others, I had problems. My industrial marigolds[2] were caked in mud and the moment I touched my phone it acted like a magnet to the gunk. In the end, I resorted to taking my gloves off (a mistake!) as my phone's screen refused to respond to my rubber-clad fingers. In hindsight, using digital maps of the mine turned out not to be such a good idea. Before entering the old mine, we'd surmised that we were being innovative and efficient by not bringing a traditional laminated map which seemed like a cumbersome thing to carry, but it turned out we were wrong. Using a digital map was nearly impossible.

Figure 3.2 Lamenting the loss of a phone.

Just before I set out to make the climb myself, I noticed Mayhem fumbling with something at the top of the slope – his DSLR camera. The entire time we'd been down Odin Mine he'd been trying to take photographs of our trip, but he hadn't had much luck. As I dug my fingers deep into the mud in a bid to stop myself from sliding, I could hear him swearing because he couldn't clear his lens of a thin layer of condensation. Each time he wiped it, he would coat the lens with dirt before it fogged back up. Eventually, he gave in and put the camera away for good. He was disappointed, but not enough that it marred the exploration. In fact, I would argue that eventually putting our cameras and phones away made us much more aware of our surroundings. Even Mcnally put his phone away despite having been convinced a short while earlier that he'd had a bar of signal appear.

The Underside of Modernity   57

With all the unnecessary gear stashed away, we pressed on. There was something about the narrow rift ahead, which we assumed had been an old mineral vein that made it impossible to stop. We were tired by this point, but we couldn't resist exploring more of the mine. An ultimate unknown was luring us forward, a powerful force that promised wonder and excitement if we continued. Although the old passageways of Odin Mine have been carefully mapped and named, until each one was experienced in our mind's eye and by our bodies, this truly was a voyage into the strangeness and wonder of a brand-new world.

Something about our familiar selves changed too. The interplay between us and the cave led to an interchange occurring, an interchange somewhere between reality and imagination, and we found ourselves more appreciative of simple discoveries – of odd-looking stones, of our immediate company and of suddenly having complete awareness of our surroundings. It wasn't until we reached the third pitch, just beyond Weasel Pit that it dawned on me how ignorant of my surroundings I normally am in the everyday world. Always needing to be somewhere, or with my head buried in some form of electronic device, I realised I live in the constant shadow of blissful obliviousness and unfamiliarity. Here, though, things were different, and for the first time in a very long while I noticed other things all around me. More crucially, I not only fully appreciated these things, I was also able to begin making sense of them.

Removed from the flow of everyday life, our trip to Odin Mine altered our day-to-day routines. In no uncertain terms, compulsions that we do not normally think of or about were suddenly prohibited. On this point, it was interesting to watch Mcnally habitually reach for his phone to check for any kind of update, whether it be an email or Snapchat. Later, he confessed his irritation that he had been so detached from the surface world he had tried to convince himself a bar of signal had appeared on his screen tens of metres below the ground. In reality, he knew the bar was a mere figment of his imagination, albeit a desperate one. His reaction is perfectly understandable though, for this was the first time in a long time, perhaps even in his entire life since he is younger than me and Mayhem, that Mcnally had found himself completely unconnected from a networked life. What he encountered, therefore, were feelings of unfamiliarity and strangeness, feelings that made him feel incredibly awkward and uncomfortable at first.

Thinking a little deeper about why Mcnally acted in the way he did, it is worth considering how the internet is something that provides a space for the exploration of identity. This is something Turkle (1995) highlights in her earlier work, the idea that the virtual space of the internet allows people to customise and experiment with new identities in ways that are less possible in the 'real' world. As Turkle (2017) has gone on to argue, in many ways a life lived in the virtual places of the internet feels like a better place to explore identity because it is possible to hide ourselves away behind avatars and carefully modified profile pictures. And yet, while the virtual world would normally allow Mcnally to experiment with different ways of being himself and the fantasies of who he wanted to be, in the natural underground none of this was possible. Suddenly, Mcnally was vulnerable;

he was dressed all wrong and unsure of himself, and in his embarrassment had nowhere to retreat to. To borrow Turkle's (2017) way of putting it, he felt less of a person, less prepared for the unsettling proximity of his circumstances and the perceived emptiness (or so he thought at first) of his physical surroundings.

Another thing that was difficult to adjust to at first was our inability to use our cameras. As Lynn Leeson (2013) points out, forms of technology such as cameras have become extensions of our bodies in our everyday lives. What this signals, as Donna Harraway (1991) suggests, is that there has been a blurring of the distinction between where humans end and machines begin. In many ways, these ideas are reminiscent of Marshall McLuhan's (1962) classic expose on 'extensions of man', and the idea that digital technologies and organic bodies are becoming merged to the point that digital functions accelerate normal functions of the body. Thinking about these ideas in relation to Mayhem and Mcnally, it is important to note that in their minds whatever they could capture on a camera inside Odin Mine would directly impact their 'celebrity status' in the surface world, especially on online platforms such as Instagram, TikTok and YouTube where they could expect to receive new likes and followers for doing something different. Problems occurred, however, when it became impossible for Mayhem to take photos due to fluctuations in temperature which caused his camera lens to fog up. Likewise, Mcnally reached a point where he found that he was unable to get his camera out due to the amount of mud he had caked on his glove.

Much more could be said on the subject of digital technology, but at this point, I want to concentrate on what there is to be gained from suddenly being unable to use devices such as phones and cameras. In his critique of society becoming a totalitarian 'technopoly', a world where everyday life can only be understood through the technologies we use, Neil Postman (1992) argues that there is the risk of life being reduced to finding meaning only through machines. What he argues is that certain devices establish sovereignty over all aspects of human experience simply because we assume they can do things better than we can. What we discovered in the natural underground, however, is that this is not always the case. In fact, when forms of technology become unusable, whether the cause is mud or a cracked screen, we quickly learn that we are quite capable ourselves of having face-to-face conversations, that we do not need platforms such as Twitter to voice opinions, and that an electronic device is not the best way to capture the essence and feeling of the underground. In other words, the moment technological devices are absent, it dawns on us that we can rely on our senses and imaginations to understand the world around us. And, as Jean-Paul Sartre (1968) suggests, better understanding the world around us through the physical analogon helps us better appreciate artistic creativity, intellectual culture and the development of interpersonal relations.

To expound further on this last suggestion, attention can be turned to our experience of trying to navigate Odin Mine. As the last section of the episode revealed, it was impossible to keep our phones clean enough to zoom in on specific features and details of our map. Our thick, mud-covered marigolds did not help matters of course. Likewise, although each of our devices was GPS compatible, this feature immediately became redundant and could not be used as it normally might on the surface to navigate roads or footpaths. Drop and scratch-resistant screens which were normally reasonably durable in day-to-day life made no difference either and meant we were unable to check the map in certain crawl sections and other awkward spots. In short, the whole experience of trying to use technology to navigate turned out to be an exasperating ordeal. Nevertheless, key advantages were quickly noticed when we finally gave up relying on it, the main one being that we were forced to think for ourselves as we might well have done in a pre-digital era. What this allowed us to do was direct our focus to our immediate surroundings and in no uncertain terms live in the moment. Without the digital map, we found we were much less distracted and that we paid more attention to each another. I was more attuned to my surroundings as well which made me feel as though I had a better understanding of the natural underground and improved confidence in my ability as a navigator.

What we also gain through technology being unusable is the attenuation of performative tendencies. Following Erving Goffman's suggestion that people are not unlike actors on a 'social stage' when they encounter other individuals, it has been argued that when placed in front of a camera human beings have an even greater desire to project a certain image of themselves (Hill, 2015). David Lyon views this as being especially true for younger people in the twenty-first century as a growing number 'believe that unless you're on social media you don't exist' (2017: 832). In other words, 'liquid' modern people manipulate their appearance, the settings in which they perform, and their emotional demeanour all to 'act up' and play to the camera. Keeping up appearances and projecting an idealised image of oneself, however, is challenging, especially when audiences are on the constant lookout for flaws, mistakes and contradictions in performances (Hill, 2015). What this means is that acting up to the camera can be a highly demanding task, one requiring the suppression of feelings of embarrassment or shame and the general acceptance, as Serpil Kir (2019) points out, that exhibitionism is increasingly seen as a normal part of life.

Yet, with our cameras off and our connections to the outside world effectively severed, it began to dawn on us just how much they impact our day-to-day lives. To borrow Mcnally's way of putting it, 'you don't realise how much they [cameras] control your lives, but the reality is they're there all the time. You can't escape it'. This was indeed our first reaction, but there was more to our experience than mere reflections. It seemed there was a shared sense of relief between the three of us, relief that recording had ceased and that we no longer had to worry about our material being poured into the hands of Instagram, Facebook and other social media platforms. What we discovered is that we were suddenly able to speak freely and that we felt more inclined to be open with one another in our conversations or when pangs of fear were suddenly experienced. What this suggests in other words is that the natural underground was discovered to be a site of revival for attributes that make us human, attributes that face the real threat of being lost in a world where digital technology is always on.

Summary

What this chapter highlights is the idea that modernity brings with it certain consequences. Foremost among them is relentless change which produces the sour taste of impermanence and uncertainty. Consumer capitalism is the driving force behind this turn, a turn that appears to be transforming people into what Herbert Marcuse judiciously described as one-dimensional beings. For many people, those of us who are fortunate enough to live market-mediated lives at any rate, this is not necessarily a bad existence since consumer living gives us more freedom than most people ever would have experienced or even imagined in the era of 'solid' modernity. A setback, however, is that the dazzling lights and glamour of consumerism strip away and make us forget about simpler things that are uncommodifiable, especially things that are modest and unperverted.

Amid the noise and chaos of permanent connectivity and hyper-mediatisation, the magic of the natural underground is an example of something that has been forgotten or at the very least is overlooked in our day-to-day lives. Yet, there are some people, including me, who would attest that there is something important about the call of the caves. There is something in their mundane qualities and also in how they provide a means of changing how we think and feel. At a distance from the disenchantment and disillusionment of consumer capitalism, then, it is the natural underground that can help us reassess what is important in the world.

As the remainder of this book goes on to discuss from the perspective of an interpreter, inside the kingdom of the dark explorers find themselves able to leave the everyday world behind. Away from the instability, precariousness and uncertainty of 'liquid' modernity, bodies not only become immersed in patterns of thought and movement but a wide variety of different sights, scents, sounds and feelings that occupy the mind so completely it is to the exclusion of everything else. It follows, therefore, that it is not the mere physical beauty and magnificence of the natural underground that is being unpacked in this book, but the existential experience that is sometimes social but always deeply personal. Although physical beauty and magnificence certainly play a part in the experience, what this book sets out to uncover is something deeper, something in the natural underground that penetrates the body, the conscious mind, and the profound, ineffable emotional depths of the subconscious. It is with this in mind that we can move now to the next chapter which begins to explore the significance of intimacy and what I have termed the 'scotopic' experience.

Notes

1 Hazardous Area Response Teams, more commonly known as HART, are teams based within each of the UK's NHS Ambulance Trusts. These teams work closely with fire and rescue services to help save lives in difficult circumstances and high-profile incidents.
2 An industrial version of rubber gloves that were originally developed in the 1950s for washing up.

References

Agger, B. (2013). *A Critical Theory of Public Life: Knowledge, Discourse and Politics in an Age of Decline*. Oxon: Routledge.

Bauman, Z. (1992). *Intimations of Postmodernity*. London: Routledge.

Bauman, Z. (1998a). Identity: Then, Now, What For? *Polish Sociological Review*. 123: 205–216.

Bauman, Z. (1998b). *Globalization: The Human Consequences*. Cambridge: Polity.

Bauman, Z. (2000). *Liquid Modernity*. Cambridge: Polity.

Bauman, Z. (2005). *Liquid Life*. Cambridge: Polity.

Bauman, Z. (2011). *Socialism the Active Utopia*. Oxon: Routledge.

Bauman, Z. (2016). This is a 'liquid modern' World: Zygmunt Bauman in Conversation with Nicholas Gane. In: T. Blackshaw (Ed), *The New Bauman Reader: Thinking Sociologically in Liquid Modern Times*. Manchester: Manchester University Press, 91–112.

Bauman, Z. and Lyon, D. (2013). *Liquid Surveillance*. Cambridge: Polity.

Bauman, Z. and Raud, R. (2015). *Practices of Selfhood*. Cambridge: Polity.

Bingham, K. (2021). A Short Ethnography of Twenty-first Century Consumers: On Retail Rage and One-dimensionality. *Journal of Consumer Culture*. [Online First]. DOI: 10.1177/14695405211039614

Blackshaw, T. (2005). *Zygmunt Bauman*. Oxon: Routledge.

Blackshaw, T. (2017). *Re-Imagining Leisure Studies*. Oxon: Routledge.

Carnicelli, S., McGillivray, D. and McPherson, G. (2018). *Digital Leisure Cultures: Critical Perspectives*. Oxon: Routledge.

Cin, S., Mustafaj, M. and Nielsen, K. (2021). Patterns of Media Use and Leisure Time Among Older Adults. *New Media and Society*. [Online First]. DOI: 10.1177/14614448211062393

Crane, R. and Fletcher, L. (2015). *Cave: Nature and Culture*. London: Reaktion Books.

Dowd, M. (2015). *The Archaeology of Caves in Ireland*. Oxford: Oxbow Books.

Freeman, J. (1920). *Poems New and Old*. London: Selwyn and Blount.

Freud, S. (1920). *Beyond the Pleasure Principle*. London: Hogarth Press.

Fromm, E. (1991). *The Art of Listening*. New York: Open Road.

Giddens, A. (1984). *The Constitution of Society: Outline of the Theory of Structuration*. California: University of California Press.

Giddens, A. (1991). *Modernity and Self-Identity: Self and Society in the Late Modern Age*. Cambridge: Polity.

Gillett, J. (2002). *Of Caves and Caving: A Way and a Life*. Lincoln: Writers Club Press.

Hanson, J. (2007). *Caves*. New York: Chelsea House.

Harraway, D. (1991). *Simians, Cyborgs, and Women: The Reinvention of Nature*. Oxon: Routledge.

Heap, D. (1964). *Potholing: Beneath the Northern Pennines*. London: Routledge and Kegan Paul.

Hill, A. (2015). *Reality TV*. Oxon: Routledge.

Hurd, B. (2003). *Entering the Stone: On Caves and Feeling Through the Dark*. New York: Houghton Mifflin Company.

Jameson, F. (1991). *Postmodernism, or, the Cultural Logic of Late Capitalism*. Durham: Duke University Press.

Kir, S. (2019). Voyeurism in Social Networks and Changing the Perception of Privacy on the Example of Instagram. In: S. Kir (Ed), *New Media and Visual Communication in Social Networks*. Hershey: IGI Global, 255–269.

Lash, S. (1994). Reflexivity and Its Doubles: Structure, Aesthetics, Community. In: U. Beck, A. Giddens and S. Lash (Eds), *Reflexive Modernization: Politics, Tradition and Aesthetics in the Modern Social Order*. California: Stanford University Press.

Leeson, L. (2013). Romancing the Anti-Body: Lust and Longing in (Cyber)space. In: A. Kroker and M. Kroker (Eds), *Critical Digital Studies: A Reader*. London: University of Toronto Press, 85–100.

Lovelock, J. (1963). *Life and Death Underground*. London: G. Bell & Sons.

Lyon, D. (2017). Surveillance Culture: Engagement, Exposure, and Ethics in Digital Modernity. *International Journal of Communication*. 11: 824–842.

Macfarlane, R. (2020). *Underland: A Deep Time Journey*. London: Hamish Hamilton.

Marcuse, H. (1964). *One-Dimensional Man*. London: Routledge & Kegan Paul.

Massola, J. (2019). *The Great Cave Rescue*. Richmond: Duckworth Books.

McLuhan, M. (1962). *The Gutenberg Galaxy: The Making of Typographic Man*. Toronto: University of Toronto Press.

Office for National Statistics. (2017). Young People Spend a Third of Their Leisure Time on Devices: Is Technology Making Us Less Sociable? A Look at How Technology Has Influenced Our Leisure Time. [Online]. Retrieved from: https://www.ons.gov.uk/peo plepopulationandcommunity/leisureandtourism/articles/youngpeoplespendathirdofthe irleisuretimeondevices/2017-12-19

Office for National Statistics. (2020). Internet Access: Households and Individuals, Great Britain: 2020. [Online]. Retrieved from: https://www.ons.gov.uk/peoplepopulationand community/householdcharacteristics/homeinternetandsocialmediausage/bulletins/int ernetaccesshouseholdsandindividuals/2020

Postman, N. (1992). *Technopoly: The Surrender of Culture to Technology*. New York: Knopf.

Sartre, J.-P. (1968). *The Philosophy of Jean-Paul Sartre*. Ed. R. Cumming. London: Methuen.

Spracklen, K. (2015). *Digital Leisure, the Internet and Popular Culture*. Basingstoke: Palgrave.

Tabor, J. (2011). *Blind Descent: The Quest to Discover the Deepest Place on Earth*. London: Constable and Robinson.

Turkle, S. (1995). *Life on the Screen: Identity in the Age of the Internet*. New York: Simon & Schuster.

Turkle, S. (2017). *Alone Together: Why We Expect More From Technology and Less From Each Other*. New York: Basic Books.

Wajcman, J. (2015). *Pressed for Time: The Acceleration of Life in Digital Capitalism*. London: University of Chicago Press.

Wei-Haas, M. (2022). Descending into One of the Deepest Caves on Earth. *National Geographic*. [Online]. Retrieved from: https://www.nationalgeographic.com/science/ article/descending-into-one-of-the-deepest-caves-on-earth

Chapter 4

The Poetics of Caving
Rediscovering Intimate Things

Introduction

To begin my exploration of the natural underground I first want to turn the reader's attention to Robert Macfarlane's suggestion that 'sometimes in the darkness you can see more clearly' (2019: 55). In many ways, this short statement encapsulates the central purpose of this book and my belief that the kingdom of the dark can change the way we view and experience the world. Keeping this in mind, next I want to turn the reader's attention to Friedrich Nietzsche's warning that 'when you gaze long into an abyss, the abyss also gazes into you' (1973/2003: 146). One of Nietzsche's points, I think, is that the abyss represents a void whose sheer breadth cannot be crossed nor its true depths ever reached. This is a space of such scale and magnitude it is at the same time hostile to life but somehow manages to also harbour it. On the one hand, the abyss can make us think about the emptiness and nothingness of the world beyond the human sphere, yet on the other it contains such power it can make us question every single one of our existing beliefs, our all-too-human particularities and our numbness to things that exist at the very edges of everyday life. In other words, Nietzsche is reminding us that the unknownness of darkness can terrify us and cause us to look away but also, like Macfarlane is suggesting, that it can contain passions, meanings and knowledge we perhaps know exist yet have never taken the time to try and understand or appreciate.

It is with the above ideas in mind that this chapter sets out to produce a meditative and at times poetic interpretation of the natural underground that transcends the problems and pitfalls associated with the first reading of Nietzsche's dark abyss. With the view that some people have lost faith in the course present modernity has taken, the present chapter is a means of showing how caves can be thought about and experienced in such a way that they help certain individuals find reprieve from the everyday world. My starting point lies with the idea of the intimate immensity of the natural underground. As I will go on to argue, it is not just a sense of noiselessness some people are in search of, it is rather a feeling of tranquillity that imposes itself upon the mind and body so powerfully it can produce an unrivalled sense of emancipation and freedom.

DOI: 10.4324/9781003301752-4

The Intimacy of Caving

Bright sunshine punctuated the walk from Bullpot Farm to the entrance of Lancaster Hole in the Yorkshire Dales. We were carrying large coils of rope which seemed to become heavier as the terrain switched from footpath to trackless moor. Growing frustrated that the walk was further than we'd expected, and that the gradient of the moor seemed to be growing ever steeper, I became increasingly aware of my heart thumping deeply in my chest, and of hot blood pulsating uncomfortably around my body. Panting hard, we eventually reached the lidded entrance of Lancaster Hole in amongst a group of limestone boulders. Fighting the urge to rest, we removed the metal lid and set about rigging our first pitch from a large block close to the entrance tube (Figure 4.1).

Figure 4.1 The entrance to Lancaster Hole.

The Poetics of Caving   65

To help Mcnally gain more experience in rigging, we let him set up the first anchor. I inspected this scrupulously before beginning my descent to a rebelay positioned within the first few metres of a concrete pipe. After setting up a second anchor, I descended further to reach a large, exposed balcony ledge where I could set up a Y-hang for the next 28-metre pitch down the entrance shaft. Relying on my cowstails to take my full weight, I placed two steel maillons into two nearby fixed bolts. I then attached the rope using a double figure of eight knot and threw the remainder over the balcony into the shaft below. The rope hummed gently as it fell, the noise amplified by the great open space. The pitch was set, and I was ready to invite the others to join me, but I paused for a moment to enjoy my position hanging over the balcony edge.

Gazing down, the view was striking. The shaft below, glistening and precipitous, seemed to suck me inside. The light from my torch, and my subsequent ability to see, was consumed by the immense darkness. At this point, it dawned on me that I was surrounded by silence. Every now and then, I would adjust my position in my harness to try and get a little more comfortable and it would creak with the motion, but otherwise the great abyss breathed everything else inside. Stillness ensued and I found myself somewhere between feeling quite alone and yet very close to the rock encompassing me. The longer I remained in position over the ledge, the more I grew comfortable with precarity and solitude. I stared calmly into the abyss for a while, absorbing the refreshing state of equanimity.

Noises from above soon disturbed my contemplation. An erratic light illuminated my position as a silhouette descended upon me. The sound of material rubbing against rock filled the cavernous space, mixed with the clanks and clicks of metal equipment being worked. The spell of the cave broken, it was time now to welcome the others to Lancaster Hole.

—

There are some places where silence becomes less of a subtle phenomenon. The natural underground is such a place for it is here it is more easily heard. If the reader has ever sat alone in a quiet house, you will be familiar with what I am talking about here. When you listen intently and there is nothing to be heard, the sound of silence becomes almost deafening.

Lancaster Hole breathed this very same type of silence, so effectively it seemed to permeate the cavern walls as I descended the first 4 metres to reach a large natural balcony. Beneath me lay 28 metres of abyss and rising from within its depths was the presence of a silence so huge it rang loudly in my ears. As the most experienced rigger of the group, I had gone first and for all the effort required in the setting up, I quickly discovered it was worth the additional bit of exertion. As I waited for the others, hanging off my cowstails from a pair of bolts inserted firmly into the rock, the silence persisted. Like a morning mist, it was thick and motionless, quickly invading the ledge and the vast space around me. Fear of slipping and falling into the abyss soon subsided as the mist closed in all around me. To borrow a famous quote from the poet Charles Baudelaire, for the first time in a long time 'the tyranny of the human face [had] disappeared' (cited in Kaplan,

2009: 57) and I could feel the pure intimacy of my setting. By the time the others joined me, however, the silence had faded. It was shattered by the sound of Mcnally's body being forced through the constricted entranceway, and the metallic clicks of his descender battling against the friction of the rope.

To be clear, my experience of intimacy is not a new area of study nor a particularly novel finding since it has interested human beings since time immemorial. The word itself is derived from the Latin term *intimus*, which can loosely be translated to mean 'inner' or 'innermost'. Philosophers such as Plato and Aristotle were among the first to explore and discuss the idea in detail and what they were concerned with in particular were its ties to love and friendship, especially the depth of interpersonal understanding and concern (Sexton and Sexton, 2012). This popular interpretation of intimacy still holds strong in the twenty-first century and social psychologists have developed a range of theories to help us understand closeness with other human beings. We can take the work of Ingrid Smyer (2013) as one example which breaks intimacy down into four key types: physical, experiential, cognitive and emotional. What ties each of these categories together are themes such as love, kindness and sensitivity. The problem, however, is that this is not the kind of intimacy I experienced in the natural underground.

Another common understanding of intimacy according to Sexton and Sexton is in the idea that it is 'an awareness of the innermost reality of one person by another' (2012: 1), something private that has been disclosed in the confidentiality of a special interpersonal relation. In other words, from this perspective, there is something innately social about intimacy (Jamieson, 2011). The feeling is not created through compulsion or even a result of desire, it is rather generated naturally through mutual consent and knowing another person in such a way that they can be viewed deeply and internally (ibid). Once again, however, I am inclined to argue that my experience of intimacy was starkly different.

My own interpretation of intimacy is perhaps more closely aligned with the later work of Gaston Bachelard where he argues that unfurling levels of meaning and reality can be found within a space or structure. To further explain what I mean here, attention can be turned to his seminal text *The Poetics of Space*. Crucially, this book reveals a dramatic shift in Bachelard's thinking as he moves from the field of science to poetry, and it is this shift that enables him to guide his readers very carefully through the phenomenological object of the *home*. For Bachelard, the house represents a space of intimate being that is a person's own 'corner of the world' (1957/2014: 4), a space used as a repository for memory and to provide lodging for the soul. Central to this idea is the point that the house is the key to uncovering an inner self because it can be used to journey into a private place of contemplation, self-discovery and reassurance. As Bachelard (1957/2014) reveals, each room is capable of stirring a different sensation, of igniting imagination and of revealing endless dimensions of existence. Of course, this way of imagining space may seem overly romantic and perhaps a little too 'touchy-feely' for some people. Yet, it does encourage us to think about embodied

The Poetics of Caving   67

relational states of openness which in turn opens our eyes to the broad possibilities of virtually any surrounding space.

Although Bachelard (1957/2014) encourages us to think about architecture and human-made spaces, his ideas are arguably just as applicable to the natural underground since you can just as easily read a cave and use it to move in and out of imagination as you can a house or flat. Crucially, what Bachelard teaches us is that if we immerse ourselves deeply in the soil of everyday life and the wide array of places we encounter, we can uncover an 'intimate relation with the concrete realities of nature' (Gilson, 1963: xiv). As the episode above demonstrates, the cave, a place of silence and mystery, can be brought into focus and limited only by daydreams, memories and longings and can easily become an inner landscape from which new worlds can be created.

What is required first, however, as Bachelard (1957/2014) reveals, is an 'unlearning' of rationalistic modes of thinking. As he observes using his example of a cellar, we tend to gaze into dark voids with a sense of trepidation and apprehension which suggests it is a rational fear of underground space, one caused by the incomprehensibility of such space, that makes us associate it with death and horror (Meijenfeldt, 2003). As Bachelard (1957/2014) notes, uncertainty and darkness are frequently set against the light and hope of an attic space or skylight on the roof. It is unsurprising, therefore, that a feeling of instability overwhelmed me at first as my mind taunted me with thoughts of slipping and tumbling over into the abyss. To truly appreciate the space around me and the intimacy of my circumstance, then, it was vital I made some effort to push my rational feelings to one side. Hence, when I gazed down into the abyss beneath me, I fought hard to refute the idea that my own mortality could be waiting for me below.

When I eventually did gain control of my fear of the unknown space beneath me, I found myself slowly settling back into my harness with my full weight supported by the pair of steel bolts protruding from the rockface. The experience transformed as I waited for the others to join me, from an adrenaline-fuelled descent down the length of Lancaster Hole to an exploration of the hallways of my mind and the intricate details of the space around me. Just as I know which boards creak the loudest in my house at night, I started to notice the tiniest features in the rock. In other words, the cave around me was no longer mysteriously inert or a terrifying space because it began to acquire form and familiarity. Suddenly, I felt safe from the outside world, from the normal worries and problems encountered on the surface, as if I had entered a repository of intimacy. I should note that this is a feeling I have experienced before, when I have sheltered inside abandoned buildings for example, so it is not a feeling limited to the natural underground. My point is that certain places can, slowly but surely, become havens of intimacy, places where it is possible to be temporarily immobile, contemplative and protected. Nevertheless, I should stress that I am convinced no other place has ever felt quite as intimate as the natural underground.

Scotopia

The above discussion notwithstanding, I want to be clear that there is more to intimacy than entering different hallways of the mind, and to noticing otherwise inconspicuous details of a surrounding space or place. As I will now attempt to explicate, intimacy also involves the stimulation of senses and emotions, especially those that are generally absent in the humdrum of everyday life. There is a name for this kind of intimacy, one I have discussed elsewhere in a paper detailing one of my visits to the Paris catacombs (see Bingham, 2020). I refer to it as *scotopia* or a *scotopic experience*. What I want to argue in the remainder of this chapter is that scotopia is an essential part of any exploration of the natural underground, but I want to go further by also unpacking its central systems. To help me do this, more narrative interjections follow.

Before I go on to unpack the concept of scotopia, I realise a short introduction explaining the origins of the idea would be useful. The starting point of our discussion, therefore, begins with the detail that the term 'scotopic', from which scotopia derives, originates from two Greek words: *skotos* which refers to 'darkness' and *opia* which signifies 'a condition of sight'. It was ophthalmologist, John Herbert Parsons (1984), who first introduced the term, using it to define vision and sensitivity of the eye in conditions of low light intensity. In other words, Parsons was interested in 'dark adapted' vision after adjustment. The term has also been used by Helen Irlen (1991), an expert in the field of visual processing problems, to refer to a condition of the brain that increases a person's sensitivity to light. What Irlen argues is that scotopic sensitivity may be a neurological condition that prevents the brain from being able to interpret colours and light and therefore hinders a person's ability to process visual information in the normal way.

As important as both understandings of the term scotopic are, a key problem is that they are literal interpretations. That is to say, both Parsons and Irlen do no more than contemplate how a normal bodily function (sight) is distorted or impeded in conditions where light availability is limited or reduced. What this uncovers is that there is scope to think in an alternative way, one that is perhaps more sociological and considers how the other senses are shaped and enriched when people experience decreased visual acuity. It is precisely this path, the sociological route, that this chapter sets out to follow.

Keeping the above points in mind, the term scotopia is used in this book as a way of describing a state of *being-in-the-world* that takes into account how important bodily senses are when engaged in forms of leisure (or sport) such as caving. The crux of the argument is that a scotopic experience is one where sight has lost its position as the dominant sense due to the limited availability of light in the natural underground. More on this will be discussed shortly. For now, it is enough to note that when conditions of sight are made more difficult or vision is completely lost other sensory systems that are more easily ignored and overlooked are brought to life. Substituting our preferred sense for other sensory systems

The Poetics of Caving   69

allows us to experience senses that are much less familiar or, for some people, virtually unknown. This same point is explained well in the work of French romanticist François-René de Chateaubriand. In his book *Voyage to America* (1826/2015), he points out that when a campfire appears to die out and is reduced to red-hot embers silence follows, but it brings with it a multiplicity of other ways of perceiving the fire which are potentially evocative and emotive. What this signifies is that by addressing those unfamiliar and otherwise unnoticed aspects of life, and by developing a new receptiveness to everyday sensations, explorers of the natural underground are more likely to feel empowered to reorder, reinterpret and reimagine subterranean space.

To fully expound my definition of scotopia, I have taken inspiration from Michel Foucault's (1984) concept of heterotopia and broken it down into a series of key principles. First, as it was mentioned above, our ability to see things visually must be limited or absent. This follows the idea that knowledge attained exclusively through sight is likely to result in an insufficient and erroneous visually based epistemology that restricts our descriptions, analyses and subsequent understandings of the world around us (Bull and Back, 2020). It is natural, therefore, that scotopia is very likely to occur in subterranean spaces since they are one of the few places that can be completely impervious to light.

Second, it is important to note that scotopia is not something that occurs because people suddenly notice the noises, smells, tastes and feelings that are part of the ignored rhythm of the everyday. As I have argued elsewhere, it is aroused specifically when people find themselves immersed in certain shapeshifting, undesignable and imperceptible worlds of leisure where imagination can be allowed to prosper (Bingham, 2020). In other words, scotopia is a phenomenon in and of leisure. In no uncertain terms, it belongs to leisure.

A third point is that scotopia involves the discovery (also the rediscovery for some people) of other sensual aspects of social, cultural and personal experience that tend to either be the exception above ground or which are not present in everyday life (Bingham, 2020). That is to say, senses that are strange or even at odds with social, cultural and personal norms can be discovered when scotopia is experienced. These are feelings or sensations that can vary between being unpleasant and uncomfortable or invigorating and calming.

A fourth principle of scotopia is that it stimulates memories, emotion and nostalgia. Scotopia does this by operating between three discrete poles,[1] which can be referred to as the *mundane*, the *spectacular* and the *melancholic*. Generally, a scotopic experience begins with accepted mundanity as familiar sounds, smells, tastes and feelings of the natural underground spring to life (Bingham, 2020). The average cave, for example, has a familiar earthy odour and the air is damp and cold. By contrast, in wet caves with active streamways, the air usually smells clean and feels fresh against bare skin. As for dry arid caves, the lack of humidity causes smells to disappear, and they produce dust that can cause a subtle prickling sensation at the back of the throat. Regardless of any differences, these are the ordinary, comfortable and repeatable aspects of scotopia. When they emerge, they are a reminder that the familiar sensations of the underground world have reappeared.

Occasionally, a scotopic experience can enter two additional poles. The spectacular is the moment scotopia really comes to life and the senses are ignited in such a way that they become more profound and have an intensity that is nothing short of intoxicating. In other words, the spectacular is a moment of excitement and pleasure, one 'capable of resurrecting past memories and ontological feelings that elicit greater nostalgic power' (Bingham, 2019: 16). The downside to the spectacular side of scotopia is that it is always short-lived. This is not a major problem though since it actually serves to make us fiercely nostalgic and more desirous to experience the same or similar sensations again. In short, ephemerality is what makes the spectacular truly spectacular. By contrast, the melancholic pole is a reminder that scotopia cannot help but comprise certain undesirable sensations. This occurs when the feelings and emotions associated with the scotopic experience become too intense and result in the scotopia reaching the end of its life (Bingham, 2019). This is not to suggest that the melancholic pole prevents good feelings and sensations from ever being rekindled. In time memory and nostalgia revive certain smells, feelings, tastes and sounds and so, like red-hot embers, they retain an unextinguishable enchantment.

The fifth and final principle is that each system of scotopia is intersensory and cross-communicative. What this means is that senses are not often stimulated by individual modalities or experienced in isolation. In reality, as Mohan Matthen (2015) argues, senses are either in tension or they work together and augment one another. This is something Fiona Macpherson (2011) reminds us, that senses often interact in ways we might not have predicated.

To summarise the ideas presented so far in this section, what is significant about experiencing scotopia is that it encourages people with critical minds to think about their immediate reaction to stimuli. These are moments where people not only sense new things but are also likely to feel flooded by new sensory information. In other words, there is more to scotopia than the idea of dark space, or that it is about leading readers through unfamiliar environments. Unpacking experiences of scotopia is about developing reciprocity with the world around us and challenging the idea that there is ever a sensory experience that is passive or inert. With these ideas in mind, what follows in the remainder of this chapter is an insight into a leisure world where the noises, smells and textures of the ignored rhythm of the natural underground can be found, a world where imagination prospers and different possibilities are realised.

Before I can continue, however, I wish to address why the gustatory system is conspicuously absent in this chapter. By no means do I mean to imply it is not an important component of scotopia, because it certainly can be. I have for example explored its significance vis-à-vis a trip to the Paris catacombs (see Bingham, 2019). However, its role in this chapter would be extremely limited since nothing in Lancaster Hole excited my taste enough to give me anything serious to discuss. I will simply point out at this juncture, therefore, that a scotopic experience does not necessarily have to comprise the provocation of all our senses together – one or two will suffice.

Systems of Scotopia

Everybody will have had moments when the visual cortex is unable to carry out its normal role, when the primary cortical region of the brain cannot receive, integrate and process visual information being transferred from our eyes. This could be when we turn out the light before going to bed, when we wake up cocooned in a sleeping bag unsure where to find the zip, when we walk down an unlit path or when we enter a basement to fix a tripped circuit breaker. We know what happens next. Our brains and senses become hypersensitive to all sorts of stimuli, both internal and external, as our attention shifts to the power and richness of the other senses. There are several scholars who have pointed out that hallucinations occur as sight deteriorates, but we are reminded that this is merely the human mind struggling for form, meaning and concepts that help us imagine, understand and create (Sacks, 2020). In other words, this is the first step before we become what the famous theologian John Hull (1990) has described as a 'whole-body seer'. This is something Hull investigated following the deterioration of his own sight to the point of blindness, the idea of shifting his centre of gravity to other senses and being able to accord his attention to a whole new landscape. Take his discussion of rain as a starting point, for what he writes in his experience of deep blindness is that:

> [it] has a way of bringing out the contours of everything; it throws a coloured blanket over previously invisible things; instead of an intermittent and thus fragmented world, the steadily falling rain creates continuity of acoustic experience ... presents the fullness of an entire situation all at once, gives a sense of perspective and of the actual relationships of one part of the world to another.
>
> (1990: 26)

Following Hull's mention of the acoustic experience as a point of departure, we can now move to consider how the natural underground sharpens our other bodily senses. What happens is that a different kind of intimacy with the subterranean world is found and felt, one paired with an intensity of being-in-the-world that happens to be superior to anything known through sight. Blindness, therefore, reveals an entirely new order, an alternative mode of human being that reshapes us both intellectually and imaginatively.

The Auditory System

Mcnally joined me on the balcony just as I began clipping into the rope. I spoke to him briefly before checking my gear one last time, then I leaned backwards over

72 The Poetics of Caving

the ledge. An all-too-familiar feeling of disconcertment joined me as I waited for the Stop to take my full body weight. When it took, I looked down from my precarious position hoping I might see the bottom. Naturally, I couldn't. My headtorch barely did anything to stir the dark abyss lurking beneath me. Instead, the shaft yawned with mysterious silence and sounds yet to be made intelligible. Focusing back on my gear, I reversed my tying off of the descender and then eased some tension onto the handle of the device to begin lowering myself past the balcony lip. I did this until I was suspended in mid-air over the main shaft.

Adding more tension to the descender's handle, I started to slide down the rope at a steady rate. The rope hummed gently as I gained speed. The abyss below was still pitch black, so I began to look to my left and right to gain some sense of my surroundings. This was the moment my headtorch began to flicker and it suddenly dawned on me that I'd not replaced the battery from the previous day. This explained why the cave up until this point had been so damn dark. I continued to descend, hoping to reach the bottom before my torch died completely. At this point, I started to notice the sound of the rope a little more. I also became aware of something flapping noisily above me. I was certain a winged creature was nearby, but my light was so dim I only had shadows and a beating sound to help me fathom whether it was real or not. I was only able to ponder these sounds for a moment or two more. Before I could get too philosophical, my light switched off.

Other than the faint pinprick of Mcnally's headtorch far above me, I was plunged into complete darkness. All of a sudden, I was aware of feeling very alone. I felt near to the rock, but I was unsure how close it actually was. I could certainly smell it, its dampness. I could also hear water gushing somewhere on my left-hand side, but in reality I no longer had any perception of space whatsoever. My legs jolted involuntarily when my body realised I was suspended in mid-air with no clue as to my distance from the walls or floor. Then my mind caught up, and battling a transitory moment of terror I strained to listen for something that would give me some inkling of spatial awareness. For a moment there was utter silence, but the longer I listened the more the silence took on a new form.

The rope below me thwacked against the wall, presumably because of me having kicked it with my jolt. This motion filled the shaft with the echoes of the sharp snap. The sound of water suddenly seemed stronger now, almost as if it should have been touchable, but I noticed I wasn't getting wet. Beyond the odd drip, I remained completely dry. I rested in my harness for a moment, beginning to feel comforted that the silence I had entered was alive with sounds of the natural underground. After a while my confidence grew, and the fear began to subside. I released the tension on my descender once again to drop smoothly through the blackness. As I gathered speed, I began to feel as though I was dropping in free fall. Imagined walls were whooshing past and the roar of wind joined me. What sounds and what a sensation! I began to brake when I sensed the noises around me change. I couldn't see the floor, but I felt it arriving rapidly as the echoes I was

The Poetics of Caving   73

causing changed subtly. I landed with a clatter onto a bed of stones in a shallow streambed, welcomed by a sense of now knowing where the ground lay.

It is Marshall McLuhan (2005) who has argued that auditory space has traditionally been viewed as something that is contained in nothing and, equally, contains nothing. This point follows the suggestion that sound can be regarded as being totally invisible. Consequently, for some people, especially those who are comfortable remaining visually orientated, it can be perceived as something that is unintelligible and therefore difficult, if not impossible, to comprehend. However, as McLuhan (2005) reminds us, no architect can risk being ignorant of the auditory system because noise is an essential part of participational experience, especially in an increasingly fluid world that has increasingly fewer margins and a growing number of centres. According to McLuhan, teenagers were among the first to resolve the problem of the organisation of space by print and digital media culture as they adapted to create private auditory spaces that work well to disrupt visual surroundings. As he indicates, music and radio are prime examples of interpenetrative things that have altered perceptions and awareness of space. They not only allow individuals to embrace the act of hearing in a visually dominated world, but they also encourage people to appreciate how sound can change the everyday world and inspire different thinking.

The above points notwithstanding, it is important to consider the idea that sound has had something of a turbulent past since it has been considered by many people to be more of a disturbance rather than something that provokes imagination or enjoyment. As Michael Bull and Les Back (2020) remind us, sensitivity to sound has long been dictated by cultural norms and class-based influences. What this means, particularly in cultures that favour 'private' space, is that the production of noise has often been deemed uncivilised and a nuisance. From the likes of Charles Dickens who petitioned against street musicians for disturbing the flow of his thoughts to the planners of the English countryside David Matless (2016) is concerned with who condemned the sounds of cars and working-class invaders, intolerance to auditory stimuli has been widespread. On this point, scholars have long depicted the urban spaces of our cities and towns as places of overstimulation and commotion, particularly in the twenty-first century where technology has turned the volume up even further with public smartphone use, powerful sound systems and uninterrupted internet streaming (Olds and Schwartz, 2009; McLuhan, 1994). Nevertheless, this is merely one way of viewing sound.

To return to the idea of paying attention to auditive experience, when it becomes the dominant sense in places such as the natural underground what is important is that it enables people to experience things a little differently. The first thing that changes, according to Bull (2016), is that sound appears in a more transitory sense, as opposed to vision which imposes order by fixing objects in their place. To elaborate on this idea, if the reader were to stand at the base of a cliff in broad daylight, the cliff would become a fixed object with its various cracks, arêtes, crimps, slopers and chalk marks. By contrast, when I reached the bottom of Lancaster Hole and glanced around the chamber I could see nothing visually, certainly no definitive features, and so I was instead relying heavily on my hearing to make sense of my surroundings. Unlike sight which offers a singular perspective, the sounds all around me, from the noise of the rope thwacking against the rock to the sound of water gushing somewhere on my left-hand side, produced a space temporarily permeated by plurality.

The work of Georg Simmel (1997) can be used to explain the above idea further for he argues that anything auditory can be perceived as being simultaneously egotistical and democratic. What Simmel means by this is that our ears tend to greedily draw everything within their vicinity into them, as mine did from the very moment I began my descent into Lancaster Hole. However, our ears also have no control or choice over what is taken in, a lack of discrimination in other words, which means 'hearing is by its very nature supra individual' (Simmel, 1997: 116). It also means the auditory system transmits a wide variety of individual moods and feelings and the momentary flow and expression of impulses and thoughts. In short, hearing is more erratic and unpredictable than sight and, as Simmel reminds us, temporally limited to the moment. On this point, I have no doubt that when Mayhem and Mcnally descended after me they tuned into a range of newly emerging sounds, or that they perceived similar ones I had heard in different ways. As an example, with it being his first major descent Mcnally had been panicking the entire time he was lowering himself, so his attention was focused on the unfamiliar sounds of the metalwork and the creaking of his harness rather than the space around him. My attention, on the other hand, had been attuned to the imperceptibility of darkness as I attempted to break in and uncover everything it was hiding.

Another thing I noticed while I was being guided by the auditory system is the despatialisation of the area around me. Had I been abseiling off a cliff on the surface, my vision would have given me good awareness of space since vision is a robustly spatial perceptual modality (Huntmacher, 2019). That is to say, vision enables us to become aware of things that are independent of ourselves. Hearing, however, might be described as aspatial for it cannot tell us for certain anything about volume, depth or distance. Instead, it becomes the responsibility of our imaginations to perceive space auditorily. As Paul Noordhof (2018) explains, this can be achieved through a combination of 'active sensuous imagining' (a mental image informed by sensuous content) and 'suppositional imagining' (an entirely imaginative projection or product).

There are some scholars, of course, such as Michael Bull (2016) and Casey O'Callaghan (2010), who have suggested that the above way of thinking is too simplistic since it overlooks the argument that sound can be a medium for spatial centredness through the reconstruction of narrative and place. There is also the debate, as found in the work of Matthen (2015), that while hearing may be more prone to error than vision, we can discern some sense of direction and the knowledge sounds are being experienced in the same shared environment as ourselves. Underpinning the arguments presented by Bull (2016), O'Callaghan

(2010) and Matthen (2015), then, is the important warning that suggestions about despatialisation are all-too-often reliant on abstract analyses rather than empirical knowledge or experience. The point raised is an essential one, and certainly in the surface world links can be established between cues and perceptual mechanisms that arrange spatial sounds in a particular location, direction or even at a certain distance. If a knock is heard at my front door for example, or if I hear student footsteps approaching my office, I have a good idea where the sound is coming from based on empirical knowledge.

Nevertheless, what the above perspectives overlook is the earlier point I raised about the striking effect audition has on the imagination, especially in natural underground spaces that do not conform to the same order or logic as spaces created by human beings. As Barbara Hurd (2003) points out, in spaces where the mind lacks normal stimuli, it eventually begins to compensate by creating sensuously informed sounds and images where they might be or where there are none. One of the key consequences of the mind being left to fill in blanks is that it easily becomes confused which means it becomes difficult to gauge what is real and what is not (Hurd, 2003). What happens next, therefore, is that visual and auditory illusions transpire. These are slightly altered states of consciousness that provide feelings of great expansiveness, waves of deep tranquillity, and intensified feelings and emotions that are difficult to find anywhere else (Hurd, 2003).

As I made my descent down Lancaster Hole, I relied largely on my auditory system to make sense of the surrounding space. With my light flickering, I slowed the speed of my abseil and started to notice an intensification of sound. It began with the steady hum of the rope moving through my Stop, before shifting to the sound of falling water somewhere nearby. Something above my head flapped, perhaps a bat, or so I thought at the time, and the space around me seemed to grow larger. When my light went out completely, in the total absence of light I lost all sense of spatiality, all awareness of my depth and the true size of the Lancaster Hole. In my imagination, the cave could have extended for miles because the sounds seemed to be everywhere I was not, sounds that were audible but always beyond my reach and perception. Any sense I had of my position, of my place in the cave, was suddenly invented and so I chose to embrace it until I could change the batteries in my headtorch. This continued for a while, me listening to sounds I could not be certain were even real, until my legs made an abrupt connection with the ground. At this point, I melted back into the cave and some sense of spatiality swiftly returned.

Before I move on to discuss the next system of scotopia, it is important to include a warning about my focus being centred entirely around the imagination in this section. I am conscious that encouraging a retreat into the mind may prevent a reader from thinking about locations outside the imagination. In other words, I want to point out that I am aware the auditory system can be spatial, and perhaps ordinarily it is, but in my isolated experience of Lancaster Hole this is not something that occurred.

The Olfactory System

Although smell is incredibly useful to human beings as it compliments other senses, provides warning against danger and contamination and can cause aphrodisiac effects, twenty-first-century individuals are generally eager to remove or eliminate anything that might be deemed a bad or unfamiliar odour. As Zygmunt Bauman (1993) reminds us, smells have become something that should be closely monitored and managed in present modernity. This is a point Richard Kearney (2021) explores and what he argues is that smells change according to cultural and social circumstances and therefore can take on new connotations over time. What this means, as Kearney explains, is that it is important to be mindful of the cultural and social conditioning of the nose because it is responsible for eliciting our emotional responses to smells which in turn contribute to our interpretations of the world around us. With this in mind, because the olfactory system is so closely controlled and monitored in the twenty-first century it has arguably become the least intimate and intense of all the sensory systems which in turn means it is likely to be regarded as the least important sense (Spence, 2015).

Regardless of any negative connotations associated with smell in present modernity, there is still something special about it that is at risk of being overlooked. As Douglas Porteous (2006) argues, unlike vision and sound, it can be described as an emotional, arousing sense that involves increased cognition (ibid). This is a point Alastair Bonnett (2016) has unpacked, the idea that poignant smells can act like powerful cataracts and stimulate deeply meaningful emotions and memories. The smell of a favourite meal may carry a person back to their childhood and their mother's cooking for example, or bibliosmia (the smell of a good book) may remind us of the times we have enjoyed a good novel in a quiet library or a favourite armchair. Our own homes are another useful example for each one has its own smell that is immediately recognisable to a visitor and apparent to us after having been away for a lengthy period of time. Of course, the intensity of smells quickly declines after a period of extended exposure as people become habituated to them, but once they are revived they quickly regain their power (Porteous, 2006). It is primarily this revival I am interested in and part of my argument in this chapter is that the (re)stimulation of memory and nostalgia is integral to the scotopic experience of the natural underground. With this in mind, our attention will now return to the narrative episode running through this chapter and the three discrete poles that were mentioned earlier – the mundane, the spectacular and the melancholic.

Before I continue, however, one more key point needs to be made. It should be noted that all of our sensory systems are capable of stimulating memories and nostalgia but olfaction has been chosen to unpack these ideas because it appears to have the closest relationship to sentimental longing and wistful affection than any other sense (Henshaw, 2014; Arshamian et al., 2013). As Dove describes it, '[smell is] the pathway to the memory of a person' (2008: 17).

—

After congregating at the bottom of Lancaster Hole, we followed an obvious path westward towards a short climb. This led to a large passage with a narrow groove running the entire length of the floor until we reached a hole we had to carefully avoid. Just ahead was a slope of boulders that dropped away from us and opened out into a huge chamber known as Bridge Hall. Following boot imprints in the mud, we slowly made our way to the bottom of the hall, passing under a gigantic natural bridge of rock spanning the length of the chamber from one side to the other.

As I waited for the others to carefully negotiate a steep section of the boulder slope, I paused for a moment. Although I had never visited it before, the smell of Bridge Hall was familiar. Like an abandoned building that has a recognisable musty smell to it, the natural underground also has a recurring scent, especially when mud is present. It is rich and earthy, a moist smell that seems to linger pleasantly in the nostrils. It immediately reminded me of the cave we had entered some months earlier via the Victorian culvert, alive with a fresh, subtly salty aroma. I breathed in deeply, filling my lungs with the smell of every muddy cave I had ever entered. I seemed to gain a powerful sense of familiarity and nostalgia as the smell alone was enough to transport me back to the moment we had first discovered the natural underground. There was something strangely comforting about the feeling.

The smell of mud didn't last for long. It was broken the moment I began to make my way down the slope because another smell erupted. It was that of sweat, mixed with the general unwashed stench of an unwashed oversuit. Although there was a hint of vinegariness to it, I can't say it was bad because it too evoked good memories. Bizarrely, the odour made me feel more at ease with the space around me, so much so it began to seem more welcoming and comfortable. I may have been in the presence of danger and the unknown, but I felt strangely reassured and comforted by the idea I was on safe, recognisable ground. Realising I had stopped once again having been distracted by my olfactory system, I continued with my descent until I reached a spot where Mcnally and Mayhem had dropped their tackle bags (Figure 4.2).

Following a narrow rift in the left-hand wall from Bridge Hall after taking a short break, we walked for a short distance until we were forced to proceed on hands and knees through a section filled with what Eyre and Ashmead have described as a 'syrupy mixture of mud and water' (1967: 70). I can confirm that little has changed since the 1960s. The mud is still there, and it is just as sticky. In fact, I would go so far as to suggest that Arthur Gemmell and Jack Myers' 1952 description of the same passage remains accurate – it was exactly how I would imagine 'a Flanders dugout in November' (1952: 89). Part of the way through the passage, we encountered a section requiring a flat-out crawl to pass beneath a block of rock obstructing our path. From the back, I could hear groans up ahead. As Mayhem's boots disappeared from view, I prepared myself for the inevitability that I would soon be dragging myself through the veritable quagmire.

In the end, the flat-out crawl wasn't as bad as I'd imagined. In truth, it was enjoyable, and it dawned on me that the groans I'd heard from the others weren't of frustration or distress. They were instead of the oxymoronic kind, alive with the anticipation of excitement. As we congregated at a small pitch we would

Figure 4.2 Mayhem consulting the maps while we rest.

need to negotiate as our next obstacle, a shared feeling of ecstasy stirrer. So much mud was smeared across Mayhem's face, the three of us burst into a fit of uncontrollable laughter. When we eventually calmed ourselves, Mayhem breathed in deeply and began to speak:

> Gonna sound weird saying this, but that's the shit right there. Mmm. That's a powerful aroma that like, proper earthy n' that. I like it. I dunno about yous [sic], but that smell gets me excited every time. Like the mud. You get me? Do yous both get the same?

Mcnally and I both nodded in agreement. He was absolutely right. The strange smells erupting from my beard were oddly electrifying as the mud mingled satisfyingly with sweat and traces of beard oil. What I liked especially, just like Mayhem, was the modest aroma of earth at the centre of everything. Somehow it smelt earthier, saltier and richer than earth would normally smell. In a word, it was nothing short of spectacular.

The smell of the cave changed once again as we negotiated our way into a larger, cavernous space. I wouldn't have thought it was possible as we'd been crawling through the mud, but it smelt even more strongly of earth in this chamber. A sense of exhilaration grew as we spotted enormous blocks of limestone scattered around the floor of the cavern. The blocks had clearly fallen from the ceiling as there were recesses directly above us of similar size and shape. We walked around the largest of the slabs and soon found ourselves in a large space decorated with brown stalagmites. The floor was soft and loamy in here, dark enough to absorb all the light from our three headtorches. This made it difficult to gain any sense of the shape and size of the chamber. What we did notice, however, is that each stalagmite formation adorned a white top which gave us a good indication that they were still growing. The reason for the name of the series (the Graveyard Series) was now clear in any case as the scene was not unlike an ancient burial site with crude headstones reminiscent of those that might be found in the Kela Mazin cemetery in Kurdistan (Figure 4.3).

As we gazed at the stalagmites, we became increasingly aware of the presence of water. There was a change to the previously muddy aroma. Following our noses to the source, we reached a muddy ditch with a stream running through

Figure 4.3 Stalagmites and stalactites inside the Graveyard Series.

it. Jumping down into the gully, we followed Mayhem as he began to trace the water upstream into a passage. We proceeded with the passage gradually becoming lower and narrower, until we were forced to our hands and knees. We continued for a short while longer until the route ahead finally became impassable. By this point, the smell of mud had become almost absent as the water had washed most of it away. The new aroma which was fresh and wet stirred something in all three of us. We began to fear that the tiny space we occupied might flood at any second and this made us feel uneasy. Mayhem then reminded us that he'd read something about the Graveyard Series being prone to flooding during periods of wet weather as water can enter the system from avens in the roof of the series. Spurred by the sudden olfactory reminder of water and our short conversation, our imaginations went wild. A surge of adrenaline kicked in next, caused by our instinctive feelings of trepidation, and it was at this point we decide to scramble back to the safety of the main chamber as quickly as possible.

Back in the main chamber of Graveyard, we crossed a natural bridge to reach a steep mud bank. We skirted around this, dodging a cluster of taped-off stalagmites to reach a low crawl in the far corner. Inside the crawl, we passed several more stalagmites growing tall on a mud floor that had dried in such a way it looked as though somebody had attempted to lay down crazing paving slabs. Beyond this, we reached a boulder choke but found ourselves able to worm our way down through several levels to reach a tight rift. Mayhem led from here, slowly squeezing his way through the incredibly narrow passageway. After a few minutes of trying to keep up, Mcnally and I gave up. We'd reached a section that would involve dragging our bodies sideways through a narrow 'V'-shaped crack at the base of the passageway as this was now the widest point of the rift. Reluctant to move any further for fear of becoming stuck, we decided to leave Mayhem to the reconnaissance.

Lying flat out in the mud, we soon began to cool down. Since we were damp with sweat and water from the streamway, we began to feel chilly to the point of discomfort. We started to become aware of odours once again as well. This time, though, they'd become foul. Consequently, the natural underground no longer seemed to incite feelings of homeliness, and any nostalgia we'd felt previously was rapidly waning. What had once been a pleasant aroma of mud mixed with the tang of bodies being worked was now becoming something cold, unpleasant and dirty. In close proximity to one another, I started to notice that Mcnally smelt a little ammonia-like, probably because of stale urine (he'd struggled to relieve his bladder before entering the cave and had ended up with some of the contents dribbling down the inside of his oversuit). Mixed with a sour alcoholic stench from the beers he'd drank the night before, the air around us seemed less natural now. It was stained by a livelier odour of human grease and mustiness. Suffused in each other's odours, the pair of us shifted uncomfortably and eventually grew frustrated that Mayhem was taking so long. By now we were ready to surface. Our stench was becoming too intense and we were rapidly descending into an obvious state of melancholy.

—

The Poetics of Caving 81

In my experience of caving, the olfactory component of scotopic experience typically begins with smells that are commonplace and mundane. What I mean by this is that a variety of familiar smells associated with and of the natural underground have the potential to be relived each time it is visited. As Blackshaw (2003) puts it, these are the great 'truths' that accompany all leisure worlds.

To elaborate further on this idea, often when we first enter a cave the available space is imbued with the satisfying smell of dampness. This is not the damp smell of students who are yet to master how to dry their clothes properly or an abandoned building type of damp, this is a refreshing and reinvigorating type of damp. Cool air races through the nostrils, moist and virtually odourless, and it carries with it a feeling similar to the one you get when you breathe in menthol or mint. To be clear, I am not referring to the smells of menthol or mint in a literal sense here, I am merely likening the feel of these things to that same pleasant cooling effect you catch when you smell the cold on a winter's day. Scholars such as Thomas Hummel and Andrew Livermore (2002) have referred to this as trigeminal perception which forms part of the integrated experience of an odour and includes sensations of touch, pressure and pain. According to Hummel and Livermore (2002), trigeminal perception involves the stimulation of the trigeminal nerve which in turn is responsible for sneezes when we smell pepper or tears when we chop onions.

The ordinary smell of a cave changes the moment you find mud. A rich, subtly salty but fresh aroma arrives, one that might better be described as a form of petrichor (the scent of the air following rainfall). Using two Greek terms *petra* (stone) and *ichor* (blood of the gods), it was Isabel Bear and Roderick Thomas (1964) who originally coined this term. They went on to suggest that the smell of petrichor is trapped oil in soil and rocks in dry places, an oil secreted by plants to prevent seeds from germinating, or geosmin in moist areas which is a chemical produced by a soil-dwelling bacteria. Neither the oil nor bacteria are really of any concern to me here since I have little interest in the chemicals they produce. What interests me instead is how the smell of mud inside the natural underground speaks a special language. It speaks to me of petrichor, but also of familiarity and comfort, a revival of memories of other muddy caves I have explored which includes the first one we ever entered inside the Victorian culvert. Interestingly, the memories of the mundane smells of caves never fade. In fact, they seem to last much longer than memories of sounds or sights, and they always emerge more vividly for the very reason that they are charged with recollection and meaning.

The mundanity of the olfactory system does not end with the usual smells of the natural underground, it continues over the course of a trip. The odours emanating from our oversuits and gloves for example are another source of familiarity that pinch our nostrils when we are underground, especially if they have not been properly hosed down after a previous trip. As I described above, for me an all-too-familiar vinegary odour rises from deep within my suit. Every movement seems to stir it loose. Curiously, though, it is not unpleasant. What it evokes instead is a strange sense of warmness and familiarity, a reminder that the body is being worked hard which is itself always a good feeling. In many ways, there is something reminiscent of childhood in the smell for it is not unlike one of those odours children either tolerate or find perfectly normal. As Porteous (2006) reminds us, children are generally more accepting of basic body smells such as excrement and sweat, until they adapt to various social and cultural norms at least. To be a caver, then, is to regain this childlike tolerance by pushing aside all social and cultural conditioning. Indeed, even around Mcnally and Mayhem who were both wearing unwashed 'boil-in-the-bag' suits (unbreathable PVC overalls), I was unaffected by their aroma in an unpleasant way. It was, rather, something I took to be a welcoming part of the natural underground. Even now as I write, I reflect fondly on this smell and the good memories it restores.

In addition to the mundane, there is also what Blackshaw (2003) refers to as the spectacular. That is to say, as the scotopia really gets underway, the olfactory system produces additional spectacular feelings and emotions. To borrow Alain Corbin's way of putting it, 'like voyeurism, some olfactory behaviour patterns permit a new conduct of the rhythms of desire' (1986: 207). These are feelings and emotions that are more profound because 'they are capable of resurrecting past memories and ontological feelings that elicit greater nostalgic power' (Bingham, 2019: 16). In other words, these are the kind of smells that are intoxicatingly nostalgic. To unpack this point further, I encourage the reader to think about the episode above once again.

As Mcnally, Mayhem and I entered the Graveyard Series for the first time, almost immediately the rich odour of mud coalesced with our growing excitement and increasing sense of anticipation. Following a narrow rift from Bridge Hall, we quickly found ourselves proceeding on all fours through soft, syrupy earth. It was thick and stuck to anything that made the slightest contact. At one point, as I mentioned above, it even managed to get into my beard where it quickly developed into a powerful, earthy aroma mixed with the remnants of my rum-scented beard oil. The scent came in waves, surging through my nostrils briefly before disappearing again. Each time it returned it seemed more earthy than the last, more natural and more invigorating. Strangely, this excited me as the rules and smells of the everyday were immediately cast aside. This allowed new rules and smells to become acceptable. As Mcnally pointed out in the immediacy of the event, he 'love[ed] the smell of mud on [his own] clothes and hair' since it reminds him of the necessary dirt of adventure. Mayhem also spoke fondly of the mud, particularly when we'd exited the cave. To borrow his exact words, he suggested that 'adventure without dirt isn't adventure at all ... the feel and smell of dirt's the coal or wood, that spicy bit of adventure you need to keep the fire burning'. In short, then, it was the smell of mud clinging to us that reminded us of its significance for it is (at least for us) part of the magic of experiences that are daring or unusual.

The spectacularity of the experience did not end with us getting mud in our beards, it escalated as we ventured further into the Graveyard Series. For example, when we negotiated a set of boulders and the smell became waterier, our fear began to intensify. It was the vividness of our memory that was responsible, stirred by the mysteriously indescribable smell of the water. The subtle change in smell reminded us that water often enters the Graveyard Series in periods of wet weather which in turn gave us vivid images of water pouring down from the avens directly above us. Despite the fact that pure water has frequently been described as being odourless since the time of Aristotle (2018), the noticeable change in the smell of the air reminded us of other stream caves we had entered and those intense feelings of trepidation that follow when you know the space might flood unexpectedly at any moment. By no means do I mean to suggest that any of us wanted to be caught in a potentially lethal situation, but the olfactory reminder that it could happen was so hair-raising it was utterly sensational. It was, in a word, spectacular.

The final pole to be discussed is the melancholic. This is the suggestion that any scotopic experience cannot help but encompass certain undesirable elements, or elements that gradually become undesirable. With this in mind, I would argue that a Freudian assessment is needed at this point to draw out the idea that Eros (the pleasure instinct) and Thanatos (the death instinct) are in a constant struggle against one another in the natural underground. As Freud (1963/2008) argues, the latter of the two naturally seeks to destroy the former and this is perhaps achieved when the intensity of odour in a cave becomes too intense. What happens next is that the mundane smells of the scotopia begin to break down to the point that they are abhorred. To put it another way, smells in the natural underground can reach a point where the novelty or the magic they once created wears thin. When this occurs, melancholia takes over which, according to Freud (1963/2008), is governed 'silently' and 'elusively' by the Nirvana principle (a forceful yearning for a state of oblivion). This compulsion signals that the end of scotopia is in sight and with it comes a peculiar, almost inexplicable urge to end it for good.

To elaborate further, it was as we worked our way deeper into the Graveyard Series that I became aware the scotopia was wavering. After worming our way through a series of tight crawls, we found ourselves wedged in a tight rift. Here, Mcnally and I decided to wait while Mayhem, the skinniest of the group, scouted out the route ahead and it was while we were resting that our moods began to sink. Mcnally pointed out that he was cold first, and then began to complain that he also 'stank like shit'. Still recovering from a few too many pints the night before, he was now suffering from 'beer farts'. Whenever one was released, it would linger for several minutes or so inside his PVC suit. He joked that we should not risk lighting a match, but he was probably right since one of them was so egregious it made him gag. Like Mcnally, my mood was starting to shift. Mixed with the stench of Mcnally, I was beginning to feel the adverse effects of being caked in mud and wearing an unwashed oversuit after sweating from exertion. The same smell of body odour I mentioned earlier no longer seemed to stir pleasant memories. Instead, it made me feel irritable and keen to retreat to the surface. By the time Mayhem returned, Mcnally and I were completely silent.

84 The Poetics of Caving

Without a single word being uttered, we doubled back and started crawling in the direction of Bridge Hall.

Although it would appear that the melancholic pole is the inevitable destroyer of scotopia, there is more to be said because what has not been discussed yet is the dialectical interplay that occurs between the Eros and Thanatos. What happens, as Andrew Cutrofello argues, is that the constant battle between the two life instincts typically culminates in '[Eros] somehow bind[ing] Thanatos to its own ends' (2005: 129), which means it appeals to our desire to reproduce and recreate. In other words, in due course, whether it is a few hours, days or weeks after scotopia comes crashing to an abrupt end, the loss of its familiar smells can cause strange pangs of nostalgia, especially when those smells happen to be rediscovered. What happens is that the smells are revitalised and transformed into something that seems familiar and desirable once again. In the end, the melancholic pole makes us realise that beyond the unsatisfactoriness of the everyday world, there is a sense of place that has its own fantastical odours that cannot be experienced in the same way anywhere else.

The Tactile System

Another sense that was stirred during the scotopic experience of the natural underground was touch. Before I go on to unpack it further, however, it is important to note that the tactile system is different to the other systems that have been discussed so far. While it is classified as one of the five traditional senses, it is unique since touch does not have a single sense organ (Todd, 2014). This is not to suggest that our other senses cannot partner themselves with more than one sense organ (in scotopia they often do), it is to point out that ordinarily they can be active independently via a single medium. Touch on the other hand relies on the skin as its primary sense organ, but, as Todd (2014) points out, the skin itself is in fact not sensory. Rather, the skin contains a multiplicity of sensory systems that can cause a wide range of feelings from pains, tingles and itches to more complex sensations such as pressure and vibration.

Indeed, great philosophers have long recognised that the tactile system is something special. If we turn to Aristotle for example, in particular his major work *De Anima* (On the Soul), what he argues is that tactility is the most universal and intelligent of all the senses. By this he means our bodies are at the same time sensitive and always on, making them permanently susceptible to things such as movement, noise, temperature and pressure. As Aristotle (1941) declares, wisdom is first attained through touch, mediated directly by the flesh and can be thought of as a reading of the world that allows us to make distinctions and register differences. In other words, for Aristotle (1941) to touch well is to live well for it is the essential link between the human and non-human, self and other, and indeed inside and outside.

Nevertheless, as it was mentioned earlier in the chapter, vision has typically been viewed as the superior sensory system and myriad scholars have encouraged people to view all of our other senses as inferior. On this point, although Aristotle was one of the first scholars to draw attention to the importance of touch, his ideas have generally been side-lined for the past 2,000 years by those of Plato who was an early advocate for sight. According to Plato, 'vision ... is the cause of the greatest benefit to us, inasmuch as none of the accounts now given concerning the Universe would ever have been given if men had not seen the stars or the sun or the heaven' (1925: 47a). It is this view that has been widely adopted and accepted across the Western world. Indeed, Richard Kearney (2021) reiterates this point in his argument that Western philosophy has in the main been characterised as optocentric (sight-centred) which consigned all other senses, particularly touch, to the lower realms of perception.

It was the development of existential phenomenology that revived the original Aristotelian appreciation for tactility. As Kearney (2021) reminds us, phenomenology is about viewing 'truth' as something that is present in everyday reality and in lived experience. However, to realise these 'truths', individuals must come to their senses and not only learn to reflect on primary carnal experiences which evoke sensations, emotions and moods but also suspend, if only temporarily, ingrained prejudices. Inspired by the revolutionary effort of key phenomenologists such as Martin Heidegger, Jean-Paul Sartre and especially Merleau-Ponty who explicitly focused on the phenomenon of touch, the remainder of this chapter goes some way towards unpacking the significance of the tactile system and its role in the scotopic experience. With this in mind, I begin with Merleau-Ponty's observation that 'touch is formed in the midst of the world and as it were in the things' (1968: 134). In other words, neither I nor the world around me completely determines my experience of touch independently because it occurs reciprocally by means of a mutual relationship between my own body and flesh and the body and flesh of the world around me. I will go on to explore this point shortly, but before I do I invite the reader to consider another short episode.

—

After growing cold waiting for Mayhem, we decided it was time to resurface when he returned. As well as being low on motivation and strength at this point, we remembered that we had to be back out in good time to avoid my wife sending a callout to Cave Rescue. So, retracing our steps, we left the remainder of the Graveyard Series for another time.

The crawl on the return journey was more arduous, and I began to notice that my body was starting to feel bruised and battered from the strain of dragging myself over rock. Similarly, Mayhem and Mcnally were becoming aware of how painful their knees felt as the hard ground was unrelenting in the way it poked and prodded their unprotected flesh. The same thing was happening to my knees. The cave floor felt hard against my kneecaps and the growing pressure in my joints was so great both knees were beginning to feel weak. Each movement seemed worse than the last, but we pressed on desperately trying to find a space big enough to stand up, even just a little bit.

The sounds of our puffing and grunting filled the passage. Even though it only contained basic medical supplies, food and water, our tackle bag had grown heavy now and each haul seemed to sap our energy to the point of exhaustion. Our bodies felt cumbersome now due to the persistent exertion, yet we continued to force ourselves forward until the passage eventually grew in size, enough that we could walk upright again. Mayhem's knees, which were still on the mend from an injury he'd sustained climbing, clicked audibly as he stood and this made him groan. Grimacing, he turned to face me and Mcnally to point out that 'he'd neva even thought about wearing knee pads, since you don't think of shit like that when you see snaps of Lancaster on Insta or YouTube'. He limped forward, searching for a suitable place to sit and rest. Mcnally paused for a moment with a look of contemplation on his face, then responded:

> It's strange, like the pain n' that, coz it's bad but I kinda like it, weirdly. Do yous get wadda mean? ... I've not experienced this before, it's different. It's, like, real innit. Sounds cheesy that, don't it, but it makes you feel alive, don't it? Me knees wouldn't be feeling this way in any uvver circumstance, would they ... Yer being a fairy you, Ford, mate. Enjoy it, you'll be back to normality soon, lad.

—

It has been argued by Kearney (2021) that touch might be thought of as being a portal that is impossible to close, a connection that is at all times highly sensitive to everything foreign and not itself. However, since we have entered a world of digital culture, hyperconnectivity and hyperreality, the tactile system has been excarnated meaning twenty-first-century individuals have fallen out of touch with incarnate experience. More importantly, to borrow Kearney's point about Alice entering the rabbit hole, there is the risk of 'find[ing] a labyrinth of looking-glasses – with no way back' (2021: 125).

If the reader thinks back to the earlier discussion in Chapter 3 about the influence of technology in present modernity, we can begin to reflect further on the idea that illusion created by technology replaces lived experience. Essentially, this point follows one of Jean Baudrillard's (1983) key ideas – the argument that reality has disappeared as it has gradually been replaced by simulacra. At the heart of this suggestion is the realisation that everyday people are becoming increasingly reliant on electronic devices and digital platforms that connect them to virtual worlds but at the same time disconnect them from the real one. To borrow David and Ann Gunkel's (1997) way of putting it, as attempts are made to transcend bodily flesh by means of virtual profiles what is accomplished is a violent erasure of humanness and this comes at the price (among others) of tactile experience. To accentuate this point, it has been estimated that nearly three billion people worldwide use Facebook (Datareportal, 2022), that over two billion people are users of YouTube and that there are approximately one billion users of Instagram (Ceci, 2022; Dixon, 2022). As Kearney (2021) points out, it is platforms such as these that allow users to collaborate in the creation of exaggerated personas that serve to mask, and in some cases completely transform, the realities of our tangible selves.

The Poetics of Caving   87

Thinking about the above points helps explain Mayhem's reaction to the pain he felt in his knees as he crawled his way out of the Graveyard Series. As he pointed out, grimacing with pain as his already injured knees were poked and prodded by jagged pieces of rock, he'd 'neva even thought about wearing knee pads, since you don't think of things like that when you see snaps of Lancaster on Insta or YouTube'. In other words, what Mayhem reinforces is the idea that the virtual world cannot help but create a vicarious sense of safety precisely because it lacks the feeling and emotion that accompanies tactile experience. This is a point Baudrillard (1996) famously tried to explain in his argument that global hostilities are increasingly becoming global spectacles or 'TV Wars' that lack feeling and emotion because they are fought screen to screen rather than hand to hand as they were in the past. Ultimately, what this allows us to do as observers (those of us who are fortunate enough to live in countries that are not war-torn at least) is view images of battle action from a distance without ever touching it ourselves or ever gaining a sense of the true atmosphere of the places we see.

The question to be asked here then, based on the discussion so far, is how twenty-first-century beings get back in touch with themselves (and each other) in an era of exponential excarnation. What I want to suggest by drawing on Kearney's (2021) dynamic of the double sensation is that the natural underground is a space that enables people to reconnect with their tactile systems because it is first and foremost distanced from the digital eye that dominates our world. Nevertheless, it is important to note, and we may say seemingly paradoxically, that the tactile system is also unavoidably intertwined with the digital eye. This is the suggestion in other words that tactility in the natural underground, and the incarnate action involved, is dependent upon the dominance of digital culture and the virtual fantasies it creates. By shocking our bodies into unfamiliar feeling, the natural underground not only offers a temporary means of escape, it encourages us to think about the simulation crisis above ground. In turn, we are reminded of the importance of re-identifying and reopening spaces that allow us to inhabit the world through our tactile system.

Keeping the above discussion in mind, we can turn next to Mcnally's response to Mayhem. This was interesting because he pointed out that the pain in his own knees was bad but that he liked it since it made him feel more attuned to the world around him. As he explained, it was different to anything he had experienced before, namely because it was so real. In other words, as opposed to everyday life where it becomes easy to replace two-way sensibility – which is important because it allows us to strike a balance between our own selves and something 'Other' – for one-way sensationalism (Kearney, 2021), this offered him a very tactile way of retracing his steps from deep within Alice's rabbit hole.

There are of course many examples of two-way sensibility being replaced for one-way sensationalism in the twenty-first century, especially in contemporary literature and film. The film *Don Jon* is a prime example as it portrays a hardcore pornography addict who decides he favours virtual stimulation over the real act. Likewise, Tom Perrotta's (2017) novel, *Mrs Fletcher* explores the life of a divorcee in her mid-forties who goes through a sexual awakening of sorts as she develops a habit of watching MILF porn which sends her into a world starkly different to her real life. However, what examples such as these frequently emphasise as well, in line with Mcnally, is that bodies are not always lost to the fantastical and the make-believe because human beings are not only capable of reflexivity (Giddens, 1991), they are also able to relate to or denote sensations. Moreover, as Martin Barker (2014) points out, human beings are rarely satisfied leaving things entirely to imagination. Instead, many people (Mcnally included) are inclined to use virtual mechanisms and representations to remind themselves or become aware of the possibility of tactile experience and doing so helps them discern precisely what interests, excites and arouses them. What this signals is that the world of simulation and simulacra is absolutely essential if the tactility of places, and indeed scotopic experience itself, is to be discovered in places such as the natural underground because it prompts us to think about what is not available in our day-to-day lives.

Summary

Exploring the natural underground is as much about seeking a space of intimacy as it is entering what I have termed scotopia. While scotopic experience is of course inherently intimate, what I have attempted to show is that it corresponds to a kind of intimacy that is a little different to traditional interpretations of the same term. As I have argued, it involves the elicitation of multiple complex feelings and senses as opposed to interpersonal concerns, deeply isolated psychological hallways of the mind, or suddenly being able to notice the fine intricate details of physical space.

In short, scotopia is a state of *being-in-the-world* that involves an eruption of bodily sensation, but it can only be reached if certain preconditions are met. As I pointed out, it must occur in darkness, hence why the natural underground is at the centre of my discussion, and it is aroused specifically in spaces or places of leisure. Furthermore, scotopia involves sensual experiences that are generally at loggerheads with social and cultural norms belonging to the surface world, and it typically entails the stimulation of powerful memories and nostalgia that operate between three distinct poles – the mundane, the spectacular and the melancholic. Lastly, the very existence of scotopia relies on the close interaction of intersensory experience. That is, senses must augment or create tension between one another for a scotopic experience to be properly felt.

Essentially, what I have attempted to show is that once the basic preconditions of scotopia have been met, a person is able to become a 'whole-body seer'. This is an individual described by John Hull as being capable of shifting their centre of gravity away from sight towards other senses which reveal whole new landscapes of experience and knowledge. The intimacy of the kingdom of the dark, then, appears to lie deep within our senses, exciting and stimulating them in various ways from its muted position within the body rather than some mysteriously located soul.

Note

1 The poles known as the *mundane* and the *spectacular* were originally coined by Tony Blackshaw (2003) in his book *Leisure Life*. The *melancholic* is an additional pole I included (see Bingham, 2019), one that accounts for the less desirable aspects of memory and emotion.

References

Aristotle. (1941). De Anima. In: R. McKeon (Ed), *The Basic Works of Aristotle*. New York: Random House.

Aristotle. (2018). *On the Soul: And Other Psychological Works*. Trans. F. D. Miller. Oxford: Oxford University Press.

Arshamian, A., Iannilli, E., Gerber, J., Willander, J., Persson, J., Seo, H-S., Hummel, T. and Larsson, M. (2013). The Functional Neuroanatomy of Odor Evoked Autobiographical Memories Cued by Odors and Words. *Neuropsychologia*. 51(1): 123–131.

Bachelard, G. (1957/2014). *The Poetics of Space*. New York: Penguin.

Barker, M. (2014). The 'problem' of sexual fantasies. *Porn Studies*. 1(1–2): 143–160.

Baudrillard, J. (1983). *Simulations*. New York: Semiotext(e).

Baudrillard, J. (1996). *The Gulf War Did Not Take Place*. Bloomington: Indiana University Press.

Bauman, Z. (1993). The Sweet Scent of Decomposition. In: C. Rojek and B. Turner (Eds), *Forget Baudrillard?* London: Routledge, 22–46.

Bear, I. and Thomas, R. (1964). Nature of Argillaceous Odour. *Nature*. March 7: 993–995.

Bingham, K. (2019). The Foul and the Fragrant in Urban Exploration: Unpacking the Olfactory System of Leisure. *International Journal of the Sociology of Leisure*. 3: 15–36.

Bingham, K. (2020). Rethinking Utopia: The Search for 'topias' in the Paris Catacombs. *Leisure/Loisir*. 44(4): 521–546.

Blackshaw, T. (2003). *Leisure Life: Myth, Masculinity and Modernity*. Oxon: Routledge.

Bonnett, A. (2016). *The Geography of Nostalgia: Global and Local Perspectives on Modernity and Loss*. Oxon: Routledge.

Bull, M. (2016). Sounding Out the City: An Auditory Epistemology of Urban Experience. In: M. Bull and L. Back (Eds), *The Auditory Culture Reader*. London: Bloomsbury, 73–86.

Bull, M. and Back, L. (2020). Introduction: Into Sound… Once More with Feeling. In: M. Bull and L. Back (Eds), *The Auditory Culture Reader*. Oxon: Routledge, 1–18.

Ceci, L. (2022). YouTube – Statistics and Facts. *Statistica*. [Online]. Retrieved from: https://www.statista.com/topics/2019/youtube/

Chateaubriand, F-R. (1826/2015). *Travels in America*. Lexington: The University Press of Kentucky.

Corbin, A. (1986). *The Foul and the Fragrant: Odor and the French Social Imagination*. Leamington Spa: Berg.

Cutrofello, A. (2005). *Continental Philosophy: A Contemporary Introduction*. Oxon: Routledge.

Datareportal. (2022). Facebook Statistics and Trends. [Online]. Retrieved from: https://datareportal.com/essential-facebook-stats

Dixon, S. (2022). Instagram – Statistics and Facts. *Statistica*. [Online]. Retrieved from: https://www.statista.com/topics/1882/instagram/

Dove, R. (2008). *The Essence of Perfume*. London: Black Dog Publishing.

Eyre, J. and Ashmead, P. (1967). *Lancaster Hole and the Ease Gill Caverns, Casterton Fell, Westmorland*. Ledbury: The Cave Research Group.

Foucault, M. (1984). Of Other Spaces. Trans. J. Miskowiec. *Diacritics*. 16(1): 22–27.

Freud, S. (1963/2008). *General Psychological Theory: Papers on Metapsychology*. New York: Touchstone.

Gemmell, A. and Myers, J. (1952). *Underground Adventure*. London: Blandford Press.

Giddens, A. (1991). *Modernity and Self-Identity: Self and Society in the Late Modern Age*. Cambridge: Polity.

Gilson, E. (1963). Foreword. In: G. Bachelard (Ed), *The Poetics of Space*. Boston: Beacon Press, xi–xiv.

Gunkel, D. and Gunkel, A. (1997). Virtual Geographies: The New Worlds of Cyberspace. *Critical Studies in Mass Communication*. 14(2): 123–137.

Henshaw, V. (2014). *Urban Smellscapes: Understanding and Designing City Smell Environments*. Oxon: Routledge.

Hull, J. (1990). *Touching the Rock: An Experience of Blindness*. London: SPCK.

Hummel, T. and Livermore, A. (2002). Intranasal Chemosensory Function of the Trigeminal Nerve and Aspects of Its Relation to Olfaction. *International Archives of Occupational and Environmental Health*. 75(5): 305–313.

Huntmacher, F. (2019). Why Is There So Much More Research on Vision than on Any Other Sensory Modality? *Frontiers in Psychology*. 10: 2246.

Hurd, B. (2003). *Entering the Stone: On Caves and Feeling Through the Dark*. New York: Houghton Mifflin Company.

Irlen, H. (1991). *Reading by the Colours: Overcoming Dyslexia and Other Reading Disabilities Through the Irlen Method*. New York: Penguin.

Jamieson, L. (2011). Intimacy as a Concept: Explaining Social Change in the Context of Globalisation or Another Form of Ethnocentricism? *Sociological Research Online*. 16(4). [Online]. Retrieved from: https://www.socresonline.org.uk/16/4/15.html

Kaplan, E. (2009). *Baudelaire's Prose Poems: The Esthetic, the Ethical, and the Religious in the Parisian Prowler*. Athens: The University Georgia Press.

Kearney, R. (2021). *Touch*. New York: Columbia University Press.

Macfarlane, R. (2019). *Underland: A Deep Time Journey*. London: Hamish Hamilton.

Macpherson, F. (2011). Taxonomising the Senses. *Philosophical Studies*. 153(1): 123–142.

Matless, D. (2016). *Landscape and Englishness*. London: Reaktion Books.

Matthen, M. (2015). The Individuation of the Senses. In: M. Matthen (Ed), *The Oxford Handbook of Philosophy of Perception*. Oxford: Oxford University Press, 567–586.

McLuhan, M. (1994). *Understanding Media: The Extensions of Man*. Cambridge, MA: MIT Press.

McLuhan, M. (2005). Inside the Five Sense Sensorium. In: D. Howes (Ed), *Empire of the Senses: The Sensual Culture Reader*. London: Routledge, 43–52.

Meijenfeldt, E. (2003). To Be and Not to Be. In: E. Meijenfeldt and M. Geluk (Eds), *Below Ground Level: Creating New Spaces for Contemporary Architecture*. Berlin: Birkhäuser.

Merleau-Ponty, M. (1968). *The Visible and the Invisible*. Trans. A. Lingis. Evanston: Northwestern University Press.

Nietzsche, F. (1973/2003). *Beyond Good and Evil: Prelude to a Philosophy of the Future*. Trans. R. J. Hollingdale. London: Penguin.

Noordhof, P. (2018). Imaginative Content. In: F. Macpherson and F. Dorsch (Eds), *Perceptual Imagination & Perceptual Memory*. Oxford: Oxford University Press, 96–129.

O'Callaghan, C. (2010). Perceiving the Locations of Sounds. *Review of Philosophy and Psychology*. 1: 123–140.

Olds, J. and Schwartz, R. (2009). *The Lonely American: Drifting Apart in the Twenty-First Century*. Boston: Beacon Press.

Parsons, J. (1984). *Diseases of the Eye*. London: Churchill Livingstone.

Perrotta, T. (2017). *Mrs. Fletcher*. New York: Scribner.

Plato. (1925). *Plato in Twelve Volumes, Vol 9*. Trans. W. Lamb. London: William Heinemann.

Porteous, J. D. (2006). Smellscape. In: J. Drobnick (Ed), *The Smell Cultural Reader*. Oxford: Berg, 89–106.

Sacks, O. (2020). The Mind's Eye: What the Blind See. In: D. Howes (Ed), *Empire of the Senses: The Sensual Culture Reader*. Oxon: Routledge, 25–42.

Sexton, R. and Sexton, V. (2012). Intimacy: A Historical Perspective. In: M. Fisher and G. Stricker (Eds), *Intimacy*. London: Plenum Press, 1–20.

Simmel, G. (1997). *Simmel on Culture: Selected Writings*. Eds. D. Frisby and M. Featherstone. London: SAGE.

Smyer, I. (2013). *Relationship Within*. Bloomington: Balboa Press.

Spence, C. (2015). Just How Much of What We Taste Derives from the Sense of Smell? *Flavour*. 4(30): 1–10.

Todd, R. (2014). *Themistius: On Aristotle, on the Soul*. London: Bloomsbury.

Chapter 5

Unsilencing Fear in the Natural Underground

Introduction

When I first began writing a draft of this chapter, I brooded for a while over the idea that human beings have an innate fear of silence. It is something that grips us because, as Maurice Maeterlinck (1900) describes, it has a 'sombre power' that causes deeply rooted feelings of dread to fester. Certainly, it is possible for human beings to tolerate silences, such as the silence of isolation, but it often bears an inexplicable weight that can unsettle even the bravest and toughest of individuals (Corbin, 2018). As the famous pessimist poet Alfred de Vigny reminds us across much of his work, unhappiness speaks in silence (Bonhomme, 2003). This may explain why human beings are so keen to avoid or escape those places where silence seems to reign, places such as the natural underground which for many people is little more than an immense black void containing a profound level of danger.

After much deliberation, however, I changed my mind. What struck me is the thought that in fearing silence (together with many other things), twenty-first-century individuals have become the creators of the silencing of fear. That is to say, fear has become something to be ignored and it seems that 'liquid' modern people do the best they can to avoid it. This is not to suggest that fears have disappeared in present modernity, it is to point out that our entire lives are filled with continuous fear – perhaps more than humans have ever faced before – but also that we take all kinds of ingenious detours that help us temporarily shift our attention away from the sources of fear (Bude, 2017). Indeed, this is something Zygmunt Bauman (in Bauman and Tester, 2001) reminds us, that life in 'liquid' modernity is less about the long haul or reaching a secure destination than it is about hopping between interim stations or inns along the way. It is my concern for human ignorance, therefore, that steers the direction of this chapter.

With the above ideas in mind, this chapter begins with a section that unpacks fear in the twenty-first century and how we have ultimately entered a culture of heightened fear and fear avoidance. In the second part, I attempt to explore the suggestion that human beings should reconnect themselves, when opportunities present themselves, with sources of fear. At the risk of sounding a little too much

DOI: 10.4324/9781003301752-5

Unsilencing Fear in the Natural Underground 93

like a self-help author, what I am arguing in line with the stoic philosopher Lucius Annaeus Seneca is that instead of turning fears silent and being avoidant of them there is much to be gained if we face up to them. As Seneca (2016) argues, when ignorance of fear takes over it can be ruinous. Not only does it rob us of our ability to think clearly, but it also causes us to become self-defeating and resigned to the belief that our lives are governed by anxiety and unhappiness (ibid). It is true that fear can be useful, for in certain situations it can help us survive, but it is just as true that we can become too fearful to live fruitful lives (Altheide, 2017). What the natural underground has taught me, then, is captured well in the work of Seneca:

> It is likely that some troubles will befall us; but it is not a present fact. How often has the unexpected happened! How often has the expected never come to pass! And even though it is ordained to be, what does it avail to run out to meet your suffering? You will suffer soon enough, when it arrives; so look forward meanwhile to better things.
>
> (2016: 27)

The full significance of Seneca's point will be explored in greater detail later in the chapter. Before that, though, as I mentioned above, it is time to consider fear in the twenty-first century and how it is at the same time exasperated yet made silent.

Facing a Dialectical Dilemma: Culture of Fear and Fear Avoidance

According to Ulrich Beck (2009), threats and insecurity have always plagued humankind, especially in the past when people faced the greater danger of disease, famine and poverty. Piousness and confidence in Gods typically provided some relief of course, but as belief in religion has steadily declined the world has developed an entirely different relationship with risk (Inglehart, 2021). What this means, in a nutshell, is that human lives are no longer guided or protected by the power of deities and their overarching wisdom. A consequence of the transition into a world marked by the absence of creators of the universe and sources of all morality is that risk unfolds in more terrible and ambiguous ways.

As Beck (1992) explains, the changing nature of the world means we have begun to transition away from traditional societies into *risk societies* that are increasingly preoccupied with the future. Hence, risk in present modernity becomes a mediating issue that must ultimately be negotiated using new technologies and the judgement of scientists. The paradox of course is that the more technology and science are relied on, the more they transform the world by creating new and improved risks. As Beck (2009) reminds us, these are risks produced on the back of modernity's successes that cannot be controlled. Subsequently, a steady decline of confidence in 'expert' authority has ensued and as it has waned problems of uncertainty, insecurity and trust have begun to dictate our lives. This in turn means fear is written on the world (Pain and Smith, 2012).

To be clear, our *risk society* operates on the basis of fear. Fear that something could happen, not that it will. Fear, therefore, which is indelibly connected to risk, is tied more closely to possibility than it is reality, meaning it is a phenomenon that is largely invented. Indeed, Elemér Hankiss (2001) makes this point that human beings are a particularly hyper-anxious species despite being creatures that have much less to worry about in comparison to other animals living in perpetual states of uneasiness and alertness as they endeavour, day in, day out, to resist death. From concern over global threats such as nuclear catastrophe, environmental changes, terrorism and epidemics, and everyday concerns such as financial security, body image and health, hypothesised fear is everywhere for human beings. Yet, while fear clearly has a significant impact upon human lives, it can be argued that we have throughout history been reasonably successful in producing ways of protecting ourselves against it (Hankiss, 2001). Certain belief systems, institutions and behavioural patterns are examples of just a few methods of protection.

Keeping the last point in mind, what becomes clear is that *fear avoidance* has been a principal method of seeking protection against fear, so to further unpack this theme a useful place to start is with Thomas Mathiesen's idea of 'silent silencing'. According to Mathiesen (2004), this is a means of silencing people without them realising they have been silenced. As he goes on to point out, many subtle and undetectable methods of eradicating opposition have in fact existed over the course of human history, and they have been cleverly incorporated into everyday people's lives without them ever truly noticing. In a nutshell, it is precisely because its mechanisms are noiseless in character that the silent silencing of human beings has been so successful and pervasive. As Mathiesen (2004) argues, noiselessness helps to legitimise each mechanism, and once legitimacy is gained they become, one by one, increasingly trusted and relied upon.

One of the most dominant mechanisms of fear avoidance was mentioned at the beginning of the chapter. What I am referring to of course is religion. Interestingly, few major sociological figures have ever explored the relationship between fear avoidance and systems of faith and worship in the Western world in great depth (Hankiss, 2001). Max Weber, however, is one notable exception since he devoted some of his work to the effect of religion and how it has occupied a central role in relieving people of fear. As Weber explains, religion has always helped to redeem people:

> From distress, hunger, drought, sickness, and ultimately from suffering and death … [and also from] political and social servitude … from being defiled by ritual impurity … the senseless play of human passions … from radical evil and the servitude of sin … from the barriers of the finite … the threatening punishment of hell … [and from] the senselessness of the universe.
>
> (1915/2017: 280–281)

What is especially interesting about Weber is that he goes beyond religion in his discussion of fear and anxiety and how it has shaped our world. By this I mean he addresses how the extreme inhumanity of Calvinism, the branch of Protestantism that accentuates the authority of the Bible and the sovereignty of God, played a major role in thrusting us into the practice, spirit and culture of capitalism. As Weber (1930) explains, Calvinism not only created spiritual isolation and made countless people suffer the agony of inner loneliness; it caused many individuals to fear for the salvation of their souls and, ultimately, experience severe anxiousness over the thought of death. Although capitalism was created unintentionally on the back of the protestant work ethic, in the end it grew to undermine religion in society. In many ways, capitalism emerged as a form of reprieve and it ushered in a new version of civilisation, one that turned out to be much more effective at disguising fears and anxieties. Of course, capitalism is still a source and a cause of fear, the point is that it is more effective at making us ignorant of the fears we possess (Hankiss, 2001).

Since Weber, scholars such as Bauman have gone to great lengths to scrutinise the influence of capitalism in present modernity, particularly the effects of consumer capitalism for this is what has dominated Western lives since the mid-twentieth century. As he points out, consumer capitalism is the latest attempt to incapacitate fear (Bauman, 2006). After all, in the twenty-first century, the distraction of consumer society is the reason human beings have become so idiosyncratic and seemingly free. Nevertheless, Bauman (2006) is quick to remind us that it is this idiosyncrasy and the perceived freedom it brings that dictates what people believe in and how they behave. What this means is that people who inhabit present modernity are prompted to buy their way into distraction by giving in to the allure of a wide array of gadgets, gizmos, deals and trends. The main consequence of this is that only one certainty is made possible in the world we think we know and understand, the certainty of uncertainty, changeability and insecurity. This kind of life is a liquid one. It forces people to continuously flow from one short-lived episode to the next, from one challenge to another, and so it brings with it brand new dangers and threats (Bauman, 2006). Life, therefore, continues much in the same way it always has, as one continuous search for expedients and strategies that temporarily stave off the imminence of threats and dangers.

What the above discussion serves to do is remind us that human ignorance remains much the same since we continue to use mechanisms such as consumer capitalism to temporarily distract ourselves from fear. What it also signals is that fearfulness remains a way of life in the twenty-first century. The problem, as I have argued, is that distraction techniques rarely work in the long term which is why fear remains part of the common currency of present modernity. The question I consider now then is how fear, instead of being strategically ignored, can be experienced and embraced, and whether facing up to it improves our overall condition of living. Before I can begin the reversal of the silent silencing of fear, however, I sense it is time now to continue with my underground story. It is set this time in the limestone plateau of the Peak District.

Giant's Round Trip

Something flashed in my rear-view mirror. I glanced up to see a car appearing at the top of the hill, its headlights blaring as it began to follow a dirt track towards where I was parked. I'd arranged to meet a guy called Luke Hellewell from work since he'd expressed some interest in caving earlier in the week. He had very little experience of the natural underground, but as a keen climber and general enthusiast for the outdoors, I was confident he'd have it in him to tackle the 'Round Trip'. As a Peak District classic, I thought Giant's Hole would be a good way of introducing him to caving.

After changing and answering a dozen of Luke's burning questions in a small parking area, we made our way up a nearby valley in an easterly direction. Taking care to keep a dry-stone wall to our left, we walked until we reached an obvious 10-metre-high opening on our right (Figure 5.1). Before we made our way down

Figure 5.1 The entranceway to Giant's Hole.

to the stream that would guide our way, I turned to Luke and asked if he was ready. Clearly more apprehensive now, he nodded and paused for a moment. Then he replied, 'You're in charge, lad. You lead the way. I'm totally appih t' be undah instruction, pal'.

With me leading the way, we passed through the swallet entrance into a roomy streamway passage. We continued to follow this with ease, enjoying the sight of various calcite formations along the way until we reached the head of the famous 7-metre pitch, Garland's Pot. This point marks the true beginning of the rest of the cave. Luke peered over the edge while I rigged it. Like me, he was struggling to catch sight of the bottom as the beam from his headtorch was obscured by cascading water. I sent Luke into the pot first, keeping an eye on him as he fumbled with his descender and began his bumpy descent into the dark hole. Once he reached the bottom, he quickly detached himself from the rope and moved towards a narrow slit in the rock behind him to avoid the worst of the waterfall's spray. I joined him a few moments later.

From the base of Garland's, we entered the next section of the cave called the Crab Walk. For the next half a mile or so, we would have to emulate crabs by walking sideways down a tight, twisting passageway. Our progress was slowed because of the awkwardness of the tackle bag we were hauling which contained a rope, some basic medical supplies and a little bit of food, but after much puffing and panting we eventually reached the very tight bit at the end. This particularly narrow constriction is commonly referred to as The Vice.

There are two ways of passing this obstacle. The first involves contorting the body through the upper reaches of the squeeze. The second route, found at ground level, is more suited to slightly larger people, but it entails slithering through a pool of cold water. Having passed through the upper section of The Vice several times before, and gone through the terrifying experience of thinking I was stuck on my first-ever attempt, I encouraged Luke to give it a try. I explained to him that it was an experience not to be missed. Like I had done the first time, he soon found himself firmly wedged and unsure of what he had to do to free himself. There was very little to pull on with his hands, and his legs were all but useless while his chest was in the crux of the pinch. I sensed that fear was starting to creep its way into his body, the same feeling of fear that had gripped me in that exact position. However, he managed to retain his calm as I talked him through what to do next. As coolly as possible, I told him to take a few breaths, then exhale to make himself smaller. After that, I explained he had to push forward with a vigorous burst. Luke followed my instructions perfectly. He grunted involuntarily and a split-second later was through. I gave him a moment to enjoy his feeling of relief before picking up the bag to signal it was time to start moving again.

The next section of Giant's Hole required us to descend Razor Edge Cascade and then a short-laddered section in Comic Act Cascade. After this, the passage suddenly transformed and became easy-going as we entered the aptly named Great Relief Passage. This took us to the Eating House where we took a right-hand turn leading to Maggin's Rift. Knowing an intimidating section lay just ahead, it was here I suggested we take a quick break.

For a while, the pair of us chatted as we munched on a couple of cereal bars I'd stashed inside the tackle bag. It wasn't long, however, before we had to move again. Cold was beginning to seep through our damp underlayers, spurring us back into action. Quickly passing through Letterbox Passage and Ghost Rift, we found ourselves at the entrance to Giant's Windpipe. This is a low passage that must be crawled through and is mostly filled with water. Following bad weather, the route is sometimes completely sumped meaning a return journey back up the Crab Walk must be made, but this time, despite it being early winter, we were fortunate there was a small gap between the surface of the water and the ceiling of the passageway.

I entered first, crawling on all fours, to begin with until the level of the ceiling became so low I was forced to slither across the rocky floor. The water was icy cold, and I gasped as my body slid beneath the surface. It was a strange, disconcerting feeling being pushed against the ceiling due to air trapped in my oversuit while battling to keep my head tilted sideways above the waterline. I had to be careful moving forward since any rapid movement stirred a miniature wake which would cause the water to swell above my nose and mouth. Even though I had completed this route several times, I still found it unsettling to notice how close I was to that threshold separating life and death. Doing my best to push such thoughts to the back of my mind, I eventually made it to the other side. I breathed a sigh of relief and then called for Luke to begin making his way through, listening carefully just in case he encountered any problems.

Quite quickly it was clear he too was gripped by fear. I could hear frantic movements and fast, panicked breathing as he struggled to keep his head above the waterline. When something he was wearing became snagged on a protruding rock, he called out to himself in sheer panic. Understanding precisely what he was feeling, I urged him to keep moving. I peered into the darkness of the Windpipe, hearing him move ever closer until he finally emerged with a look of desperation written across his face. He hauled himself free and immediately slumped against a small mound to regain his strength and sense of calm.

After another quick break, we travelled a bit further down the passage to reach the roof of Crab Walk. A nervous-looking Luke watched as I set up a retrievable abseil from a bolted in hanger. Once again, he asked several dozen questions, mostly about the fixed bolt and the hanger we were using and how we were meant to abseil safely down a rift that was visibly very tight. Dismissing most of his questions with a casual, 'we'll be alright', I explained why the abseil was necessary. As I told him at the time, we'd be descending directly into Crab Walk, meaning our journey to the exit wouldn't take too long from this point.

Finished with the rigging, I watched once more as Luke prepared himself for the abseil. Despite his nervousness and all the questions, I was surprised to find he was much more confident setting up this time, a much different character than he'd been at the head of Garland's. He even took care to lock-off the dead rope this time as he tested his weight on my set-up. Satisfied it would hold, he eased back into his harness and began feeding rope steadily through his device.

I waited for a short while, listening for his call to signal I was free to follow. It soon came and moments later I found myself back inside the cramped space of the streamway. All we had left to do now was recover the rope and make our way back towards Garland's Pot and then the main entrance. After detaching myself from the rope, I gave it a firm tug. It plummeted down dutifully into a shallow pool making coiling easy.

Searching for Fear through Edgework

Although I have argued that fear avoidance is becoming more prevalent in the twenty-first century, what I have not yet addressed is the idea that some people intentionally choose to adopt riskier lifestyles or leisure lives. In other words, because responsibility for managing risk and fear has become an individual task, certain occupations and leisure activities have become both a possibility and a source of fascination for some people and, therefore, have gained cultural significance in present modernity. Thinking back to Seneca's quote I drew on at the beginning of this chapter, it might be suggested that the people involved in such occupations and activities heed his advice, albeit unwittingly. Knowing we reside in a world of uncertainty, unpredictability and risk, and that we are likely to suffer its consequences anyway, these are individuals who decide to 'look forward meanwhile to better things' (2016: 27). With this in mind, my suggestion in this chapter is that the natural underground attracts people of this nature. In fact, I would argue that for anybody involved in caving, confronting and responding to the silencing of fear is something that is valued. Crucially, what cavers realise, providing they have sufficient skill, grit and determination, is that a place of the 'betwixt and between' can be reached if fear is embraced and this plunges them into a world of imagination and pure possibility.

There is a name for the kind of activity I am talking about here and it begins to give us an insight into what people gain when they welcome fear into their lives. For many scholars and adventure enthusiasts, what I am perhaps referring to has been described as *edgework*. Borrowing the idea from Hunter S. Thompson, the edgework model was originally introduced by Stephen Lyng (1990) to explain why there has been substantial growth in the number of people who engage in high-risk sports and activities in the past few decades. While edgework research was centred around the realm of leisure to begin with and activities such as skydiving, rock climbing, scuba diving, hang gliding and motor racing (Lyng, 2005), it quickly expanded into other domains and academic interest areas. For example, some researchers such as Jeffrey Kidder (2006) and Granter et al. (2018) have argued that high-risk jobs such as bike messengering and ambulance work hold the same appeal or intensity as high-risk leisure. Another area where edgework has been applied is the field of criminology. The work of Jack Katz (1988) for example, specifically his book *The Seductions of Crime*, laid the foundations for thinking about certain forms of criminal behaviour as a special kind of edgework. There are other scholars, too, who have applied the concept to newly emerging phenomena such as chemsex which is the term used to describe organised gay sex sessions that are experienced under the influence of illegal psychoactive drugs and can last several hours or days (Hickson, 2018).

At this point in the discussion, I would argue that the link between the concept of edgework and caving in the natural underground seems almost seamless. Edgework is any kind of human activity or experience that must involve, at the very least, one of three key conditions. As I will illustrate below, each one could easily be significant while exploring the natural underground. I will try to demonstrate this by reflecting on the episode above. As I explain how exploration of the natural underground may be a form of edgework, the reader should acquire a sense of why cavers would dare to challenge the silencing of fear in the first instance and what it is they gain from it.

First, edgework is said to involve an activity that poses a clear threat to a person's well-being, life or sense of ordered reality (Lyng, 2005). This much was certainly true on my first visit to Giant's Hole, especially when I reached the section known as The Vice. As I wormed my way into the tight rift for the first time, my mind was racing, alarmed by the notion I might not be able to return the same way. The instant my chest felt wedged between the rock is precisely the moment my sense of reality became distorted. Firmly lodged, I was left with an important decision to make. I could give in to those urges and rational thoughts pushing me to return, knowing it would be a disappointing end if I left the 'Round Trip' incomplete. Alternatively, I could force myself to stay calm, exhale to empty my lungs of air, and thrust myself further into the gap with absolutely no certainty I would not become stranded on the other side, or worse, find myself fully stuck. Wanting to avoid disappointment, I knew I had to continue and play against the potential outcomes waiting for me on the other side of The Vice. Just as I shifted my weight and committed to pushing myself further into the rift, a feeling of fear like no other struck me. At that moment, my safety, my sense of normalcy and in my mind at the time potentially even my life were out of my hands.

Second, Lyng (2005) points out that the negotiation of some kind of boundary must take place. At the most abstract level, what he means by this is that the border between consciousness and unconsciousness, chaos and order, form and formlessness, sanity and insanity, or life and death must be found. The point is that people must strive to get as close as possible to the edge without actually crossing it (Lyng, 2005). Thinking back to the episode above, the reader might agree that Luke's experience of Giant's Windpipe is particularly useful for unpacking this condition a little further.

As Luke crawled towards me through the flooded passage, panic quickly ensued when he discovered how deep the water was. There was roughly a 4 cm gap between the surface and the ceiling, meaning his head had to be turned sideways to breathe. I listened carefully to his frantic movements as his will to live desperately fought to stave off death. I could hear him calling out in fear. These calls were not to attract my attention, they were instead entirely reactive and instinctive. This was his body's way of telling him that he was negotiating the boundary. With no knowledge of the length of the passage or how deep the water was up ahead, and no way of turning around, he could do no more than remain firmly rooted on the edge. What kept him there, as he reported afterwards, was the knowledge that I was through. I was a reminder that he was unlikely to cross the line and drown. He affirmed this once he made it through. With sheer relief written across his face, he turned to me and said, 'It were mental not knowing what were ahead. I was shitting me-sen coz I were convinced it were getting deeper … What kept me goin' were knowin' you'd made it t'utha side alive like'.

Third, it has been suggested that edgework requires an ability to understand and define the limits of performance or actions (Lyng, 2005). Of course, edgework involves individuals pushing themselves to the outer limits of their capabilities, but they still manage to remain in complete control in situations that feel uncontrollable. To once again use Luke as an example, as we were setting up a retrievable abseil from a single hanger to lower ourselves from the roof of Crab Walk back into the base of the rift, he seemed nervous and laden with questions. Having done very little rigging training or practice underground, when it was time to drop in, Luke was suddenly forced to abandon himself to two things – his natural ability to pick things up quickly and whatever overlapping climbing knowledge he had at his disposal. Overall, this was enough for him to understand and control the risk involved and to know what to do to reach the bottom of Crab Walk. Unsurprisingly, his descent was not the most elegant, but he had the relevant competencies to be able to concentrate under pressure, lock-off the descender safely whenever he needed to force his body through tighter sections of the rift, continuously command his body to act and ultimately not plummet to the ground. In other words, to borrow Lyng's way of putting it, Luke had 'the right stuff' (2005: 126) about him to enter an edgework experience and be insured against a grizzly injury or death.

Notwithstanding the significance and usefulness of the concept of edgework for unpacking how the natural underground might be used as a means of defying the silencing of fear in present modernity, what I want to argue next is that certain problems accompany the idea. The main issue is that whenever the concept is applied scholars tend to reinforce the idea that risk is generally minimised and controlled through careful skill and mastery. As Lyng (2005) points out, edgework is a rational and restorative practice, one that not only helps people respond to the helplessness of living in a risk society but also enables them to regain a sense of personal control over their lives by means of the pursuit of action. In other words, edgework seems to be more about reducing anxiety, chaos and, ultimately, fear (O'Grady, 2017; Bunn, 2017; Lyng, 1990). What this suggests is that becoming an edgeworker suddenly seems more like another strategy of fear avoidance, albeit it is an artful one, which is problematic because there is a lot more to caving than this. As it was discussed in Chapter 3, the natural underground is a place that more easily resists control and manipulation which means unexpected risks can frequently occur. It also means that fear in the natural underground can take people by surprise before any risk has been

102 Unsilencing Fear in the Natural Underground

managed or negotiated. The concept of edgework, therefore, does not quite fit the bill when we are trying to understand how the silencing of fear can be reversed.

Another crucial problem with the concept of edgework is that it is only used to emphasise the positive attractions of leisure activities that are deemed high risk (Lyng, 2008). To borrow Zinn's (2008) way of putting it, risk-taking and reaching the edge is about weighing up the gains and losses and always being in favour of whatever there is to be gained. The obvious issue here is that experiences of the edge might also be negative, even when a dangerous leisure pursuit is skilfully practised with the right amount of control, mastery and emotional intensity. Indeed, the reason for engaging in the risky activity in the first place may have been associated with significant gains, but a person could ultimately arrive at a negative experience. In such instances, the fine balancing of the edge – that liminal space that lies somewhere between safety and danger – would have been transcended rendering the experience uncomfortable and dangerous to the point of being life-threatening. Yet, in my mind, there is something messy, complex and difficult to deal with here because that negative experience – essentially a direct experience of raw, unveiled fear – might push people to value that feeling and appreciate how rare encounters are in our everyday lives. In short, something has been gained but little to no importance is attached to it because the concept of edgework is unable to account for it or make much sense of it.

To reiterate my earlier point, after analysing the concept of edgework more closely it becomes increasingly obvious that there are limitations to overcome when trying to form an interpretation around the unsilencing of fear in the twenty-first century. Our attention, therefore, will now be turned to a different concept, one that is perhaps more suited to helping us understand what there is to be gained if fear is embraced.

Unsilencing Fear through Limit Experience

Another concept that can be used to unpack my and Luke's experience of fear is Michel Foucault's notion of *limit experience*. While it may seem that both limit experience and edgework are synonymous concepts, I want to be clear that they are not since they have subtle variances which I will endeavour to explain further in the remainder of this chapter. In addition to explaining the differences, what this last section also does is unpack how limit experiences help to reconnect people with feelings of fear as it provides a place for me to explain what there is to be gained when such feelings are experienced. Before I can do either of these things, however, I will begin by providing a brief definition of limit experience. Of course, as is usually the case with anything written by Foucault, the definition has been teased out of his work since it cannot easily be taken from one single source.

In *L'ordre due discours* (The Order of Discourse, 1971), Foucault describes a space of untamed exteriority, a space replete with energy, turbulence and even chaos. What he is referring to is the possibility of seeking out transformative experiences, and what is significant, as Jay Miller (1993) points out, is that the man behind the writing, Foucault himself, was such a seeker of clandestine knowledge and mysterious states of intense disassociation from the world. As Miller (1993) suggests, it was the intoxication of sex that fascinated Foucault the most, and it is his knowledge and understanding of having been plunged into the passion of this kind of 'limit' experience that enables him to give us an idea of its role and purpose in our lives. Part of the introduction to Foucault's second volume of *History of Sexuality* comes close to capturing his lust for limit experience:

> As for the motive that compelled me, it was very simple. In the eyes of some, I hope that it will suffice by itself. It was curiosity – the only kind of curiosity, in any case, that merits the pain of being practiced with a little obstinacy: not the kind that searches out in order to digest whatever is agreeable to know, but rather the kind that permits one to get free of oneself ... There are times in life when the question of knowing if one can think differently than one thinks and perceive differently than one sees is absolutely necessary if one is to go on looking and reflecting at all.
>
> (1990: 8)

One of the central goals Foucault had in mind when he introduced the idea of limit experience was to challenge the privileging of the 'lived experienced' by phenomenologists. What Foucault wanted to draw attention to instead was 'unliveable' experience. To quote Foucault directly, this kind of experience involves 'the maximum of intensity and the maximum of impossibility at the same time' (2000: 241).

Having defined limit experience it is useful first, before we move on to explore how such practices potentially upset the silencing of fear in present modernity, to remind ourselves of some of the key features of the concept of edgework. What must be echoed is that edgework is used to refer to various instances of positive boundary negotiation that are carefully navigated and controlled. These are encounters that involve *transcendence* into some kind of liminal realm (a threshold) as the edge is reached as closely as possible (Lyng, 2005). Furthermore, edgework generally involves activities where the consequence could, in principle, be lethal (i.e. result in injury or death) if something were to go wrong and someone strayed over the edge (ibid).

Limit experiences are different since they involve *transgression* rather than transcendence, and the primary focus or goal of any transgression is that normative boundaries can ideally be crossed and recrossed with non-lethal consequences (Lyng, 2005). Additionally, transgressions are infringements or violations of rules, codes of conduct or laws which means attention does not have to be limited to a singular set of margins that separate life and death. A common misconception, one found in the work of Chris Rojek (2000) for example, is that limit experience is bound to the search for so-called higher pleasures and that individuals are willing to risk their own self-destruction, or indeed that of others, to reach it. In reality, however, limit experiences are much more than this and what Foucault provides is an alternative interpretation of a type of practice that is an act of 'liberation' involving 'work carried out on ourselves by ourselves as free beings' (1984: 47). With these ideas in mind, what is being challenged with the concept of limit experience are the limits imposed by structures of power-knowledge such as consumer capitalism (i.e. the controlling and manipulation of fear). What I want to reiterate, then, is that Foucault's limit experience is more about liberating oneself from powerful forces that not only operate in every aspect of our everyday lives but also cause us to surrender hard-fought freedoms.

To elaborate on the significance of this last point, at the time of writing Luke presented a good example of an individual who seemed more familiar with the direction, control and management of commercial outward bounds centres and indoor climbing walls, and the rules and practices adopted by their instructors. In other words, his knowledge of adventure was mostly derived from a structure of power (consumer capitalism) that generally holds a monopoly over fear. However, in the natural underground he was momentarily liberated by a limit experience because he transgressed into a different reality that involved his feeling of fear becoming his own. This is something he pointed out as we rested briefly immediately after passing through Giant's Windpipe: 'Jesus, you can't buy the kinda panic I felt there, not that I was actually gonna die or owt, but I've not felt that before. That were propa anxiety that'. What this accentuates is the point that most forms of leisure have been turned into consumer goods and therefore prevent us from being able to experience what leisure really has to offer (Baudrillard, 2016). Normally we are willing to accept this, but I would argue that in certain instances, as with Luke's experience, it is possible to successfully alter knowledgeability and open our eyes to an entirely different way of viewing the world. This last idea is one that filters nicely into the next point of discussion.

Another reason why the concept of limit experience is better suited when it comes to unpacking feelings of fear in the natural underground is that it can be experienced negatively (Miller, 1993). To elaborate on this point, in addition to the obvious display of relief Luke was feeling after exiting the Windpipe, a few days after the trip we were talking about it with other work colleagues in our office and Luke admitted he would 'not be revisiting anytime soon'. When probed why, his exact words were, 'Nothing about it were pleasant. Nevah before in ower life have a shit me-sen so much'. As it was noted earlier, this is something edgework does not make allowance for, unless the edge is poorly negotiated and stepped over. In this instance, though, as Lyng reminds us (1990), edgework would no longer be edgework. Limit experience on the other hand was used by Foucault, particularly in his earlier work, to explore forms of life that are pushed to the fringes of society. What Foucault had in mind specifically were negative domains such as criminality, madness, poverty and suffering, domains that 'embody cultural values that support the very gestures of exclusion' (Tirkkonen, 2019: 452). In other words, what Foucault was able to do over the course of his career was draw out the hidden dimensions of dominant institutional regimes and discourses by orientating his work around negative domains. Essentially, each domain was viewed within a dominant discourse system as defying the order of things and, therefore, could be described as being at the limit of understanding.

To return to the central point of the discussion, in a world that encourages people to silence fear through avoidance or treat it as something that needs to be made positive what Luke was able to do in the natural underground is experience its true unpleasantness. This kind of fear was raw and at the limits of understanding, a type of fear that has been made inexplicable and incomprehensible because it cannot be sold or exploited by consumer capitalism. In other words, it is a type of fear that has no real place in present modernity. In transgressing the normal protection he would usually have in the surface world then, Luke perhaps for the first time in a long while was able to see the world in an entirely new light.

Another way limit experiences are useful for realising and revitalising fear in the twenty-first century is in the way they become a vehicle for exploring the broad possibilities of the body. What I mean by this is that while edgework is about understanding and defining the limits of performance or actions, limit experience is something more since it is about overcoming practices of subjectification, individuation and alienation. As Foucault (2002) puts it, limit experience is about gaining power to refuse products of present modernity which can be in the form of concealed subjectivities or even individuality itself. By contrast, edgework is very much about developing the appropriate skills, practices and knowledge to be able to negotiate the edge, often utilising specialised equipment, well-defined rules and the right kind of appearance, which in turn causes every edgeworker to embrace their own special kind of performative identity (Walby and Evans-Boudreau, 2021). Expanding on this point, what Tony Blackshaw and Tim Crabbe (2004) remind us is that in our consumer society, performative edgeworker identities are increasingly characterised by the need for instant gratification and immediacy which signals that they in fact live surface lives as opposed to anything more authentic just like any other consumer. In other words, edgework might be seen to be an amplification of a pre-existing or surface self that can be used for purposes relating to transcendence while limit experience refers to a process Foucault (2002) describes as 'self-creation' that is created in the moment.

According to Foucault (2002), what is fundamentally different about a limit experience is that it renders any constraints found in everyday life irrelevant and makes it possible to discover new possibilities of embodied existence. In other words, new ways of being that have previously been unknown or remained unrealised are revealed. On this point, there are few occasions where I have encountered a situation that requires absolutely no identity or subjectivity, but on my own first visit to Giant's Hole, while I was consumed by the task of passing through The Vice, I surpassed all and every need for these things. It did not matter that my usual self dissolved and became inconsequential. Steered entirely by fear, my body transformed as I entered an unfamiliar, almost uncontrollable, state where I was more conscious of my rapid heartbeat as it was being pressed against cold rock, and the uncomfortable coarseness lingering at the back of my throat. I no longer cared what anybody else thought about my character since my task became one of exploring the limits of my fear. Suddenly positioned at the helm, I was free to identify new possibilities of being and doing. For Foucault (1991), this is the point of any limit experience – they serve to '[tear] the subject from itself' (31–32) and ensure that when they return the person involved does not remain the same individual as they were before.

One final thing to note about limit experience is that it is not something that is limited to the individual. Before continuing with this point, it is important to be clear that I am not suggesting edgework weakens patterns of collective identification since the opposite has been argued by several scholars (Mellor and Shilling, 2021). In Cronin et al.'s (2014) work for instance, which is an examination of the 'creeping edgework' involved in spells of 'carnivalesque consumption', it is reasoned that a sense of collectivity compels people not to lose control since it would break their responsibility to the group. Nevertheless, it cannot be overlooked that Lyng and others like him have accentuated the point that in disrupting the voice of society edgework is typically found to be very attractive to individuals wanting to call out 'an anarchic self' (1990: 878). What this means is that in seeking edgework experiences what people are often left with is a residual self that is egocentric and prone to narcissism (ibid).

Keeping the last point in mind, we should return our attention to limit experience. Although there has been an exclusive focus on the first-person perspective so far, it is important to note that limit experiences are also intersubjective which means they cannot help but alter how people relate to others or influence the kinds of relationships they build with one another. As Tirkkonen (2019) argues, certain limit experiences that shatter customary inhibitions can rouse a collective energy that leaves little room for separate ambition or egotism, and this creates something similar to a cultural system of classification and order. As Foucault (2006) points out using the example of mental illness, when the mode of being is altered anyone involved is able to speak about the conditions of being (i.e. schizophrenia or hysteria) within a context that is both special and unique to themselves. We might call this process of intersubjectivity as *being-in-common* with one another, and this typically takes place in situations that are otherwise unknown – and indeed cannot be known – to all outsiders.

Thinking back to a conversation that took place at work a few days later, what I recall vividly are the blank looks we received from other colleagues listening to Luke as he explained in substantial detail the Giant's Hole 'Round Trip' to them. To anybody who had not experienced the cave or at least something similar in the same way we had, his account of fear meant absolutely nothing to them. Without the limit experience, they could only do what most people do when the natural underground is mentioned and disregard the whole ordeal as something irrational and illogical. In other words, what Mathiesen's (2004) refers to as 'silent silencing' was hard at work that day in our office as each one of our colleagues acted as all 'liquid' modern consumers must. Having never sampled it, embraced it or understood it as a form of limit experience, they simply turned a perceived source of fear silent. Only one other in the office understood us, Jed 'the outdoor guy', for he too had visited Giant's Hole and the sections Luke was talking about (The Vice and Giant's Windpipe). As someone who had welcomed the chance to reverse the silencing of fear, then, he was we might say another *being-in-common*.

Summary

What this chapter has explored is Ulrich Beck's assertion that we live in an era that is riskier than ever before. In response, many twenty-first-century individuals attempt to avoid or veil their fears of risk by means of consumer capitalism. Although consumer capitalism is a mechanism of control that seems to produce more fears than it does alleviate them, for most people it offers some distraction and even temporary respite from the stresses and pains of present modernity.

Responding to some of the problems twenty-first-century individuals face, numerous scholars have employed Stephen Lyng's concept of edgework to argue that there has been an increasing demand for skills and knowledge that not only enable people to disrupt the silencing of fear but also embrace it as part of their leisure lives. Crucially, when fear is embraced through edgework, it is said to offer all kinds of sensations that are otherwise unavailable in everyday life, alongside feelings of escape. It is precisely with these ideas in mind that the present chapter set out to examine whether exploration of the natural underground is potentially another form of edgework that allows practitioners to exploit fear as a means of reaching a place of 'betwixt and between'.

Nevertheless, there were several issues with the concept of edgework. Foremost among them is the suggestion that edgework is an elaborate form of fear avoidance and that it is, as a concept, limited in scope as it is only used to deal with the positive aspects of risk-taking. In response to these problems, what the chapter suggests is that Michel Foucault's notion of limit experience may be better suited when it comes to forming an interpretation around how and why cavers use the natural underground to reconnect themselves with feelings of fear. Of course, it cannot be ignored that several scholars have linked Foucault's concept with his willingness to test the limits of sexuality, and the idea that he may have knowingly endangered other sexual partners with the HIV virus, but to only view it in this way is to ignore the greater significance of the idea. Looking beyond those arguments that describe limit experience as an attempt to risk self-destruction (or that of others), what this chapter argues is that certain spaces and forms of leisure provide a means of liberating oneself from limits imposed by structures of power-knowledge. In other words, while consumer capitalism might hold a monopoly over fear in the twenty-first century because exploration of the natural underground frequently involves limit experiences individuals are able to confront and potentially reverse the silent silencing of fear.

108 Unsilencing Fear in the Natural Underground

To recap, limit experiences that take place in the natural underground allow individuals to transgress everyday boundaries, which means they are infringements or violations of normal rules and codes of conduct. They are, to once again borrow Foucault's way of putting it, acts of *liberation* from mechanisms of fear and control that involve 'work carried out on ourselves by ourselves'. Limit experiences are also useful because they allow the negative aspect of fear to be known, the raw unpleasantness and the undesirable domains that have no place in consumer societies. There is no need to hide them for they are often an integral part of limit experience. What limit experiences also do is help individuals explore the broad possibilities of the body. This means a limit experience involves a process of 'self-creation' that is created precisely in moments when fear is encountered and embraced. As Foucault explains, such experiences serve to 'tear the subject away from itself' and make it so they discover entirely new possibilities of being and doing. Finally, as they are intersubjective, limit experiences allow people to develop collective understandings of fear. As it was argued above, this is a process of *being-in-common* with others that typically takes place in situations that remain unknown to outsiders, situations for instance that occur in the natural underground.

References

Altheide, D. (2017). *Creating Fear: News and the Construction of Crisis*. London: Routledge.

Baudrillard, J. (2016). *The Consumer Society: Myths and Structures*. London: SAGE.

Bauman, Z. (2006). *Liquid Fear*. Cambridge: Polity.

Bauman, Z. and Tester, K. (2001). *Conversations with Zygmunt Bauman*. Cambridge: Polity.

Beck, U. (1992). *Risk Society: Towards a New Modernity*. Trans. M. Ritter. London: SAGE.

Beck, U. (2009). *World at Risk*. Trans. C. Cronin. Cambridge: Polity.

Blackshaw, T. and Crabbe, T. (2004). *New Perspectives on Sport and 'Deviance': Consumption, Performativity and Social Control*. Oxon: Routledge.

Bonhomme, D. (2003). *Alfred de Vigny: The Rosetta Stone of Esoteric Literature*. Victoria: Trafford.

Bude, H. (2017). *Society of Fear*. Cambridge: Polity.

Bunn, M. (2017). Defining the Edge: Choice, Mastery and Necessity in Edgework Practice. *Sport in Society*. 20(9): 1310–1323.

Corbin, A. (2018). *A History of Silence*. Cambridge: Polity.

Cronin, J., McCarthy, M. and Collins, A. (2014). Creeping Edgework: Carnivalesque Consumption and the Social Experience of Health Risk. *Sociology of Health and Illness*. 36(8): 1125–1140.

Foucault, M. (1971). The Order of Discourse. *Social Science Information*. 10(2): 7–30.

Foucault, M. (1984). What is Enlightenment? In: P. Rabinow (Ed), *The Foucault Reader*. New York: Pantheon Books.

Foucault, M. (1990). *The Use of Pleasure: Volume 2 of The History of Sexuality*. Trans. R. Hurley. New York: Vintage Books.

Foucault, M. (1991). *Remarks on Marx: Conversations with Duccio Trombadori*. Trans. R. J. Goldstein and J. Cascaito. New York: Semiotext(e).

Foucault, M. (2000). *Power, Volume 3 of Essential Works of Foucault: 1954–1984*. Ed. J. Faubion. New York: The New Press.

Foucault, M. (2002). *The Essential Works of Michel Foucault, 1954–1984. Vol. 3: Power*. Ed. J. Faubion and R. Hurley. London: Penguin.

Foucault, M. (2006). *Madness and Civilization: A History of Insanity in the Age of Reason*. New York: Vintage Books.

Granter, E., Wankhade, P., McCann, L., Hassard, J. and Hyde, P. (2018). Multiple Dimensions of Work Intensity: Ambulance Work as Edgework. *Work, Employment and Society*. 33(2): 280–297.

Hankiss, E. (2001). *Fears and Symbols: An Introduction to the Study of Western Civilization*. Budapest: CEU Press.

Hickson, F. (2018). Chemsex as Edgework: Towards a Sociological Understanding. *Sexual Health*. 15: 102–107.

Inglehart, R. (2021). *Religion's Sudden Decline: What's Causing It, and What Comes Next?* Oxford: Oxford University Press.

Katz, J. (1988). *Seductions of Crime*. New York: Basic Books.

Kidder, J. (2006). "It's the Job That I Love": Bike Messengers and Edgework. *Sociological Forum*. 21: 31–54.

Lyng, S. (1990). Edgework: A Social Psychological Analysis of Voluntary Risk Taking. *American Journal of Sociology*. 95(4): 851–886.

Lyng, S. (2005). Sociology at the Edge: Social Theory and Voluntary Risk Taking. In: S. Lyng (Ed), *Edgework: The Sociology of Risk-Taking*. Oxon: Routledge, 17–49.

Lyng, S. (2008). Edgework, Risk, and Uncertainty. In: J. Zinn (Ed), *Social Theories of Risk and Uncertainty: An Introduction*. Oxford: Blackwell, 106–135.

Maeterlinck, M. (1900). *The Treasure of the Humble*. London: George Allen, Ruskin House.

Mathiesen, T. (2004). *Silently Silenced: Essays on the Creation of Acquiescence in Modern Society*. Winchester: Waterside Press.

Mellor, P. and Shilling, C. (2021). Edgework, Uncertainty, and Social Character. *Sociological Research Online*. 26(4): 959–975.

Miller, J. (1993). *The Passion of Michel Foucault*. New York: Simon & Schuster.

O'Grady, A. (2017). Introduction: Risky Aesthetics, Critical Vulnerabilities, and Edgeplay: Tactical Performances of the Unknown. In: A. O'Grady (Ed), *Risk, Participation, and Performance Practice: Critical Vulnerabilities in a Precarious World*. Cham: Palgrave, 1–32.

Pain, R. and Smith, S. (2012). Fear: Critical Geopolitics and Everyday Life. In: R. Pain and S. Smith (Eds), *Fear: Critical Geopolitics and Everyday Life*. Aldershot: Ashgate, 1–20.

Rojek, C. (2000). *Leisure and Culture*. Basingstoke: Macmillan.

Seneca, L. (2016). *Seneca's Letters from a Stoic*. Trans. R. Gummere. New York: Dover Publications.

Tirkkonen, S. (2019). What Is Experience? Foucauldian Perspectives. *Open Philosophy*. 2(1): 447–461.

Walby, K. and Evans-Boudreau, A. (2021). Gender and Edgework Paradoxes in Tree-planting in Canada. *Gender, Place & Culture*. 29(5): 715–735.

Weber, M. (1915/2017). *Max Weber's Economic Ethic of the World Religions: An Analysis*. Ed. T. Ertman. Cambridge: Cambridge University Press.

Weber, M. (1930). *The Protestant Ethic and the Spirit of Capitalism*. London: Unwin Hyman.

Zinn, J. (2008). Introduction: The Contribution of Sociology to the Discourse on Risk and Uncertainty. In: J. Zinn (Ed), *Social Theories of Risk and Uncertainty: An Introduction*. Oxford: Blackwell, 1–17.

Chapter 6

Life and Death Underground

Mortality, Immortality and Other Survival Strategies

Introduction

Up to now, my exploration of the natural underground has revealed that spaces of intimacy and scotopic experiences can be found in the kingdom of the dark. My exploration has also unpacked the idea that caves are a perfect place to embrace fear through limit experiences. What has not been mentioned yet is the significance of mortality. Given that caves are generally considered to be fear-provoking, and that most people would agree they should be avoided because of the danger they pose, it seems only logical that my attention should now turn to life and death underground. Before I can do this, however, I want to start by considering how death is perceived in the surface world and what kind of strategies people employ to ensure their survival. Once I have done this, my attention will return underground so that I can consider whether death is perceived in the same way and whether a different set of survival strategies are needed to prevent mortality.

Living with Death

For most of us, the inevitable transience of life cannot help but remain traumatic. It is difficult to imagine existence without any feeling and thought, a type of existence where consciousness simply dissolves into nothingness. If we try to imagine our own deaths for instance, it quickly becomes obvious how irremovable we are from the process of imagining since it is our minds that do the conceiving. What this means, as Zygmunt Bauman declares, is that death can seem like 'the ultimate defeat of reason' (1992: 16). Not only does death undermine reason, but it also saps our confidence and trust in it. In no uncertain terms then, the prospect of death is something that is absurdly frightening. As Herman Feifel (2014), Clive Seale (1998) and Philip Mellor (1993) all point out, the prospect of death is so terrifying it has become a taboo subject for many people, something unpalatable or repulsive, because it betrays our eagerness for life. It is no surprise, therefore, that death, much like fear, is something that is frequently averted, obscured or hidden in our everyday lives. Unfortunately, it is not something that

DOI: 10.4324/9781003301752-6

can be denied or made completely secret, but what is important is that a variety of strategies exist to make it seem less threatening or unnoticeable in our day-to-day lives.

To begin thinking about survival strategies in the surface world, our attention can return to an idea I briefly discussed in Chapter 3. It was there I argued that a distinctive feature of twenty-first-century living is that people try to buy *ontological security* by means of experiences or material goods. Arguably, this same point is applicable now. Sharing this view, Peter Berger (1969) describes structures such as consumer capitalism as a means of providing a 'symbolic canopy' that guards people against the sheer terror of absence. Without this protection, Anthony Giddens (1991) argues that individuals would be left alone to face the pervasive worry about death and the great question that disturbs us all if we think about it for too long, the ultimate meaningfulness (or indeed meaninglessness) of everyday life.

Of course, consumer capitalism espouses a certain kind of celebration of existence and being, one amplified first by an obsession with beauty, youth and longevity and second by the subsequent suppression of the inevitability of maturation or finality (Stark, 2020). Appearing youthful is something that is glorified while the process of ageing is something that is more frequently made to sound dirty and unnatural (ibid). In other words, the body, as Jean Baudrillard (1998) reminds us, has become the finest consumer object, an object requiring salvation. As he explains, bodies are worn much like a dress or a suit and rather than get to know it in any depth people are encouraged to invest in it in a wholly fetishistic way. On this point, Baudrillard (1998) directs attention to two modes of being termed phryneism and athleticism. Making it clear that each is valid for both women and men, he argues that they can be differentiated into 'feminine' and 'masculine' poles. In short, some people take the path of becoming icons of physical beauty and eroticism while others take the path of hyper-muscularity, speed and agility.

Regardless of the successes of the strategies of phryneism and athleticism, the prospect of dying is arguably more alarming in the twenty-first century than it has ever been since contemporary individuals are becoming progressively more deprived of meaning structures. As Mellor and Shilling put it, present modernity has 'not just emptied the sky of angels, but has emptied tradition, ritual and, increasingly, virtually all overarching normative meaning structures of much of their content' (1993: 428). We have moved beyond nineteenth-century health panics about the hygiene of cemeteries, a decisively modernist phase that exercised as much control over death as possible (Laqueur, 2015). And we have surpassed the twentieth-century mindset, one born of national grief and a deep longing for a new future following two Great Wars, which resulted in the complete silencing of death (Nicolson, 2010; Brophy, 1972). We have, rather, entered a world where people not only die noiselessly and in solitude but in ways that deny the very nature of death by attributing it to specific causes such as cancer, cardiac arrest or 'old age' (Piemonte and Abreu, 2021). It might be assumed that the medicalisation of death acts to neutralise the inherent threat and terror it causes; however, Willmott (2000) reminds us that it leaves individuals feeling uncertain and unsupported when death must finally be contended with. Subsequently, people are left with very little choice, they must sequestrate death as best as they can be armed only with the distractive mechanisms brought by consumer capitalism (ibid).

Of course, to suggest that death has been completely removed from everyday life in the twenty-first century would involve denying how ubiquitous it has become in popular culture, especially in film and television. It was Geoffrey Gorer who first brought it to the attention of scholars in the 1950s in his study *The Pornography of Death*. What Gorer (1955) argues is that because death has been rendered invisible and taboo it stirs curiosity. As a result, many individuals have become fascinated with the idea, especially in the way it is represented graphically and violently in the media. Ultimately, Gorer's (1955) thesis draws out the argument that violence, viewed from a distance and inflicted upon others, is highly effective in blunting viewers' emotions towards the profound implications of mortality in the real world. According to Philip Stone and Richard Sharpley (2008), this kind of entertainment involves thanatological-themed pleasure and it is not just found in film or television. In present modernity, it is found within the realms of dark tourism, music, the arts, dark comedy and print media (ibid).

Keeping the above discussion in mind, it would appear that a paradox is beginning to emerge. As Stone (2009) points out, on the one hand, death in present modernity is suppressed through the medicalisation of dying and the power of consumer capitalism, yet on the other it has become much more visible and noticeable in our everyday lives. I am inclined to argue, nevertheless, that any paradox is fictitious since both strategies – treating death as a commodity or a source of entertainment – have the same goal. They are both subtle ways of bringing mortality back into consciousness in a less threatening manner. In other words, death is still being sequestrated, but it is being done so in ways that cause much less trauma and anxiety. It becomes normal, and yet in the same breath remains at a safe distance. Dina Khapaeva (2017) makes this point, that depicting death as entertainment, as something that can even be humorous and pleasurable, means it effectively becomes innocuous and therefore neutralised.

Conspicuously absent in the natural underground of course are those strategies and influences of consumer capitalism that offer to 'protect' us from death in the everyday world. A perceived sense of ontological security cannot simply be purchased for use in uncommercialised caves and modes of being like those Baudrillard (1998) outlines (phryneism and athleticism) are rendered meaningless. Certainly, athleticism is required in the exploration of underground places, but it is required in a pragmatic sense rather than an idealistic or narcissistic one. In other words, caves are starkly different to the world above ground because the threat of death is much more difficult to manage and control. This is something James Lovelock (1963) stresses that tragedy and death in

Life and Death Underground   113

the natural underground are not things that can easily be forgotten or made to disappear. There are certainly many tragic stories that support this claim.

The tragedy of Floyd Collins is one example,[1] and it is an incident that could happen to anybody in the natural underground, anybody whose luck has suddenly run out. Floyd Collins was an experienced American speleologist in search of new, undiscovered caves. Having found one (Sand Cave) after excavating a suspected shaft for weeks, he entered alone to uncover where it would lead. He is said to have passed through several tight squeezes using a technique requiring him to press his arms against his sides, exhale deeply to flatten his chest, and rock his hips and abdominals to help his toes propel him forwards. Eventually, after passing through a series of body-hugging pinches, he emerged at the top of a sloping pit that dropped down into a tight horizontal shaft. The shaft itself was barely large enough to accommodate a human body, so he entered feet first to test it, leaving his hands free in the event of getting stuck.

However, as Floyd manoeuvred his body down the chute and into the shaft one of his legs is said to have knocked a boulder loose. There was no time to wriggle out of the way. It crashed down onto his ankle, and in the process of struggling to free himself he dislodged more loose rock. This caused a torrent of stone to topple around Floyd's waist and legs. Completely trapped, and without a light source since his kerosene lamp had been extinguished during the collapse, he could do little more than listen to the sound of his own breathing as he waited, desperately hoping somebody would raise the alarm when they realised he was missing.

Over 24 hours passed before the alarm was eventually raised and a rescue attempt was launched. Hundreds of people turned out to rescue Collins, from family members to fellow cavers, hardened miners, engineers and even the National Guard, but their efforts were all in vain. As the condition of the cave rapidly deteriorated due to the increased traffic passing through, drills and dynamite were eventually used to create a new shaft from the outside. In the end, it took 17 days to reach Collins, by which point it was confirmed he was dead. When the rescuers found his body, they discovered that his fingers and nails were torn to pieces. This served as a disturbing reminder of the terror Collins must have felt alone in the darkness, and the frantic effort he had made to try and free himself.

The stark reality of death in the natural underground does not end with the incident involving Floyd Collins. There have been many more tragedies, tragedies that have even involved several cavers simultaneously. The Mossdale Caverns Disaster is such an example. In 1967, six working-class cavers entered the system armed with explosives to blast through a blocked section known as Mini-Cow passage. Although the weather had initially been clear when they set off, while they were underground over an inch of rain fell over the course of three hours. When other cavers on the surface realised that the entranceway to Mossdale was underwater, alerts were sent out to local cave rescue teams. Work immediately began to dam the stream and pump out water. In total, some 10,000 sandbags were used to divert the flow of water and 19 fire pumps used to drain the cave.

As soon as it was possible, rescue teams entered the still-gurgling entranceway. It was noted immediately that flood debris was scattered everywhere, and that dirty yellow foam lined the ceiling. Debris in the form of belongings of the missing cavers was also found scattered intermittently which made search teams wonder whether gear had been intentionally stashed or was carried there by a raging torrent of water. It was not until they were much further inside the cave, at the infamous 274 metre crawl that has been measured as being 25 cm high and 60 cm wide, that the rescuers found the first of the missing bodies. One of the rescuers, Michael Melvin, provides a first-hand account of the true horror of the moment:

> As we continued yet further down Far Marathon, we realised that the chances were increasing of finding our friends waiting at the head of the climb into High Level Mud Caverns, which was now not far in front of us ... But I was brought up short when I rounded a corner and saw four neoprene-covered legs across the passage in front of me. 'They're here', I called back. 'Are they OK' replied Jim. 'No, they're dead', was my sad response ... Two bodies were jammed up into a side-rift, wedged in by what had been a desperate search for airspace.
>
> (n.d. 26–27)

To continue the search for the others, rescuers were forced to squeeze themselves over the tangled bodies. Very soon after passing them, three more were found. It would take several more return visits until the sixth body, that of John Ogden, was discovered since it had been washed into a narrow fissure that was partially covered with stones. As it was impossible to remove the bodies of the six, they remained where they were for three years. They were eventually moved by a small team of Leeds-based cavers into a nearby side passage off the northern arm of the High Level Mud Caverns known as The Sanctuary.

Keeping the harsh reality of the above stories in mind, in the remainder of this chapter I want to argue that the naturally occurring and untameable danger involved in places such as caves means people require alternative ways of dealing with death. What I want to emphasise is that the strategies employed by people exploring the natural underground are generally more creative and perhaps much less conspicuous than those we rely on in our everyday lives.

Attempts have of course been made to give a name to forms of leisure that help people contend with death in creative and less conspicuous ways. For some, they may be referred to as dark leisure (Spracklen, 2018) or dark tourism (Stone and Sharpley, 2008) and what they allow people to do is reconceptualise mortality, turning it from instinctive terror or dread into something that stimulates and educates. Dark leisure, according to Tony Blackshaw (2018), can take on several forms. It can involve leisure that is perceived as 'abnormal' or 'deviant', leisure that occurs in liminal settings that allows people to reach out to new communicative spaces, leisure that appeals to people who are fascinated with death and gothic culture, and leisure that encompasses certain moral implications (ibid). No doubt there are many more forms that could be included here, yet all of them are in fact of little concern to me because the focus in this chapter is to look beyond the objectivation of leisure and its categorisation. The central reason why is that there are many forms of dark leisure and tourism that are direct products of commercialisation, and in my mind this is something the exploration of the natural underground is generally not. There is, however, one essential value on which all the above-mentioned forms of dark leisure converge that I am interested in and, as Blackshaw points out, that is *freedom*. What Blackshaw means by this specifically is 'the freedom we have to identify and express ourselves in our own inimitable ways' (2018: 11).

What I want to argue, therefore, is that individuals enter the natural underground to survive, to show themselves they are not just alive but that they *still* are. Clear of the increasingly objective interpretations of dark leisure or dark tourism, what cavers discover are their own subjective realities where their imaginations can flourish and contend with death in an infinite number of ways. What is being suggested, in a nutshell, is that underground explorers are engaged in a form of leisure where they must constantly and independently negotiate how to manage, control and suppress death, and at the same time look beyond the fear of tragedy. As the next section of the chapter goes on to explain, people cope by using their own creativity and imagination rather than mechanisms that can be paid for. I would argue that this is a constant demand all explorers of the natural underground face as they are silently buffeted by distracting feelings of mortality which they desperately want to avoid, knowing all the while that if they are successfully avoided they can discover other things that matter. And so, it is towards some of the subjective survival strategies that help caver's reconceptualise mortality that this chapter now turns. First, though, to ensure my own experiences are being linked throughout the discussion, another episode has been included.

Into Each Life Some Rain Must Fall

Once again, I found myself in the Castleton area, this time splashing my way up an active streamway with Mayhem and Mcnally. We were inside a cave named Jackpot (sometimes referred to as P8), making our way back to the surface. Shortly after returning to the spacious chamber beneath Second Pitch, we'd noticed that the volume of water cascading down the waterfall had increased. While we had checked the weather forecast before going underground, and we had entered knowing conditions were wetter than normal, the sudden influx of water had taken us by surprise. We were aware this can happen, that rain can occur simply out of sheer back luck, but what we also knew was that there was no time to linger. Mayhem had been desperately keen to check out a section known as Stalagmite Grotto as there were supposed to be a number of fine-looking formations inside, but he quickly realised this plan would have to be abandoned (Figure 6.1).

Figure 6.1 The last photo taken before we had to make a hasty exit.

To avoid being pummelled by the water, we tried our best to climb up and around the left-hand side of the waterfall until we reached an overhanging lip. The spray coming from the fall was still violent and we ended up thoroughly soaked but doing this helped us avoid most of the main flow. From this point, however, we had no choice but to enter the cascade. To get past the lip and begin the ascension, we had to clip our ascenders onto the rope, meaning when we let go of the rock we were dragged straight into the centre of the raging torrent. Mayhem went first, making it look easy, then Mcnally followed. Mere minutes separated their ascents, but already I noticed conditions were becoming worse from my position on the other side of the chamber.

Mcnally had a rough time of it as he struggled against the force of the water. His body bounced about on the rope uncontrollably, and a couple of times he was knocked against the rock face. After much battling, he made it to the top. His voice was barely audible over the sound of crashing water, but I heard him give me the 'all clear' to clip in. Mimicking what the others had done to gain as much height as possible, I free climbed to the point beneath the overhang to attach my own ascenders onto the rope. Once I was clipped in, I allowed my body to swing out beneath the raging torrent. I was immediately battered and thrown around by the sheer force of the waterfall, so much so I struggled to lift my arm to gain height on my hand ascender. But I fought back, and gradually I began to move upwards. The head of the pitch seemed deceptively long as I was knocked about on the rope which suddenly seemed a lot more elastic than normal. Spluttering, I eventually reached the head of the pitch where Mcnally hauled me into the relative safety of the stream passage.

Conscious that the water level was still rising, we decided to leave the rope behind and tackle the next section of streamway as quickly as possible. Running now, as far as running was possible in the narrow, winding passage, we raced towards First Pitch. My heart was thumping so hard and fast I could feel it throb against my soaked oversuit. Trying my best to ignore it, I continued to run, taking care not to lose my footing in the fast-flowing water. Up ahead, I could see Mcnally struggling against the current as he leaned into a tight corner. His foot slipped and he tumbled to his knees. I yelled out to see if he was okay. Before I could reach him to check, Mayhem had already turned around and was pulling him back to his feet. We paused for a moment to make sure he wasn't injured, but Mayhem quickly grew impatient. He turned to us and uttered something along the lines of: 'The ghosts of Paul and David[2] should be keeping us on our toes, boys, reminding us not to hang around n' that. Let's get the fuck outta here'. Curiously, Mcnally protested for a moment, arguing that 'those other cavers messed up because they were careless and ill-prepared'. He finished with, 'this is different; we're different'. A *brief* moment of silence descended upon us as we ruminated on Mcnally's commentary, then we started to move again.

By the time we'd passed First Pitch and made our way into Cascade Chamber which is located just before the main entrance, we were sweating profusely. It was pouring down Mcnally's face and Mayhem was literally steaming inside his PVC suit. Still, there was no time to stop and relax. We were worried the entrance-way may have become impassable in the time we'd been underground, so we launched ourselves up the last slippery cascade. There was so much water we couldn't always see where we were placing our feet, but we managed to reach the final 3-metre climb to freedom. We paused briefly at the bottom to check on each other, then Mcnally made a go for it. He dived into the raging waterfall and within a second disappeared as the water devoured him. As we could no longer see him, we waited a moment to give him time to climb, guessing at how long it would take him to make the ascent. A minute or so went by and then Mayhem yelled at me – 'Do you think we should go?' I yelled back, 'Yes', and then told him

118 Life and Death Underground

to do it. Just before he leapt into the raging torrent, I made an attempt to reassure him – 'Go on, man', I said, 'You've got this!'

Again, I waited for a short while to allow Mayhem enough time to reach the surface before deciding it was time for me to get the fuck out. Alone now, I was shitting myself. I spent a moment psyching myself up, then I jumped up from where I was crouched and leapt into the entrance climb. I was instantly pummelled by water. Completely blind, I panicked for a moment as I struggled to find footholds. Suddenly realising I couldn't breathe, I thrust my head into a crack in the rock to my right. Fortunately, I found a pocket of air. With water drumming powerfully against my back, I spent a moment breathing deeply to regain my sense of calm. *Come on, Kev*, I thought to myself, *you're a caver and cavers do this shit*. I paused again, taking stock of my situation. *Come on, cavers do this!* A surge of fearlessness coursed through my body. I breathed in deeply and then stood up to embrace the full force of the cascade. With immortality on my side, I roared as I lifted my left foot into position. Once firmly in place, I pushed hard with my thigh to gain some height. Feeling the full power of being-a-caver, I ignored my blindness and inability to breathe, and continued to make steps one after another.

Just before I emerged from the small opening of Jackpot, I realised I could smell the surface. It was magnificent. One more movement upwards ensured my survival. Suddenly, I could feel much gentler splashes of rain against my face, and I was free. The evening air around me was surprisingly warm and damp, but it smelt deliciously sweet and heady. That's when I noticed two arms poised directly in front of me. I grabbed hold of them and felt a pull as I was drawn away from the kingdom of the dark (Figure 6.2).

Relieved to be walking freely in the night, we splodged our way back to the vehicles. Mayhem retrieved his key from its hiding place and unlocked the back of his van. Under the shelter of a quickly improvised tarp, we all sat on the edge of the van for a short while to rest and congratulate ourselves. At this point, I suggested we head down into Castleton to celebrate our survival with a pint, but the others declined and pointed out they both had to be in Manchester later that evening. Keen to stay warm as we could feel our temperatures beginning to drop, we began to peel off our oversuits, towel ourselves dry and pack up the gear. Then we went through Mayhem's usual ritual of ensuring all the tackle was properly separated to avoid his stuff being mixed with ours. I argued that it wasn't necessary and could feel a sense of irritation growing, but he was adamant it had to be done. When we were eventually finished, we had a quick glance around to check that nothing was left on the ground before finally driving off into the falling night.

Survival Strategies between Rocks and Hard Places

The Silence of Others

Human beings, according to Elias Canetti (1962) in *Crowds and Power*, are *survivors*. As he explains, the measure of the true success of a person is found in their

Figure 6.2 The entrance to Jackpot (P8) in normal conditions.

continuance. The obvious problem with this kind of success, however, as it was noted at the beginning of the chapter, is that it is never lasting. Another issue is that being successful at remaining alive is never-ending. It must be repeated continuously, which means efforts can never be suspended. If they are, the moment of death will have arrived.

Despite the challenges survival presents, Canetti's (1962) thesis is constructed around the idea that the difficult task of self-preservation is what drives human existence. This seems to follow Sigmund Freud's assertion that people have a natural, deep-rooted instinct for life (Carel, 2006). However, it is not Eros ('life energy') Canetti is referring to. What he argues is that belief in self-preservation, whether it is instinctive or made through rational choice, conceals a repugnant truth. For Canetti (1962), survival is less about a person's own self and more about that of other individuals. Since it is not possible to experience or live through our own mortality, death must be lived through other people. Meaning is derived through the deaths of others precisely because it is they who are deceased and not us. In other words, the desire for a long life which seems to play a significant role in the majority of cultures is about outliving our contemporaries. Knowing they have died, or that they are likely to earlier than ourselves, means we are doing something right and it allows us to measure our own success against others who have proven themselves to be unsuccessful.

The conspicuous silence or absence of others in the natural underground, therefore, offers a benchmark for our own survival success. Just as Canetti (1962) begins his analysis with a classification of different crowd types, we can think of ourselves – Mayhem, Mcnally and me – as creating a new crowd, one that allows us to group together the fatal errors other cavers have made. Although the death of a caver may weaken the broader collective, the so-called 'community' of cavers, what is also created is an important type of satisfaction arising from the fact that we have not been the victim of poor preparation and planning, or the unfortunate sufferer of an accident that could have been avoided. This is of course a reworking of Canetti's (1962) original idea, but the same principle applies. Impulses of survival are socially managed and employed to establish and protect boundaries.

And so, using the deaths of two cavers, Paul Fowkes and David Briggs, who had died in nearby caves in the Peak District to defend ourselves against mortality, it quickly became necessary for the three of us to distinguish 'Us' from 'Them'. In our minds, they were, to borrow Mcnally's way of putting it, part of the crowd that 'messed up'. They failed to prepare themselves for the harsh conditions of the underground, or they let the excitement of discovery get in the way of rational thought and well-being.[3] Certainly, at the heart of this attitude is a condition of *anomie*, a lack of normal ethical or social standards within a group, but it enabled us to create a perceived position of power. Mayhem's point about 'ghosts keeping us on our toes' also becomes significant here because this underlines our collective belief that 'Others' do not speak the same language as us, nor have the same habits, or a successful culture they can rely on. The 'Others' are part of a crowd belonging to something different, a crowd of the dead who are easily reducible to the idea of failure.

As insensitive as this strategy of survival may seem to an outsider, it is important to note that the death of all 'Others' in the natural underground is not a prerequisite for ensuring our own survival. Any image of a world emptied of all others might be one that testifies to our ultimate triumph as survivors but is also one that would be totally unbearable (Jones, 2020). A position of power, therefore, should be viewed as no more than an ingenious and carefully negotiated act of removal that entails the degradation of only a small number of deceased human beings. These individuals are reduced to the role of a tool or an instrument that feeds our drive to survive. This is a reminder, in other words, that survival cannot be a completely destructive or annihilating impulse since it would become just as nightmarish as death and therefore senseless.

(Im)Mortality Collectivised

According to Bauman (1992), the construction of group immortality may be viewed as another means of coping with anxiety over death. Efforts to establish group immortality may be the result of conscious action, but they can also be caused by subconscious pressure when anxiety is at its greatest. Although this might at first seem like a revival of some kind of community in a world where community is becoming increasingly harder to find, I want to be clear that it is not.

It was Ferdinand Tönnies (1955) who brought attention to the idea that our societies are transitioning away from traditional 'communities' by distinguishing between two types of social groups, Gemeinschaft (roughly translated as community) and Gesellschaft (relations of a more calculating kind). Emphasising the lack of fixity in present modernity, numerous twenty-first-century scholars have drawn on the concepts outlined by Tönnies to argue that Gemeinschaft community has been made all but redundant (Glover and Sharpe, 2020; Blackshaw, 2010; Bauman, 2001a). What has replaced it, as Blackshaw argues, are '"peg communities", "ad hoc communities", "explosive communities" and other disposable substitutes meant for an instant and one-off consumption' (2016: 132). They are not designed with depth or permanence in mind, their role is to satisfy cravings for security as and when they are required. In other words, so-called 'peg communities' appear in the bitter taste of community's own absence (Blackshaw, 2016). This is not only true in the surface world, but the natural underground as well. What this means is that there are times when the safety blanket of togetherness is needed. And when it appears, people find they can slip nicely into the certainty and security it brings. This is by no means a real community of course, it is rather a cumulative product of the imaginations of different but like-minded people (Blackshaw, 2016). In a nutshell, this kind of 'community' is a gloss that gives the illusion commitment is being made towards a group of other individuals.

In thinking about why 'community' is sometimes still needed, we can turn our attention to Bauman's (2001a) suggestion that community is a feel-good word. As he points out, if someone feels alone or is suffering, it feels good to have a community to fall on. If someone needs help, a community is there to set a person straight. In other words, 'community' is a cosy, warm and comfortable place. Metaphorically, it is like a roof that protects us against a storm, or a fireplace that thaws us out on a frosty day (Bauman, 2001a). Within a community it is possible to relax, for there are fewer dangers lurking in the darkness. What is more, everyone who is part of it knows each other well enough to trust things that are said and shared. Certainly, quarrels may arise from time to time, but they tend to be easy to resolve because togetherness is key to any community. People can be counted on and people can forgive in a community. In short, within a community a person's duty is to help one another and so it can be expected that help will be forthcoming in times when it is needed (Bauman, 2001a). It is clear then why the word 'community' feels so good. In a world renowned for its fierce competition, where it is normal to keep people at a distance and our cards close to our chests, the word is a reminder of everything that is missing in our day-to-day lives.

Keeping the ideas above in mind, 'peg communities' become especially important in the natural underground for two reasons. First, because people frequently find themselves deprived of opportunities to express their individuality, and second because individuality can become something that is debilitating. Of course, there are many benefits if a person establishes themselves as an individual in the surface world – they become unique, unrepeatable and indisposable (Bauman, 1992). Furthermore, as people discover how to exist at the centre of their own effort and labour, they find themselves able to exist according to their own principles and ideas (Foucault, 1980). The problem with individuality, however, is not only that it is a relentless task involving performativity and self-identification but that it also involves aggressive ego which is less useful for survival in the natural underground. As Ulrich Beck (1995) puts it, anyone left poking around in the fog of their ego, or the apparent freedom of performativity, must quickly deal with the consequences. In a nutshell, then, there are fundamental limits to individualism. To borrow a phrase coined by John Rawls (1971), although a thick 'veil of ignorance' can operate as a defence mechanism it can also plague individuals and cause constraints. As Bauman (2001b) explains, people who approach the world through the lens of individualism have no one from which they can seek guidance and support; the principles they agree to live by are unlikely to withstand gradual deterioration and decay; they become unsure of their wants, interests and means to an end; and hopelessness grows to be more difficult to contend with.

I would argue that the above-mentioned issues are exasperated in the natural underground. An important survival strategy, therefore, involves falling back into collective nets of perceived immortality (Bauman, 1992). To explain this point, inside Jackpot a type of 'peg community' came alive as Mayhem, Mcnally and I all came together to guide and assure one another, through shared labour and sacrifice, that we would be entering the future as a collective. This occurred most obviously when it was time to retreat from the flooding cave. Any private ambitions we held previously, like Mayhem's desire to see the Stalagmite Grotto, immediately had to be cast aside for the greater benefit of the welfare of the group. This also meant we had to wait when the fast current caused Mcnally to fall, and that we had to show willingness to pause and point out good foot placements when anyone found climbing difficult. Avoiding death in a collectivised form was in everybody's interest, it was our best chance of survival at the time, and so we readily surrendered the glory of individualism for our togetherness.

Despite providing warmness and security, the collective does not survive. Collective actions and projects cannot in present modernity, not since the world has become increasingly about individualisation (Bauman, 2006). Therefore, the moment death is no longer an immediate threat, the strategy of collectivisation becomes surplus to requirement. As Blackshaw (2010) reminds us, twenty-first-century individuals prefer to live their lives under the pretence that they do not need the backing and support of others. Having become so independent, they convince themselves they can live their lives anywhere and deal with intermittent feelings of loneliness when they happen to arise. Blackshaw summarises this condition perfectly with his point that twenty-first-century beings 'only want community the way they want community' (2010: 35).

Once we were safely out of Jackpot, things began to return to normal as our sense of danger started to subside. This was perhaps revealed when I suggested we stop off at a nearby pub in Castleton on our way home and the others declined. Rather than spend any more time together, or reflect on what happened, they were keen to make their way home. As is typically the case, both Mayhem and Mcnally had other engagements that evening, other things they needed to be doing, and they were no longer in need of the safety of togetherness. Further demonstrating the lack of community between us, the reader may recall the way in which Mayhem packed up his tackle. He was adamant that his gear, which was clearly labelled with yellow electrical tape, had to be separated without delay. Although we had all agreed to 'chip in' for tackle in the beginning and share it between ourselves, Mayhem did not like the idea of *his* equipment being mixed with the rest. For a while I argued with him that it did not matter, so long as we all cleaned and dried some of it, but his stubbornness prevailed and we spent several long minutes sorting out whose tackle was whose.

The Untouchables: Immortality as a Project of the Hero

According to Ernest Becker (1973), when denying death every human being has a visceral sense of immortality they can rely on. What Becker is suggesting is that beneath the surface people have the capacity to be utterly absorbed with themselves. This is without doubt a narcissistic trait, but it is one that is especially effective in shrinking the thought of death. Sigmund Freud's (1957) way of explaining it is that since the subconscious does not know its own death, a person can feel empowered by their own seeming immortality. As for Becker (1973), his explanation centres around our 'animal nature' to want to protect our own integrity which means we justify ourselves as being the object of primary value in the world. As he puts it, to feel immortal a person must stand out as the *hero* figure, the figure that not only seems more important than anything or anyone else but also makes the greatest contribution to the world around them.

There are problems with Becker's strategy in the twenty-first century though, the first issue being that it generally remains ineffective in our everyday lives because people are often too small and fictitious to be able to consider themselves a hero (Becker, 1973). While it is possible in present modernity to disguise ourselves as heroes by investing in performative identities, Baudrillard (1998) reminds us that such means of expression cannot help but ache of cosmetic falseness. As he argues, beneath the seemingly indestructible surface of 'synthetic individuality' there is no one there – 'the person with its passions, its will, its character (or banality) … is absent, dead, swept out of our functional universe' (1998: 88). Using the power of metaphor, Bauman (2006) echoes this point but goes further to suggest that present modernity favours only two social roles, those of the celebrity and the victim.

Consonant with both Baudrillard's and Bauman's ways of thinking, Becker (1973) suggests that if you tell a person they are a hero in our world of heavy consumption and consumerism, they are likely to feel embarrassed because big cars, impressive homes and branded clothing do not reflect true heroic worth. What this indicates, then, is that while heroism demands a similar degree of selfishness as performativity, it remains a natural act, a pent-up force that has no place in the wider world of make-believe or, as Baudrillard would call it, hyper-reality. Heroism, therefore, is better thought of as being something that occurs in response to something, a disastrous incident for instance, rather than an end in itself.

The second problem with Becker's survival strategy is that it can be difficult for a person to convince themselves of their heroism without help. As Becker (1973) explains, for a writer or an artist, perhaps even a respected public speaker, immortality can be reached through great work which will continue to have an impact upon people long after their death has occurred, but ultimately it requires the support of other people. In other words, certain individuals become heroic (and therefore immortal) over time only as their contribution to the world moves from being something that is recognised to something that is revered. Needless to say, this way of achieving heroism is unlikely to be possible for me, Mayhem and Mcnally since very few cavers are ever likely to be remembered for their exploits in the natural underground, unless of course they discover or achieve something extraordinary. Furthermore, given the demands of immediacy (i.e. trying to escape a flooding cave) immortality gained in this way would be utterly useless. Any immortality gained would arrive too late, by which point we would have already succumbed to mortality.

Notwithstanding the problems highlighted above, the drive towards heroism can still be used as a survival strategy by people in the natural underground because there are key moments when we believe in the idea that something about *us* has some vast significance. Aware that our own discrete attempts to become heroic are likely to fail, what we do instead – when it is necessary – is visualise ourselves as being part of something else that has eternal meaning. As Becker (1973) explains, in becoming part of a greater heroic machine we successfully attach ourselves to something bigger than all of us, something we deem to be influential and everlasting. Thinking about this in relation to the episode above, I want to argue that while making our way out of Jackpot we convinced ourselves we were members of a leisure class of survivors that sets us apart from the rest of society. In doing this, we were able to exaggerate our role in the larger heroic machine that is *being-a-caver*.

As Becker reminds us, a person 'cannot justify [their] own heroism in [their] own inner symbolic fantasy' (1973: 185). By this he means that people who glorify themselves only in fantasy cannot escape the 'unreality of fantasised self-glorification' (185). Convincing ourselves otherwise would require a fair degree of self-delusion and potentially lead to a dangerous kind of megalomania (ibid). It could also cause the very thing we endeavour to avoid – death. Certainly, if we had fantasised about self-glorification as we were climbing out of the Second Pitch of Jackpot, or in the main entrance passageway where we were unable to breathe, we would perhaps have been lost to our own egotism. What we were facing in other words was an unquestionably real situation that was beyond the control of a single body imagining themselves as a hero, a situation as Foucault (1980) would suggest that made us dependent upon the impersonal power-knowledge of a larger social body.

In thinking about larger social bodies, it is Bauman (2010) who reminds us that superhuman forces have been relied upon across human history to provide collectively shared certainty when there is none and support when it is lacking. As Bauman (2010) explains, human beings are remarkably effective at exploiting greater forces that tame and domesticate things that are not only beyond individual control but also our comprehension. Such forces may traditionally have been found in gods, compelling regimes or forms of nationalism claiming to have answers to our problems. Yet, none of these examples would have been particularly useful for us in the natural underground since they have become weak in present modernity and faith in them is frequently found to be faltering (Bauman, 2010). What we did have, however, as I noted above, is the superhuman force of *being-a-caver*, a force comprising all the qualities we may already possess in addition to some we perhaps still yearn to acquire. In other words, because Mayhem, Mcnally and I had managed to access a place that cannot be reached by 'normal', everyday human beings using tactics, strategies and equipment belonging to *cavers* we felt we were equipped with enough relevant knowledge, skills and resources to be able to survive and overcome our inferiority against the natural underground.

It was, therefore, under the superhuman force of *being-a-caver* that we were able to shoulder the heroic task of staying calm and collected as we battled raging water, and why we found ourselves capable of working instinctively with immediate knowingness when we deemed support for one another necessary or had to make a split-second decision. We were engaged in the project of the hero. This is a survival strategy, much like the others mentioned earlier, that occurs when the task of resisting mortality is thrust upon a person, but it works by convincing people they are momentarily untouchable precisely because they have a certain specialness about them.

Summary

While we may be unable to perceive it, human beings know precisely what death means. It is not only absolute but, as Bauman puts it, also 'an absolute nothing' (1992: 2), which makes it terrifying. More terrifying still is that it is something we cannot forget entirely or learn to unknow because it lies in waiting, slowly choosing when our turn will eventually arrive. The uncertainty fills us with horror, but what is even worse is the realisation that we will no longer be around to tell our story.

In the interim, however, the task of survival occupies the minds of most twenty-first-century individuals. Our aim is generally threefold: to push back the moment of death and extend our lifespan, give meaning to life and make our existence fulfilling. What this means in other words is that we become a little bit God-like as our task turns into one of defiance – the defiance of death to ensure something is made of life. For the most part, it is consumer capitalism that lifts death above the level of our concern. This is what governs the majority of our lives in present modernity and one of its greatest achievements, despite its own inherent ephemerality, is that it can render our own mortality invisible and transform the general idea into a source of entertainment. And for the most part, it works in the everyday world. By making us youthful and hyper-athletic, and by transforming death into forms of thanatological-themed pleasure, it neutralises mortality and helps us cope with the trauma and anxiety of our impermanence.

In the natural underground, though, things work a little differently. Extending the arguments made in Chapter 3, what this chapter drew attention to is the idea that the kingdom of the dark is much more difficult to commodify. That is to say, it is more resistant to the usual influences of consumer capitalism, influences that are found virtually everywhere in the surface world. Supporting this point is the reality that the relationship between death and the underground has always been close, so close in fact that the underground is regularly used as a symbol of mortality. Crucially, then, those practised and approved life strategies we use in our everyday lives become ineffective.

With the above ideas in mind, this chapter was an attempt to unpack three strategies of survival I witnessed and experienced while exploring the natural underground. In a nutshell, they are a means of defusing the awfulness and sheer horror of death because they offer a guarantee (really an illusion of course) of immortality. Although each one works independently, what they all have in common is their reliance upon other human beings. Each one is a collective endeavour, requiring the support of other people in different ways. For example, the survival of 'Others' might sometimes be used to inspire and give strength in the fight against mortality, but there may also be times when people find themselves justifying the need for the deaths of 'Others'. In the end, of course the type of strategy selected does not really matter. All that matters is that there are ways and means of knowing it is 'Us' who are the survivors, and this allows feast on the idea that 'We' are capable of defying the eternal grave.

Notes

1 A more detailed version of the story can be found in Murray and Brucker's 1982 book, *Trapped! The Story of Floyd Collins*.

2 Before entering Jackpot, the three of us had been discussing two caving fatalities that had occurred in the Peak District in nearby caves. The stories of Paul Fowkes and David Briggs were brought up. Fowkes died as a result of hypothermia when he got into difficulties returning up Garland's Pot, while Briggs was crushed by a boulder during a dig near Aston Hill Farm.

3 To be clear, I am not suggesting Paul Fowkes and David Briggs really were unprepared or that they were killed due to overexcitement. Whether they were or not is irrelevant. My point is that Mayhem, Mcnally and I merely had to convince ourselves (and one another) that these were the reasons they died.

References

Baudrillard, J. (1998). *The Consumer Society: Myths and Structures*. London: SAGE.

Bauman, Z. (1992). *Mortality, Immortality & Other Life Strategies*. Cambridge: Polity.

Bauman, Z. (2001a). *Community: Seeking Safety in an Insecure World*. Cambridge: Polity.

Bauman, Z. (2001b). *The Individualized Society*. Cambridge: Polity.

Bauman, Z. (2006). *Liquid Life*. Cambridge: Polity.

Bauman, Z. (2010). *44 Letters from the Liquid Modern World*. Cambridge: Polity.

Beck, U. (1995). *Ecological Enlightenment: Essays on the Politics of the Risk Society*. Trans. M. Ritter. Atlantic Highlands, N J: Humanity Press.

Becker, E. (1973). *The Denial of Death*. New York: The Free Press.

Berger, P. (1969). *The Social Reality of Religion*. Faber.

Blackshaw, T. (2010). *Key Concepts in Community Studies*. London: SAGE.

Blackshaw, T. (2016). Community. In: T. Blackshaw (Ed), *The New Bauman Reader: Thinking Sociologically in Liquid Modern Times*. Manchester: Manchester University Press. 129–140.

Blackshaw, T. (2018). Some Notes on the Language Game of Dark Leisure. *Annals of Leisure Research*. 21(4): 395–406.

Brophy, J. (1972). *The Long Trail: Soldiers' Songs and Slang, 1914–18*. New York: Books for Libraries Press.

Canetti, E. (1962). *Crowds and Power*. New York: Viking Press.

Carel, H. (2006). *Life and Death in Freud and Heidegger*. Amsterdam: Rodopi.

Feifel, H. (2014). Death. In: N. Farberow (Ed), *Taboo Topics*. Oxon: Routledge, 8–21.

Foucault, M. (1980). *Power-Knowledge: Selected Interviews & Other Writings*. Trans. C. Gordon. New York: Pantheon.

Freud, S. (1957). On the History of the Psycho-Analytic Movement: Papers on Metapsychology and Other Works. Trans. J. Strachey and A. Freud. London: The Hogarth Press.

Giddens, A. (1991). *Modernity and Self-Identity: Self and Society in the Late Modern Age*. Cambridge: Polity.

Glover, T. and Sharpe, E. (2020). *Leisure Communities: Rethinking Mutuality, Collective Identity and Belonging in the New Century*. Oxon: Routledge.

Gorer, G. (1955). The Pornography of Death. In: G. Gorer (Ed), *Death, Grief and Mourning*. New York: Doubleday, 192–199.

Jones, C. (2020). *Immortal: How the Fear of Death Drives Us and What We Can Do About It*. Oregon: Harvest House.

Khapaeva, D. (2017). *The Celebration of Death in Contemporary Culture*. University of Michigan Press.

Laqueur, T. (2015). *The Work of the Dead: A Cultural History of Mortal Remains*. Oxford: Princeton University Press.

Lovelock, J. (1963). *Life and Death Underground*. London: G. Bell and Sons.

Mellor, P. (1993). Death in High Modernity: The Contemporary Prescence and Absence of Death. *The Sociological Review*. 40(1): 11–30.

Mellor, P. and Shilling, C. (1993). Modernity, Self-identity and the Sequestration of Death. *Sociology*. 27: 411–431.

Melvin, M. (n.d.). The Mossdale Tragedy 1967. [Online]. Retrieved from: https://www.michaelmelvin.co.uk/mossdale/The%20Mossdale%20Tragedy.pdf

Murray, R. and Brucker, R. (1982). *Trapped! The Story of Floyd Collins*. Lexington: The University Press of Kentucky.

Nicolson, J. (2010). *The Great Silence: 1918–1920 Living in the Shadow of the Great War*. Canada: McArthur.

Piemonte, N. and Abreu, S. (2021). *Death and Dying*. Cambridge, MA: MIT Press.

Rawls, J. (1971). *A Theory of Justice*. Cambridge, MA: The Belknap Press.

Seale, C. (1998). *Constructing Death: The Sociology of Dying and Bereavement*. Cambridge: Cambridge University Press.

Spracklen, K. (2018). Sex, Drugs, Satan and Rock and Roll: Re-thinking Dark Leisure, from Theoretical Framework to an Exploration of Pop-rock-metal Music Norms. *Annals of Leisure Research*. 21(4): 407–423.

Stark, J. (2020). *The Cult of Youth: Anti-Aging in Modern Britain*. Cambridge: Cambridge University Press.

Stone, P. (2009). Making Absent Death Present: Consuming Dark Tourism in Contemporary Society. In: R. Sharpley and P. Stone (Eds), *The Darker Side of Travel: The Theory and Practice of Dark Tourism*. Bristol: Channel View Publications, 23–38.

Stone, P. and Sharpley, R. (2008). Consuming Dark Tourism: A Thanatological Perspective. *Annals of Tourism Research*. 35(2): 574–595.

Tönnies, F. (1955). *Gemeinschaft und Gesellschaft (Community and Society)*. London: SAGE.

Willmott, H. (2000). Death. So What? Sociology, Sequestration and Emancipation. *The Sociological Review*. 48(4): 649–665.

Chapter 7

An Uncommercial Traveller's Guide to the Art of Sublimation

Introduction

In an attempt to bolt together the key observations and ideas presented so far in this book, this chapter turns the reader's attention to two important concepts termed the *sublime* and the *differend*. As the chapter continues, it will become clearer what each term means and how they are relevant to the natural underground, but for now I will begin with the point that a particular feeling is found through the differend. The feeling, according to Jean-François Lyotard (1994), is that of the sublime.

The concept of the sublime is said to bear its foundations in literature dating back to the first century (see Longinus, 1739), but it is Edmund Burke's *Philosophical Inquiry into the Origin of Our Ideas of the Sublime and Beautiful* that provides the first detailed introduction. In fact, it was Burke's (1769/2008) treatise of aesthetics outlining what constitutes the sublime and the various qualities it possesses that provided the English Romantic movement with a theoretical footing. In a nutshell, Burke's understanding is that the sublime is not only a feeling of intense pain, danger and terror but also the strongest emotion a person is capable of feeling, one that is significantly greater than emotions caused by pleasure.

The work of Burke, however, has diminished in the shadow of Immanuel Kant's *Analytic of the Sublime*. What sets Kant's (1790/2007) sublime apart from that of Burke's is the claim that objects in nature are not sublime. While Burke (1769/2008) viewed nature as the most sublime object, and also believed it could be found in powerful forms of art such as literature and painting, for Kant it is a quality of the mind. As he argues, powerful storms, vast oceans and looming mountains are all subject to the imagination. Hence, Kant (1790/2007) describes the sublime as a mode of consciousness that occurs when a person becomes aware of divine experiences. The sublime according to Kant also features a strange form of negative pleasure:

> The feeling of the sublime is … at once a feeling of displeasure, arising from the inadequacy of imagination in the aesthetic estimation of magnitude to

DOI: 10.4324/9781003301752-7

attain to its estimation by reason, and a simultaneously awakened pleasure, arising from this very judgement of the inadequacy of the greatest faculty of sense.

(1790/2007: 88)

Working within similar parameters to Kant, postmodern scholars such as Jean-François Lyotard and Jacques Derrida were involved in the next major movement to take a lively interest in the sublime. In contrast to Romantics who relied on grand narratives or overarching master concepts such as nature, the likes of Lyotard (1994) and Derrida (1987) adopted a more sceptical attitude. What this means is that although postmodern understandings of sublimity retain some Romantic feeling for the vast and unlimited, attempts to realise it do not make any kind of reference to a higher faculty. Instead, this movement emphasises, unashamedly and without regret, the inability of reason or art to render the vast and unlimited representable. As Lyotard (1984) suggests, it seeks to sustain the 'incommensurability of reality' (79) and maintain the shock of the sublime. The sublime according to Lyotard and Derrida, therefore, is about searching for new ways in which it presents itself. The task is not necessarily about enjoying them either; it is rather, as Lyotard (1984) claims, to continue finding a stronger sense of the unpresentable.

It is beyond the scope of this book to provide a comprehensive history of the concept of the sublime. Hence, the above interpretations should merely be viewed as a means of demonstrating the point that what they all share in common is that the sublime generally refers to that which cannot be represented. It also refers to pleasure found in displeasure, disharmony, fragmentation and those moments when thought teeters on the edge of extinction or oblivion. In other words, the sublime is often juxtaposed against the beautiful which relates to harmony and unity. To borrow the succinctness of one of Philip Shaw's conclusions, 'sublimity arises when the harmony of a body of thought is brought into question' (2006: 149).

Keeping the above ideas in mind, what I want to argue in the remainder of this chapter is that exploring the natural underground, and of course using it as a means of evading the talons of consumer capitalism, is ultimately about locating the sublime feeling. It is, as Lyotard (1994) would likely have suggested, about finding a stronger sense of the unpresentable. With this suggestion, that ought really to be that. I could conclude that when it is explored the kingdom of the dark is often effective in stimulating imaginations, senses and emotions in complex ways. I could also conclude that exploration of the natural underground typically involves some degree of displeasure and disharmony, but that some twenty-first-century individuals are able to find pleasure and satisfaction nonetheless. As it happens, however, I would like to say a little more about sublimity. What I want to suggest is that there is a delicate art to finding it, an art that has been mastered by explorers of the natural underground. Such people become masters because they are adept at locating and negotiating the *differend*, something that might be thought of as a precursor to discovering the sublime feeling. If the reader is willing to bear with me for a short while longer, I endeavour now to explore this point further.

What follows in the remainder of this chapter is an insight into what it is like to be bombarded by three interweaving and cumulative sublime feelings that are produced by the differend, those of pleasure, pain, and outright trauma or terror. As the chapter will reveal, each experience of the differend (and the sublime feelings that follow) turns out to be a short-lived, one-time-only affair. Each one produces an amalgamated feeling, one dependent upon an individual being able to experience the tranquillity and noiselessness of the natural underground or their skill in gaining scotopic awareness, whether they have perhaps sampled a limit experience, or if they find themselves encountering a situation that exposes the true reality of human frailty and mortality.

When the Differend Speaks

Before the reader moves to the next episode, I feel it is important to note that while many ancient, modern and contemporary scholars have thought about and examined the sublime feeling, it is Lyotard's interpretation I draw on in this book. I have done so for a variety of reasons, the first being that Lyotard's (1994) work builds on the essential earlier work of Kant. What I find particularly useful about his carefully marshalled critique is his reversal of Kant's (1790/2007) understanding that the sublime, despite requiring human imagination to interpret it, is ultimately comprehended in an Idea of Totality (i.e. the soul, the world or God). For Lyotard (1994), the sublime does not lead to the pleasure of knowing the absolute certainty of a totality.

The second reason why I have adopted Lyotard's (1994) interpretation is that he not only explores what happens in the sublime moment but also suggests how it is found. What he argues is that it is the straining of the mind to the edges of itself and of its conceptuality that is key to finding sublimity. The word he uses to explain this is the *differend*. As I mentioned earlier, this idea forms an essential part of my discussion.

The third reason for choosing Lyotard's (1994) interpretation is the fact it does not fall into the inoperable abyss of a Žižekian kind of interpretation which purports that 'the sublime is an object which cannot be approached too closely' (Žižek, 1989: 170). From this standpoint, the sublime cannot help but become an illusion when people realise there is nothing beneath the surface. All that remains of sublimity is the sublime feeling that arises when it is realised there is nothing behind the object. Crucially, Lyotard's (1994) analysis differs and while he recognises there are difficulties involved in knowing and understanding what the source of the sublime is, he is clear that individuals can consume its meaning. In other words, Lyotard's interpretation is serviceable, not only because it acknowledges the point that the matter and presence of the sublime should be approached but also because it encourages us to question what is possible under the influence of sublimity.

132   Uncommercial Traveller's Guide to Sublimation

Now the reader has a better understanding of the direction I have opted to take, we can move on to the first part of the rolling episode that is used to make strategic interjections throughout this chapter. As the reader will see, I use this as a means of steadily unpacking the differend and, thereafter, those three sublime feelings I identified above – pleasure, pain and outright trauma.

—

There were four of us this time, Mayhem, a caver called Jim Figg who I'd met up with a few weeks earlier to explore Knotlow Cavern, a guy called Jamie Daly who was a mate of Mayhem's and fairly new to caving, and me. It was mid-August, and we were up at the crack of dawn to collect a key stashed under a rock in the small village of Castleton. The key would give us access to a cavern named Titan. Discovered in 1999, Titan is the biggest natural shaft in the United Kingdom. Sixty-two metres taller than Malham Cove, it has been measured at 141 metres. Since we'd first started exploring the natural underground, this particular cave had been the topic of many conversations. To Peak District fell walkers and locals we'd occasionally crossed paths with, the cave is well known for being indescribably big. As for experienced cavers we'd met along the way, they always seemed to recall the immense fear they felt regardless of the number of visits they might have made. It turned out that even urban explorers we know have heard of Titan because of its enormity. For us then, this was a cave that had the potential to be one of the most spectacular underground descents we could make in the United Kingdom.

After collecting the key, we made our way out to the fields above Winnats Pass. To avoid having to carry our gear for miles, we parked as close as we possibly could to Titan along an old farmer's track roughly 600 metres south of the cave entrance. Although it was forecast rain later in the day, presently we were met with bright sunshine and a blue, cloudless sky. No matter which way we looked, we could see for miles. This set a positive tone for the day as we began to carry our equipment over the short distance to the lidded entrance. It didn't take too long to locate the lid, but my immediate thought when we found it was that it seemed a little too ordinary-looking from the outside (Figure 7.1). I'm not sure why I thought it would be different, but it really was just like any other lid we'd encountered so far. Things changed, however, the moment we opened it up. It was clear we were peering into the entrance of a cave bearing much greater significance than anything we'd seen before, a cave not only capable of taunting our emotions and manipulating us but also causing our imaginations to run wild.

Before we pulled on our oversuits and struggled into harnesses, Jim and I made a hasty coffee on a gas stove we'd brought along with us. While we did this, Mayhem started to rig the entrance pitch and confirm Jamie was confident using caving gear. Satisfied with Jamie's level of competence, he finished attaching the rope to a set of metal bolts and threw the rest into the shaft below. The rope made its usual hum as it fell, but the noise was amplified this time by the concrete lining of the excavated hole. Jim then decided he would go first, so he clipped himself onto a safety line with his cowstails and sat down on the lip of the entrance to connect himself to the rope. Once attached, he eased himself into the hole to test

Figure 7.1 The entrance to Titan.

his weight on the line. Certain he was safe he then unclipped his protection and began the abseil into a horizontal passage 45 metres below ground.

While we waited for Jim to yell 'ROPE FREE', the rest of us discussed how bitter the coffee was, the rain that was forecast and whether it was a good day for doing Titan. It was clear there were mixed feelings and that a great deal of nervousness was circulating among us. Although it was still warm and sunny, Mayhem was concerned about the waterfall inside Titan and that the forecast had predicted heavy rain and potential flooding across parts of Derbyshire. As the most inexperienced member of the group, Jamie had his own worries; he was anxious about the height of Titan, and whether he would have the strength to make the ascent after reaching the bottom. As for me, I was busy worrying about why Titan is so famous, and, most crucially, why it's called Titan. It wasn't just that the ascent was said to be gruelling but also that the undertaking is typically reported to be nothing short of terrifying.

In between worrying and procrastinating, I happened to glance around and look at the others. This was the moment it dawned on me just how anxious everybody was. The demeanour of both Jamie and Mayhem bore the impression of people who didn't really want to be there. In truth, I was already aware that Mayhem was feeling uneasy. Only a week earlier while we were still in the process of planning our visit to Titan, he'd very nearly bailed on us. As he put it at the time, 'It's just too fucking dangerous man, like, I think it's too much, past the limit of what we should do sort of thing'. By this point, our conversation had dried up and we were left watching the entrance in complete silence for a short while. Fortunately, Jim's yell came before we could worry anymore. Rather than let my feelings of disconcertment stew any longer, I decided to go next so I set about clipping myself into the rope. Satisfied I was safe, I then slid out of sight of the others into the darkness below.

Locating the Differend

In his book, *The Differend: Phrases in Dispute*, Lyotard describes the differend not only as something that is missing but also as that which cannot be clearly described. To borrow his exact phrasing, he explains that the differend is 'what is not presentable under the rules of knowledge' (1988: 93), which hints it is a frantic struggle between both reason and imagination. What we are dealing with, in other words, is what Lyotard (1988) is referring to as an imposing *Silence*, or more particularly, as Dylan Sawyer puts it, 'the Silence of silence' (2014: 157). As Sawyer (2014) argues, the differend effectively represents a 'blind spot' that is at the same time inexplicable but also echoes loudly with a type of sound that is inaudible. To experience it, Lyotard (1988) suggests that it must first be witnessed and then allied feelings must be acknowledged because it is only feelings that reveal when a differend is present. What Lyotard also suggests is that it is the task of scholars to attend to this phenomenon and comprehend its infinite finalities as best as possible.

Contrary to Lyotard's (1988) suggestion about the need for scholars to unpack various instances of the differend, what I want to argue here is that explorers of the natural underground are the sort of people who are proficient at locating it. They are, as reflexive beings, able to look (temporarily at least) beyond the doxic information and influences that are part and parcel of 'liquid' modernity. What this means is that when underground explorers attend to the Silence of the kingdom of the dark, what they notice is the disappearance of real silence (i.e. nothingness) and the emergence of something far more vehement. In a sense, then, the differend might be viewed as being a form of intuition, a kind of knowingness that a presence is waiting to be heard as new feelings and emotions are primed to erupt. Simply put, what is being suggested here is that cavers know there are impermanent endings to silence in the world beneath our feet, ready and waiting to be imagined and/or discovered.

With their intuition, then, explorers of the natural underground are able to bring new, unknown feelings into existence which can be referred to collectively as feelings of the sublime. Of course, I am not suggesting that underground explorers can easily, or coherently, put into language what they are feeling, but I am conscious they are aware of those strange emotions and unfamiliar sensations they have experienced and how it is impossible to place those emotions and sensations into words in any precise way. Looking to shed some light on the topic, I now attempt to exploit my position as an underground explorer and explain, as best as I can, not just the effectual forces that are at play but what it feels like to rub up against the differend and embrace Silence.

—

The four of us gathered in the horizontal passage at the bottom of the first pitch before heading west towards the hole in the wall of Titan. The passage was partially flooded so the space echoed loudly with the sounds of splashes as we waded our way forwards. We turned left, and then right where the window loomed into sight.

Mayhem clambered through the window first. Of our group, he had the most powerful headtorch so wanted to illuminate the world of Titan for us. However, he was immediately disappointed because the beam from his light seemed insignificant against the sheer enormity of the cave. He yelled out into the dark. The echo of his voice rang out into the invisible depths of the void, penetrating much further than our lights until it eventually became unintelligible. Taking turns, the rest of us gave it a go. Our sounds alone were enough to make us feel in awe of the incomprehensible scale of the cavern. As Jim set about rigging the first 80-metre pitch, I sat down for a while and listened intently. I was fascinated as the void sucked at the sounds of his jangling metalwork and our general conversation. What struck me was not only how small our echoes made me feel, but how the steady scratch of our breathing and the shuffles of our clothing were tremendously infinitesimal against the acoustic might of Titan.

I was the last to descend and as I was waiting I felt quite alone. With the sounds of the others suddenly missing, the balcony I was perched on had grown completely silent. Other than a very faint speck of light 80 metres or so beneath me, I couldn't see the others either. When the rope finally went slack, I slid myself further out onto the ledge. The loose rope meant Jamie had just reached the halfway point and the changeover. I set to work preparing my descender, doing my best to ignore the void below that seemed to be trying to pull me into its depths. I looked down again as I prepared to ease myself into the abyss. A very thin fog was swirling around me as I felt the rope take my weight, further obscuring any chance I might've had of viewing the size and scale of Titan.

Loosening the descender, I started sliding down the rope gingerly. Fear gripped me as I inched my way beneath the balcony which turned out to be an overhang. Suddenly, I'd entered the abyss and it was, in one word, terrifying. I stared straight ahead and slowed the speed of my descent as I fought hard in my mind to regain a sense of fearlessness. With darkness looming on all sides, it seemed as though Titan was so big it would continue forever. Unable to see much at all, I began to listen instead to the things going on around me. Very little was audible at first, but the more I concentrated the more I found I could hear. An occasional drip would rattle from below, and the rope would creak gently whenever I moved. Then, I noticed something different. I became aware of the echo within. In everything I'd read about Titan, nobody had described anything like it, yet it was exquisite and different to the echoes I'd heard from the window. I paused and took care to listen more intently. Entirely devoid of distinction, it seemed to quiver up and down the cavern until it faded away into the obscurity of the space above me. The longer I listened, the more agreeable and comforting it became. In some indescribable way, it seemed to revive my hold on life, and I felt more closely linked to my surroundings than I had at any other point in the cave so far.

With my courage rekindled in some measure, I released more tension on my descender and began to drop smoothly through the air. I started to spin, but I didn't seem to mind too much. The echo within the heart of the cave, combined with the sound of my rope whizzing through my device, was almost spellbinding. Swirling, I couldn't resist a bit more speed. I was ready to rush into the gloom and hear Titan's darkness and emptiness roar with life.

—

To remind the reader, being an explorer of the natural underground involves being able to find the differend among the Silence. Once it is found, the sublime feeling is subsequently revealed (Sawyer, 2014). Before any of this is possible, however, the Silence must be pinpointed and, according to Lyotard (2011), the best way of doing this is visually as it is our dominant sensory system. Lyotard (2011) valorises sight because he feels the human eye is not limited to a single mode of presentation or representation which means it is capable of capturing many shades of meaning. Yet, as was highlighted in Chapter 4, there is an obvious problem with sight in the natural underground since the visual system loses its position of dominance. What this indicates is that we need to think more broadly about the ways in which sublimity can be found and we can do this by thinking about how the other sensory systems are just as capable of detecting it.

In the absence of sufficient light, the auditory system seemed to take over as the dominant sense. As we emerged from the excavated horizontal passage in the west wall of Titan, we found ourselves at a window in the rock, peering into the largest natural chamber any of us has ever seen. Our high-powered torches were no match for the sheer scale of the cavern; its walls continued down, disappearing towards an invisible ledge known as The Event Horizon and then even further into an endless black hole. The sounds of our voices trailed off into the abyss, fading into soundlessness long before they could become echoes. In his 1757 book *Enquiry*, Burke describes certain experiences that are sonic and forceful, contributing to what I might call the sonic sublime, and in my mind this is precisely what we experienced before we even began our descent into Titan. To quote Burke directly:

> The eye is not the only organ of sensation, by which a sublime passion may be produced. Sounds have a great power in these as in most other passions

Uncommercial Traveller's Guide to the Sublimation 137

... Excessive loudness alone is sufficient to overpower the soul, to suspend its action, and to fill it with terror.

(1769/2007: 120)

Furthermore, while Burke's bringing together of sounds produced by animals and human beings has been used to understand both the continuities and discontinuities between non-human and human environments (Buch, 2020), I would argue that the general premise of his idea is transferrable to the natural underground. That is to say, the sounds produced by us, an infinitesimal group of human beings, suddenly seemed inharmonious with the world around us. Our sounds seemed to be somewhat at odds with our surroundings and not quite compatible, and this undercut our sense of stability. The clanking of tackle and the scratches of our heightened breathing seemed curiously insignificant against the great vibration of emptiness emanating from Titan. Our sounds dissolved long before any of our humanness could gain hold of the space.

Despite problems of scale and representation, our ears were still the best tool available to make sense of the Silence surrounding us. Yet, before we could take what we were hearing and translate it into words, it was important for us to take everything auditory at face value and accept it for what it was. As I have argued elsewhere, following this rule brings about a spatial affirmation of things that are unfamiliar and unknown, and it provides a means of truly experiencing whatever is concealed in the Silence (Bingham, 2020). As Willem Elias (1997) reminds us, attempting to generate words too soon and impulsively is the wrong approach because anything committed to language implies greater fixity and structure.

Once the differend contained within the Silence has been witnessed, the next step is to identify exactly what is being felt. The problem, of course, as was noted above, is that it cannot be easily articulated. Really, the only way to explicate the differend after it has been sensed is to convey it using words (Lyotard, 1988), which may seem contradictory given the argument I made above about fixity and structure. However, as Lyotard (1988) reasons, while language may not be the most effective method of revealing something about things that are missing and inexpressible, it is the best means of detailing sensations of sublimity we have at our disposal. It will no doubt be an inadequate description and a far cry away from what the others experienced, but I will try my best in the next few paragraphs to illustrate what I felt based on the auditory event. To further strengthen the description, I also outline some of the others' descriptions of the sublime feeling which were similarly stirred by sound.

As I descended into the seemingly infinite depths of Titan, almost immediately I found myself subscribing to E. M. Forster's distinction between sight and sound, a distinction found in his novel A Passage to India. What Forster (1924/2000) suggests is that vision is typically associated with control and sound with connection, and this is precisely what went through my mind as I started to let the rope steadily whirr through my descender. Conscious that my eyes in the surface world would normally penetrate the colours and shapes of everything around me, and that I would therefore usually experience the world as an organised but distant spectacle, my attention was diverted to an auditory sensory force that was suddenly being impelled to work intensely. What dawned on me is that while sight usually helps us make superficial sense of the world as it enables people to create spaces that are sequential which means things are experienced in '[their] proper place, at the proper time, and in linear relationship' (McLuhan, 2004: 69–70), the sounds I was experiencing put me in closer touch with the chaos of a much more capricious environment. Rather than being able to understand the space around me by visualising something whole, I became what Lipari (2010) describes as a 'listening being', an individual who temporarily suspends familiar conceptions, beliefs and understandings and arrives at the presence of something that is felt rather than seen. A handful of people demonstrate this ability in Forster's (1924/2000) novel, individuals capable of locating the 'force that lies behind', but it seems to elude most others.

Enveloped in the Silence of Titan, the others and I did not make the same error as Forster's central characters, the likes of Mrs Moore and Adela who are unable to confront the true appearance of the Marabar Caves. While Forster's (1924/2000) caves are claustrophobic and disturbing, and mark the hollowness of the lives of his characters because they do not know how to listen, Mayhem, Jim, Jamie and I were able to open our ears to the sounds around us and celebrate a deeper sense of awareness and affinity with the natural underground. The sounds of Titan, therefore, for me at least, align extraordinarily well with Jean-Luc Nancy's representation of *listening*. To borrow his way of putting it:

> To listen is to enter that spatiality by which, *at the same time*, I am penetrated, for it opens up in me as well as around me, and from me as well as toward me: it opens me inside me as well as outside, and it is through such a double, quadruple, or sextuple opening that a 'self' can take place. To be listening is to be *at the same time* outside and inside, to be open *from* without and *from* within, hence from one to the other and from one in the other.
>
> (2015: 21)

For Mayhem and Jim, things were interpreted a little differently. Nevertheless, their interpretations still reveal how they opened their ears to the sounds going on around them and how this helped put them in closer touch with the natural underground. This is what they said when I spoke to them shortly after visiting Titan:

Mayhem: I couldn't see much, I just sat in silence and listened. The sound of air, not air but something invisible like air, rising up from the depths is what I remember most. That wasn't on the plans before we went in. It made me feel weirdly small but also comfortable at the same time. After listening to the, I dunno, the sort of rushing sound I started to feel like I was part of the cave for a bit. Like, from the cave's point of view. I realised how insignificant we are in comparison, but how fucking incredible our bodies actually are because we can use them to wriggle our way right into the sounds of such immense places.

Jim: I felt, right, like I'd wandered into a maze of sounds down there. Sometimes, there's one that might seem familiar, but only sometimes. I don't mean the sounds are unpleasant or anything because they're not, they're satisfying. Probably captivating is a better word. Actually, in Titan it's like you're listening to the songs of an unknown creature, but a creature that you only find underground. I don't mean an animal kind of creature, nothing like that, I'm talking about the cave as the animal.

To reiterate my earlier point, there is no easily communicable way of interpreting the feeling of the sublime, nor one sense that can be relied on to help explain it. In this instance, as I have attempted to unpack how Titan made us feel, the auditory system was used. Nevertheless, as the reader has seen, making it communicable has still been a challenging and delicate task.

Another issue I have wrestled with, one Lyotard (2006) himself reminds us about, is that when we try to form concrete descriptions of the sublime feeling they threaten the state and quality of subjectivity. As Lyotard (2006) argues, concrete descriptions not only damage creativity and individuality, but they also inhibit the differend from being identified in the first place. What this means is that the feeling should never become homogenised; it should, rather, be interpreted in more ways than one, hence why I focused on the many sounds of Titan and included a range of different auditory experiences as we descended the vast shaft. What really matters is that it is located by multiple perspectives at the centre of environments that are inimitable and a little bit chaotic. Certainly, what helps capture the heterogeneity of sublime feelings are various forms of leisure, especially those Chris Rojek (2000) describes as 'abnormal', or types of exploratory art because such things help us unveil the 'conditions of possibility' within the surrounding Silence. In this instance, exploration of the natural underground was the means. As I have found, it is a useful means of finding an excess of presence and what Lyotard (1985) describes as the *avant-garde*.

There is of course more to the sublime feeling than what I have discussed here, especially on the matter of pleasure and pain. Before we can explore it further, however, we need to return once again to the narrative episode that has been running throughout this chapter.

Pleasure and Pain: A Recipe for Seduction

Unclipping myself from the rope, I turned to look for the others and gather my bearings. I'd landed at the bottom of a pile of boulders close to the base of the waterfall. Fortunately, it was relatively dry, so I didn't get a good soaking. Following the position of their head torches, I clambered up the rocks and made my way towards the spot where Mayhem and Jim had chosen to rest (Figure 7.2).

Figure 7.2 Contemplating the journey back up, all 141 metres of it.

On this occasion, Jamie hadn't descended the whole way. Instead, he'd opted to remain perched on The Event Horizon. It seemed his fear had gotten the better of him. My first thought as I found a comfortable rock to sit on was that the bottom of Titan was a lot smaller than I'd expected. In fact, compared to the descent it was almost anticlimactic.

After chatting for a while, and excitedly exchanging stories of the descent, we realised it was time to get moving. Mayhem and Jim had been sitting around longer than me and they were beginning to feel the cold. I remained sitting as the others walked back to the waiting rope. To save time and get us out more quickly, Mayhem opted to ascend on a second rope we'd rigged as a precautionary measure

Uncommercial Traveller's Guide to the Sublimation   141

that ran straight to the window 130 metres above our heads. Jim set up on the one we'd used to descend which was anchored to a rebelay point near Jamie.

I watched as the pair clipped in and started taking in slack. They appeared excited as their feet left the ground and also entertained by the insane amount of bounce in the ropes. The elasticity in Mayhem's was noticeably greater, and to the amusement of all of us he flailed around like a madman for several minutes before he had enough tension to make any progress upwards. As the pair slowly gained height, I tried to take some photos and yell some words of encouragement – 'Go on, lads. You're doing well!' Ten metres up and still brimming with optimism and excitement, Mayhem called back – 'This is unreal, mate. Absolutely, fucking, epic'. There was a pause, then another voice – 'I won't lie though, the bounce in this rope is scaring the shit out of me'. I continued to listen in to their intermittent conversation as they slowly inched their way up the ropes. What they were saying was interesting, almost Jekyll and Hyde like, as they would oscillate between two very different feelings. In one moment, they would appear roused and inexpressibly delighted, and every now and then there would be an occasional joyous 'WHOOP'. In the next, they would become fearful due to growing fatigue and surges of panic whenever something felt out of place. Whenever this happened, 'WOAHs' of anxiety would reverberate loudly throughout the cavern.

An eternity passed, or so it felt, as I waited for one of the ropes to become free. When Jim's finally was, I quickly set up my ascenders and began the mammoth task of getting out of Titan. After sitting alone at the bottom of the pitch, I'd grown cold and eager to surface so it felt good to attach my gear to the rope and make my first few movements upwards. Of course, I didn't get very far to begin with. Like the others, I had to contend with the extreme elasticity of the rope, but I pushed on and did my best to achieve a steady rhythm. I rested in my harness after several minutes of hard work and looked down. To my disappointment, for the amount of effort I felt I'd put in, the floor didn't seem very far away. Straightaway I began to feel unsettled by the lack of progress I was making, and I began to wonder whether I'd actually be able to make it out under my own steam. I was already sweating profusely. The entrance window seemed so far away it might as well have been on another planet.

I pushed on again, battling against the rope's springiness. I counted my movements upwards, resting briefly on every tenth. Soon I became more systematic, pushing with my legs to gain height, then moving my arms upwards to regain the bite and trust of my hand ascender. As I got into the rhythm, the clicking of my gear became regular, like the ticking of an old clock. This was broken now and then, but only mildly, whenever the rope gently spun me around in the abyss. Although I found it alarming, each time it happened I tried hard to rein back in on the cyclical task at hand – push up the hand ascender/lift legs upwards, grip with my hands and pull with hand/push down with my legs. Strangely, I began to enjoy the mixed bag of feelings I was enduring along with the satisfaction of hard work. I continued to repeat this process all the way to The Event Horizon, and then beyond after I passed and derigged the rebelay.

The second pitch, which is larger than the first, was a lot more terrifying and exhausting. Peering upwards became habitual as I was becoming more and more desperate to see some torchlight. I needed it to gauge how much further I had left to ascend. The others, I thought, must have been waiting inside the passage, or had perhaps already made their way to the bottom of the excavated tunnel pitch, because the space above me remained completely dark.[1] I was resting more frequently now, trying hard to distract myself with things I could focus my attention on. I became pleasantly contemplative at this point, especially when I noticed how some nearby flowstone resembled the salivating jaws of some horrific beast, but at the same time, I was beginning to feel the frustration of feeling tragically exhausted.

Drawing on what felt like my last reserves of strength, I continued to inch my way upwards. And then, I could see something looming in the darkness. It looked like an anchor point. I paused, willing my eyes to focus. It was an anchor! Elated and in a fit of enthusiasm, I began to speed up. Suddenly I felt reinvigorated, and with each movement the anchor point moved ever closer. A few more movements and my hand ascender made contact with the knot that was bearing all my weight. Sweating and breathing heavily, I paused to rest my arms and regain some strength. Then I clipped in my cowstails and hauled myself across to the relative safety of the balcony. Overwhelmed by joy and relief, I slumped onto the ledge and laid my body out flat. My chest was moving up and down rapidly, my muscles recovering from the fire of constant exertion. I felt utterly euphoric as I gradually began to reflect on the event that had just taken place.

—

As the narrative episode reveals, the feeling of the sublime did not merely end with us reaching the bottom of Titan. The feeling continued to materialise on our way back up and it did so I would suggest with far greater intensity than we had felt on our descent. As indicated above, once they were clipped back into the ropes and making progress upwards, Jim and Mayhem experienced a great deal of pleasure and excitement as they began to enter the abyssal space again, but there was also a terrific sense of pain and anguish as their fear returned with vengeance. The stretch and subsequent bounce in the rope was particularly disconcerting as the true delicacy of the only thing separating life from death was revealed to them. Really, there was nothing wrong with the rope, the true source of disconcertment lay entirely with the differend because it was evoking powerful emotions and sensations. The other unsettling thing Jim and Mayhem faced is that once again they both wanted to express and verbalise to one another what they were feeling but found themselves incapable.

The unsettling things mentioned above of course are precisely what makes witnessing the differend so incredible. They exist because the differend always remains perfectly balanced between the *positive* and the *negative* (Sawyer, 2014). By positive and negative I mean specifically pleasure and pain, two simple ideas that are much harder to define. Indeed, Burke (1769/2007) reminds us of this point with his suggestion that people are frequently mistaken in the names they give to pleasure and pain and in the reasons they give to explain their existence.

Nevertheless, Burke (1769/2007) also points out that humans are still very good at recognising when they are feeling either sensation because the majority of people generally endeavour to live their lives in a state of indifference (i.e. in a state of neither pleasure nor pain). I would argue that anyone who explores the natural underground is willing to seek out pleasure and pain because they can be stimulating and sensational, but they are still left with the problem of misrepresentation and incommunicability.

Regardless of our inability to express ourselves, what is interesting about the feeling while ascending Titan is that the power of pleasure and pain united and became one. Interestingly, William Wordsworth was one of the first to celebrate this peculiar feeling, moving away from the vivace of joy or pleasure celebrated by his contemporaries – the idea that such things merely suggest elation and gaiety – to emphasise the point that pain and anguish join with pleasure to become part of the same sensation (Mortensen, 1998). In other words, what Wordsworth (1805/2014) seems to suggest is that pain, so long as it is not avoided or averted, does not impede the Apollonian serenity of pleasure but develops it into a deeper sensation that is found somewhere between the two. As he writes: 'Having two natures in me, joy the one; the other melancholy, and withal; a happy man, and therefore bold to look; on painful things' (1805/2014: 872).

More interesting still is Wordsworth's (1835/2020) insinuation that the intense emotion of pain and pleasure is rarely an end in itself since he sees this ultimately as being destructive and threatening. In fact, according to David Gervais (1987), he deplored the so-called cult of strong emotion valuing emotion for its own sake. What Wordsworth looks to instead, and what is the real subject across much of his writing, is relief and the gradual advent of nostalgia. In Wordsworth's (1835/2020) mind, too much internal emotion is distracting and vexatious and likely to remind the person experiencing it of the weight of the unintelligible moment so he seems to suggest that the power of pain and pleasure should be admired for its restorative effects when it has finally stopped.

This is certainly what I experienced after our ascent of Titan. While making my way up the single static line, the weight of fear, the sheer magnitude of the situation and the sensation of my muscles burning ferociously from constant exertion were enough to isolate my focus to the rhythmic clicks of my ascenders and the brackish smell of dirt engrained in the rope. When I clambered back onto the balcony overlooking Titan, I was met with a flood of relief. After that, I simply 'stood and watched, till all was tranquil as a dreamless sleep' (Wordsworth, 1890: 241) and suddenly the full force of the feeling of the sublime totally consumed me. I was joyous to the point that it could stretch no further, and at the same time inhibited by the agony of discomfort and muteness. I had a lugubrious look about me as I laid my body flat on a ledge by the window, and with the mixed chaos of blind pain and pleasure coursing through my body, I suddenly found myself shrouded by an immediate calmness. It was a strange sensation that was thick upon me because it was my own, stirring no doubt because I was at the heart of a situation 'suffer[ing] [from] the wrong of not being able to be phrased' (Lyotard, 1988: 22–23). My central point here then is that there are few things in our world that are so personal than being the sole witness to the existence of something sublime in the differend.

It stands to reason then that ascending something like Titan is something that must be experienced directly, face-to-face and in the flesh. Yet, while Lyotard (1988) points out the sublime only exists in the immediate present, in the 'sensation of the instant', what I discovered in the natural underground is that it is more powerful in the instant that immediately follows the event. And therein lies the seduction. Every time I feel it, I am desperate to witness it again, but the point is that it is a short-lived, one-time-only feeling that is both positive and negative, extremely idiosyncratic, and highly dependent on an individual's immediate powers of reflection or contemplation. Certainly, Mayhem, Jim and Jamie will be able to comprehend what I experienced to some degree since they all experienced their own kind of feeling, but ultimately my own experience of the sublime is exclusively and retrospectively mine.

When the Recipe Goes Wrong: An Experience of the Traumatic Sublime

Keeping the above discussion in mind, it is essential at this point in the chapter that another observation concerning the sublime is addressed. This observation concerns upheaval, distress and things that might be considered nightmarish. As Sawyer (2014) points out, one of the central problems with Lyotard's concept of the sublime is that it is generally used to unpack a sort of seamless balance between pleasure and pain and this can easily be interpreted as representing a position of relative safety and security. I would add, building on Sawyer's (2014) critical observation, that most scholars dealing with the sublime feeling view it in a similar way. What I want to do, therefore, is direct the reader's attention to the idea that there are instances where a more intense and traumatic side of the sublime feeling can escalate. This is a feeling that intensifies to such an extent that it becomes impossible to respond to it at all. That is to say, neither pleasure nor pain is felt anymore. What develops instead is a blank void of absolute dread and desperation followed by a feeling of nothingness. To unpack this idea further, we will turn our attention to Jamie's experience of ascending Titan.

—

From his position on an adjacent rope, Mayhem could do little more than watch as Jamie trembled. His arms and legs were visibly shaking, and he was murmuring something about not being able to grip his hand ascender anymore. The single length of static rope he was attached to was spinning him slowly, making it even more difficult to get his head together. Each time he rotated away from the superficial safety of the nearby rock face, into the pitch-black darkness of the rest of the cavern, he would freeze and let out a terrified gasp. In a bid to spur him on, Mayhem tried yelling a few words of encouragement, but they failed to raise Jamie's determination and spirit. Occasionally he would grit his teeth and haul himself upwards by a few inches, but his progress was painstakingly slow (Figure 7.3).

Uncommercial Traveller's Guide to the Sublimation   145

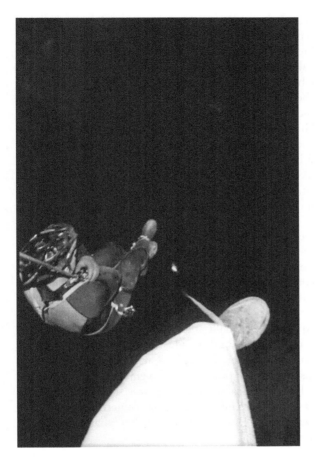

Figure 7.3 Jamie suspended beneath Mayhem.

Jamie was about halfway up the second pitch at this point, the pitch that would eventually end at the window that is used as the upper entrance to Titan. Beneath him was a drop of approximately 95 metres to the ground. The ground was invisible, and even if his headtorch had been working the jagged rocks below would have remained hidden from view because the darkness was so impenetrable to light. There was no doubt in Jamie's mind that it would be a horrific fall if any of his other equipment was to fail on him. What made things worse was that it was impossible to back out. It would have been counterintuitive to return to The Event Horizon beneath him, yet he still felt as though he was a considerable distance from the safety of the head of the pitch because the anchors above were nowhere in sight. Three words began to float around in his head at this point,

146 Uncommercial Traveller's Guide to Sublimation

'Jesus, I'm fucked'. Knowing there was nothing anyone else could do to help him, the same three words repeated themselves again and again and again. Helpless and alone, Jamie began to panic.

On the cusp of admitting defeat, Jamie's mind went into overdrive. He became convinced that he would fall to his immediate death if he released his grasp on the hand ascender. This made him grip it even more tightly. He was rapidly losing his ability to think clearly. Sheer dread and hopelessness began filling his imagination as he remained suspended in mid-air. The last thing Jamie recalls thinking is that he needed to control his breathing. Briefly, he tried focusing his attention on the rising and falling motions of his chest, but his concentration was soon broken when he realised his chest harness felt restrictive and suffocating. Almost immediately he was brought back to face the reality of his situation. This is the moment the terror became too great. He became overwhelmed by panic and the last thing Jamie remembers about the event is his mind shutting down completely.

—

The small section of the episode above is an instance where the 'most direct seeing of a violent event may occur', where the person involved 'experience[s] an absolute inability to know it' (Caruth, 1996: 91–92). For theorists such as Stephen Lyng (2005) or Ford Hickson (2018) who have unpacked and employed the concept of edgework, it might be argued that the edge is being overstepped in situations like this since a loss of control has become apparent. However, in thinking about Jamie's experience, I would argue that there is a clear disconnection between what he lived through and the idea of falling beyond the edge. Although Jamie did in fact lose complete control, what is important is that he went on to live and tell his tale. In the process, he also emerged from the event having experienced something significant. In view of this, I would argue that Jamie perhaps experienced something similar to the edge, something 'perpetually incomplete' to borrow Sawyer's (2014) way of putting it, but what he really suffered was a taste of the *traumatic sublime*.

As Sawyer (2014) argues, the traumatic sublime is a nuanced take on Lyotard's original concept. What this means is that we are dealing with a different sort of sublime to my own experience described earlier in the chapter, a derivative product that is not only unexpressed and inexplicable but absolutely unknowable during and after the moment it occurs because of the immense feeling of suffering it causes. According to Sawyer, this version of the sublime eludes all methods of representation that 'endeavour to evoke the unpresentable in presentation itself' (2014: 172). Instead, what is being felt – in this case by Jamie – 'force[s] notice of the unpresented in the unpresentable' (ibid: 173). The traumatic sublime is, therefore, an entirely foreign sensation, one that is wholly incommensurable. What Jamie experienced is a moment that is a fiercely negative experience, an instance of trauma that is so destructive it causes paralysis. Unlike Lyotard's (1988) ordinary concept of the sublime then, the feeling of the traumatic sublime is one people desperately want to end and be over. They do not crave any further stimulation and it is certainly not something that ever evokes nostalgia.

What this section of the chapter reinforces therefore is that the sublime is not something that can easily be understood. It also shows that the differend, the thing that is witnessed before the sublime feeling emerges, is likely to contain surprises that cannot be known during or even after they occur. One of these surprises is clearly the traumatic sublime and when the feeling strikes, the individual involved immediately knows they have entered dangerous territory for this is where their ability to cling onto life itself is tested.

According to Jamie, it was while sitting on the ledge known as The Event Horizon, clinging to loose rocks without a working headtorch, that the sensation first struck him. This is when it dawned on him that he was terrified beyond comprehension because he was in a world he did not understand, a world of unmitigated danger where nothing at all made sense. He had reached a place beyond the reaches of pleasure and pain, a place that had such a deleterious effect on his mind and body he was nothing but hopelessly desperate to escape. It was perhaps his haste to experience the natural underground with no real knowledge or prior experience that contributed to Jamie's feeling of the traumatic sublime. The real cause, however, can likely be attributed to his complete lack of control over how to manage the event.

Back at the cars, it seemed Jamie was trying to comprehend his experience, but it was clear he found little by way of relief. Visibly shaken and subdued, Jamie vowed he would never go caving again. Already waiting in the car, a good 15 minutes before Mayhem was anywhere near finished packing up his gear, it was quite obvious he was ready to leave caving behind him, together with the effects and memories of his traumatic sublime experience.

The Art of Sublimation

As Lyotard (1994) reminds us, many people remain puzzled their whole lives by the problem of not knowing what to think about when they encounter the sublime or how to represent it in ways that work for other people if they do spend some time thinking about it. There are some people, however, as I have attempted to reveal throughout this book, who know exactly what it is like to be a seeker of the sublime and precisely what is involved. Notwithstanding the issue of representation since it is always a difficult task (sometimes impossible), these are people who have a deep interest in mysterious, uncommercialised places and have learned to detect the presence of the sublime through intuitive knowledge and the strategic exploitation of their bodily capabilities.

To reiterate an important point I made earlier, the natural underground and the sublime feeling are both intertwined. That is to say, exploring the natural underground is all about witnessing the differend so that the sublime feeling can be detected and then experienced. Yet, there is a delicate art to experiencing sublimity, one requiring something special which is why it is not found too easily in our day-to-day lives. The specialness I have in mind is something found in cavers who are inclined to venture inside the kingdom of darkness; they must

148 Uncommercial Traveller's Guide to Sublimation

be apt at negotiating challenging situations that require just the right amount of pleasure and pain. Together and in the right measure, they are the perfect recipe for seduction. Whether it is found through the literal noiselessness and tranquillity of the natural underground, the intimacy of scotopic awareness, unique limit experiences or strategies of survival designed to resist the threat of mortality, the point is that explorers of the natural underground are shaped by the *art of seeking sublimation*. Seeking sublimation is, therefore, a literal test of the conditions of possibility and impossibility combined with an underground explorer's ability to adhere to the differend's demand. This is the demand that ways of understanding it must be adaptable and flexible enough to adjust to new and varied conditions.

What this book turns out to be, then, is a guide to the art of sublimation. It is, in a nutshell, a means of thinking about how certain leisure lives can defy conventional explanation, logic and understanding, and how those lives can feel as though they are being lived beyond the limitations and restrictions of present modernity.

Note

1 Shortly after reaching the window, Jim emerged to explain that Mayhem had dropped his phone in the flooded passage that leads to the entrance pitch. While I'd been ascending, everyone had been searching for it; hence I couldn't see their torchlights. We eventually found Mayhem's phone, much to his relief.

References

Bingham, K. (2020). *An Ethnography of Urban Exploration: Unpacking Heterotopic Social Space*. Cham: Palgrave.

Buch, E. (2020). The Sound of the Sublime: Notes on Burke as Time Goes By. *SubStance*. 49(2): 44–59.

Burke, E. (1769/2007). *A Philosophical Enquiry into the Sublime and Beautiful*. Oxon: Routledge.

Caruth, C. (1996). *Unclaimed Experience: Trauma, Narrative and History*. London: The John Hopkins University Press.

Derrida, J. (1987). *Truth in Painting*. Trans. G. Bennington and I. McLeod. Chicago: The University of Chicago Press.

Elias, W. (1997). *Signs of the Time*. Atlanta: Rodopi.

Forster, E. M. (1924/2000). *A Passage to India*. London: Penguin.

Gervais, D. (1987). Suffering in Wordsworth. *The Cambridge Quarterly*. 16(1): 1–14.

Hickson, F. (2018). Chemsex as Edgework: Towards a Sociological Understanding. *Sexual Health*. 15: 102–107.

Kant, I. (1790/2007). *Critique of Judgement*. Trans. J. C. Meredith, Ed. N. Walker. Oxford: Oxford University Press.

Lipari, L. (2010). Listening, Thinking, Being. *Communication Theory*. 20(3): 348–362.

Longinus, D. (1739). *Dionysius Longinus on the Sublime*. Trans. W. Smith. London: J. Watts.

Lyng, S. (2005). Sociology at the Edge: Social Theory and Voluntary Risk Taking: In: S. Lyng (Ed), *Edgework: The Sociology of Risk-Taking*. Oxon: Routledge, 17–49.

Lyotard, J.-F. (1984). *The Postmodern Condition: A Report on Knowledge*. Minneapolis: University of Minnesota Press.

Lyotard, J.-F. (1985). The Sublime and the Avant Garde. *Paragraph*. 6: 1–18.

Lyotard, J.-F. (1988). *The Differend: Phrases in Dispute*. Trans. G. V. Den Abbeele. Minneapolis: University of Minnesota Press.

Lyotard, J.-F. (1994). Lessons on the Analytic of the Sublime: Kant's Critique of Judgement. Trans. E. Rottenberg. The Communication of Sublime Feeling. In: K. Crome and J. Williams (Eds), *The Lyotard Reader and Guide*. New York: Columbia University Press, 254–265.

Lyotard, J.-F. (2006). The Communication of the Sublime Feeling. In: K. Crome and J. Williams (Eds), *The Lyotard Reader and Guide*. New York: Colombia University Press, 254–265.

Lyotard, J.-F. (2011). *Discourse, Figure*. Trans. A. Hudek and M. Lydon. Minneapolis: University of Minnesota Press.

McLuhen, M. (2004). Visual and Acoustic Space. In: C. Cox and D. Warner (Eds), *Audio Culture: Readings in Modern Music*. London: Continuum, 67–72.

Mortensen, K. (1998). *The Time of Unrememberable Being: Wordsworth and the Sublime 1787–1805*. Trans. W. Glyn Jones. Copenhagen: Museum Tusculanum Press.

Nancy, J.-L. (2015). On Listening. In: R. Caines and A. Heble (Eds), *The Improvisation Studies Reader: Spontaneous Acts*. Oxon: Routledge, 17–26.

Rojek, C. (2000). *Leisure and Culture*. Basingstoke: Palgrave.

Sawyer, D. (2014). *Lyotard, Literature and the Trauma of the Differend*. Basingstoke: Palgrave.

Shaw, P. (2006). *The Sublime: The New Critical Idiom*. Oxon: Routledge.

Wordsworth, W. (1805/2014). *The Poems of William Wordsworth: Collected Reading Texts from the Cornell Wordsworth Series, Volume II*. Ed. J. Curtis. Penrith: HEB.

Wordsworth, W. (1835/2020). *A Guide Through the District of the Lakes in the North of England*. Bristol: A Thousand Fields.

Wordsworth, W. (1890). *The Complete Poetical Works of William Wordsworth*. London: Macmillan and Co.

Žižek, S. (1989). *The Sublime Object of Ideology*. London: Verso.

Chapter 8

Journeying to the End and Back
Reaching a Choke

When I first told friends and colleagues at work I was interested in caving, usually their first response would be to ask why. Their phrasing of the question would generally be along the lines of, "eh, what's the point?" I understand their confusion. As a basic act, exploration of the natural underground seems like it is about reaching an endpoint inside a hole in the earth and then being successful in finding a way back out again. Certainly, when it is viewed like this, there is not much point to it. Its ontological significance carries an air of meaninglessness, and this encourages people to make the tacit assumption that it is a senseless pursuit.

Another way of viewing caving, however, is as a form of leisure that is liminal because it lies somewhere between the rhythms and routines of the surface world and the unknownness of the kingdom of the dark. When viewed in this way it becomes a lot more mysterious and interesting. Suddenly it occurs to people that another world exists beneath our feet, a world that perhaps offers a richer experience of living because it contains the wonder of sublime feelings which happen to be strangely pleasurable, painful and potentially traumatic all at once.

The aim of this book has been to provide a comprehensive investigation of the natural underground from a sociological perspective. At first glance, it might appear that the thesis emerging from my analyses leads to little more than the conclusion that the natural underground is a hellish place. If you are not damp or exhausted, you are probably lost, miserable or cold. Chances are, you are likely to experience all these things at the same time and this is perhaps why things underground should remain hidden. To view caves in such a way, however, is to ignore the magic and enchantment of a world that defies rational explanation. This is a world that requires taking what Agnes Heller (1996) would describe as an existential leap. This is a leap into awareness, self-awareness, awareness of space and awareness of the significance of social relations.

In taking the existential leap, the angle I took was that the natural underground has traditionally been investigated and controlled largely by one dominant ontological lens. My suggestion, in response to this problem, has been to become a little more fox-like rather than a hedgehog if we are to recall Archilochus's distinction made famous by Isaiah Berlin. In becoming fox-like, I endeavoured

DOI: 10.4324/9781003301752-8

to move away from the thoughts and ideas of speleologists who only have science as a means of making sense of the natural underground. My focus was instead turned to sociology and the power of imagination, senses and emotions. With these things at the forefront of my mind, I was able to turn my attention to broadening the possibilities of the sociology of caving.

My way of putting some conceptual meat onto the bones of the topic of caving was to embrace the role of an uncommercial traveller, a Dickensian figure capable of detecting things and events that might seem minor or trivial to an outsider. Being in this role meant I was able to conduct my investigation using two kinds of hermeneutics which have been referred to as hermeneutic sociology and sociological hermeneutics (see: Blackshaw, 2017). As I explained in Chapter 2, the reciprocity of this coupled hermeneutical methodology allowed me to challenge common sense doxa, understand exploration of the natural underground in relation to 'liquid' modernity and some of its big issues, and gear the book towards a sociological interpretation that manages to pull the reader into the intricate details of individual lives.

After outlining the methodology, I went on to provide an overview of the societal context in which caving is done in the twenty-first century. My thesis therefore began with the idea that the gradual transition from 'solid' to 'liquid' modernity brings with it certain consequences. Foremost among them is Herbert Marcuse's (1964) suggestion that individuals are becoming one-dimensional beings which means they cannot help but live their lives through the allure of consumer capitalism. A conclusion I drew from this is that one-dimensional lives are defined by *a-lack-of*. They lack something special, perhaps the same specialness subtly hidden in art that is difficult to commodify. My response to this first conclusion was that the natural underground is a place that allows people, for the most part at least, to leave the surface world behind. When they do this, certain things that are ignored, glossed over or not even present in our everyday lives begin to appear and this allows conditions of existence to transform for a short time. Liberated from the normal rules and traditions of present modernity, explorers of the natural underground are compelled to find their own meaning in the world, along with imaginative ways of surviving hazards and dangers that seem more literal and immediate than everyday threats of insecurity, unpredictability and uncertainty.

In Chapters 4–6, my thesis continued with suggestions as to how the natural underground stimulates imaginations, senses and emotions in unique ways. The essential conclusion to take away from this part of the book is that people who explore the natural underground 'unlearn' rationalistic habits and modes of thinking which means they are compelled to regard things differently. Entering the intimate immensity of what I have termed *scotopia* is one way of doing this. To enter scotopia is to become less reliant on vision. It is instead about becoming a version of John Hull's (1990) 'whole-body seer' by acknowledging other sensory systems. As I argued, doing so can reveal whole new landscapes of experience and knowledge.

Another way of stimulating imaginations, senses and emotions in the natural underground is to liberate oneself from the constraints imposed by consumer capitalism by seeking limit experiences. Limit experiences enable people to reconnect themselves with feelings of fear in a world where fears frequently go through a process of silent silencing.

The final way I explored the natural underground is through mortality. The task of avoiding or defying death occupies most people's attention in the surface world, yet consumer capitalism offers a variety of strategies to help render the threat invisible. What I pointed out in Chapter 6 is that the same strategies do not work in the kingdom of the dark, especially since death is harder to veil in the subterranean world. For this reason, an assortment of alternative and imaginative strategies of survival is found to be needed in the natural underground to help diffuse the awfulness of impermanence and its constant nearness.

The book's most important conclusion is found in Chapter 7. Here I argued that exploring the natural underground is actually all about *the art of sublimation*. The moment the surface world is left behind, you enter a strange place that is at the same time pleasurable and unpleasant. To borrow Edmund Burke's (1769/2007) way of putting it, the intensity of being underground strikes a person with awe. What this suggests is that entering the natural underground is always a double bind and that the person who has entered it has effectively come into contact with the agitated zone between life and death. This is a unique space that grips a person because it fills them on the one hand with great veneration, wonder and gratification but on the other deadens them as the intensity of the underground world raises the power and weight of emotions to such an extent that they cause deep misery and agony. Hence, there is immense power in the natural underground precisely because enjoyment becomes an ambivalent enjoyment. This is what Jean-François Lyotard refers to as an ontological dislocation.

According to Lyotard (1989), to be dislocated ontologically is a humbling experience because it shows a person that reality can be at play outside of dominant phrase regimes. Although Lyotard never explored the significance of leisure, the suggestion in this book is that certain forms such as caving can facilitate emancipation from language games that are more influential in controlling and channelling twenty-first-century lives. As Lyotard explains in his critique of Kant, if people dispense with consoling language games they are left with 'the naked convulsions of the differends' (1989: 341). In response to this claim, it may seem fair to suggest that Lyotard's notion of ontological dislocations points to places, despite being far removed from more usual language games, that are reducible to their own language and therefore some sense of ontological constancy or stability. However, it is here I remind the reader that any experience of the *differend* is a pure experience of dislocation since it represents a frantic struggle between reason and imagination which means it is always unique and always inexplicable. In other words, sublime feelings are felt so poignantly because of the underlying Silence at the heart of the differend that remains waiting to be found (or sometimes created) and then interpreted.

Figure 8.1 The Kingdom of the Dark.

With the above ideas in mind, my final conclusion is simple. It points to the idea that anybody following the path of the differend in the natural underground is someone who has become versed in the art of sublimation. These are people capable of disrupting the course of 'liquid' modernity because they understand how to turn their bodies into vessels that seek our strongest passions. Pushed way beyond the faculty of reason and representation, these are bodies at leisure suspended masterfully between the fullest emotional forces of discomfort, enjoyment and terror. These are bodies that simply cannot resist the delights of darkness, confusion, horror and uncertainty that are otherwise ignored, hidden or absent in our day-to-day lives. These are bodies that have entered the Silence of the Kingdom of Darkness (Figure 8.1).

The Maze Cave: Versed in the Art of Sublimation

On a cold mid-February evening deep beneath Knock Fell, the fourth highest summit in the Pennine chain, Mayhem and I reached the final northern choke point of Knock Fell Caverns. This was the end point of a dense network of narrow muddy passages known as the Inferiority Complex. After several hours of navigating the complex system, we were exhausted. Feeling utterly weak after hours

154   Journeying to the End and Back

of crawling and squeezing our way to the so-called finish, I lay flat out in the mud. Mayhem collapsed beside me with his back resting against the wall. I concentrated on my breathing for a moment as I waited for some strength to return in my arms and legs. Closing my eyes, I listened as Mayhem put into words exactly what I was thinking: 'Well, this is a bit shit isn't it. We've just literally come all this way to see some mud down a dead end'.

In that moment, the whole endeavour suddenly seemed meaningless and disappointing. The small, uninspiring chamber we were sat in exuded an emotionless air and I began to question what on earth had compelled us to reach this miserable point. A solemn pause ensued. This continued for a while, until we caught one another's eye and couldn't help but laugh at the absurdity of the situation. Eventually we were reduced to hysterics. In between laughing, our conversation went something like this:

Me: I'm having the worst time of my life.
Mayhem: Me too.
Me: [*I begin to laugh again*]. That's a dead end that.
Mayhem: I noticed, mate.
[*Laughter*].
Mayhem: Fuck. Mate, I'm literally fucked. Everything hurts and me injured knee
    feels more injured.
Me: [*Laughing more intensely*].
Mayhem: Want a cereal bar to cheer us up?
Me: Go on then.
[*Laughter as Mayhem searches the inside of his oversuit*].
Mayhem: It's broken like.
[*Hysterical laughter*].

It was just as our conversation drifted to a close that I began to realise something important. This was the moment it dawned on me that the magic of the natural underground is not found at a choke or down a sump. It is not in the act of completion or at a finishing point. Everything magical, enchanting and provoking, everything that felt truly sublime, was back the way we had come. It was behind us in the vast space of an alternative dimension, threaded wildly into the journey we had taken to get to this point. I sat and reflected on this for a while, thinking about everything we had done to reach the choke.

Our trip had begun with a 4.8-kilometre hike from the car. Having been warned against parking in the passing lanes dotted along the road running all the way up to Great Dun Fell Radar Station, we'd left the car due south on the Pennine Way. I can't say either of us enjoyed the steep walk very much, but it did give us the satisfaction that we were earning our trip underground. Needless to say, we were well and truly warmed up by the time we reached the entrance lid. Despite the temperature being in the minuses, we were sweating profusely inside our oversuits. Conscious we would begin to feel cold if we stopped for too long, finding the lid quickly became our next task. This certainly wasn't easy given that it's positioned at the bottom of a shakehole, one among many others in the area. What made matters worse was that it had recently been snowing. Having forgotten our GPS device, we were left with no choice but to scour the frozen moorland until we found the entrance. It was Mayhem who eventually spotted a metal grill by chance, half-buried beneath a layer of fresh snow. Desperate to seek reprieve from the biting cold, the pair of us acted like frenzied madmen digging it out.

My fingers were so cold they throbbed as we climbed down the 8-metre entrance shaft. The inability to use my hands made the climb more difficult than it should have been, but it did not stop the initial moment of entering the cave from being a euphoric one. I felt utter relief as I climbed away from the strong winds and grey skies above.

Any reprieve was short-lived, however, for we immediately found ourselves lost and confused at the bottom of the shaft. There were two possible routes we could take – a tight connection that leads towards the northern section of the system and an unpleasant rocky crawl to the south. We needed our compass straight away to figure out which way was which. For some reason, we chose the less friendly route to the south and soon found ourselves firmly pressed against the floor of a real-life labyrinth. As I dragged my body through the tiny passage cluttered with jagged rocks, I began to understand how easy it would be to get dangerously lost in Knock Fell Caverns. Maintaining awareness of my position was impossible as I couldn't look back and nor could I keep the map in hand. On top of this, every off-shooting passage I slithered past looked identical to the next. Thankfully, the rocky crawl wasn't too long and we soon found ourselves standing upright in an impressive chamber known as Scotch Corner Chamber. This part of the cave had an incredibly homely feel to it, starkly different from the passages we'd encountered so far, so we paused here to check the map and regain our bearing.

From Scotch Corner Chamber, we made our way towards Trans-Pennine Passage, a large rift that runs almost the entire width of the cave from West to East. We followed this as far as we could, heading for Myotis Chamber for no other reason than curiosity. At the end of the Trans-Pennine Passage, the cave suddenly became much more complex as we seemed to move up a level. Following this we faced a series of difficult squeezes. The last appeared to be so tight I was momentarily convinced it was impassable. Mayhem proved me wrong, but there was a moment of terror when he became wedged and for a few split seconds couldn't breathe. Although I'm more heavily built than Mayhem, I decided it would be a good idea to follow him once he'd reached the other side. When my chest prevented me from moving any further, I immediately regretted my decision, and when I realised I couldn't breathe I panicked just as Mayhem had. Desperate to free myself, I scraped my unwilling body against an especially rough piece of jutting rock. The cave seemed to claw at me, willing me to stay put. I was fortunate though, for in the end, it turned out I was compressible enough to be able to pass through.

On the other side, I took a moment to pull myself back together and confessed to Mayhem that I'd have to find an alternative way of returning. There was no way I'd be going back the way I'd just come. Doing our best to ignore the discomfort of having been part-grated, we willed ourselves to keep going. And we were very glad we did. Just ahead we found ourselves in a chamber, which at the time we assumed (incorrectly) was Myotis Chamber, decorated with stalactites and stalagmites. The pair of us were dazzled by these intricate formations of calcite. I would go so far as to suggest it was a fairy-tale scene, a veritable wonderland containing so much beauty it was too much to contemplate. With our powers of perception almost blown away, the magical scenery here reduced us to silence. Far away from the demands and effects of present modernity, in amongst the mud, gloom and discomfort of the natural underground, we engaged in a feast of splendour. It was a feast of pure sublimation.

References

Blackshaw, T. (2017). *Re-Imagining Leisure Studies*. Oxon: Routledge.
Burke, E. (1769/2007). *A Philosophical Enquiry into the Sublime and Beautiful*. Oxon: Routledge.
Heller, A. (1996). *Ethics of Personality*. Oxford: Blackwell.
Hull, J. (1990). *Touching the Rock: An Experience of Blindness*. London: SPCK.
Lyotard, J-F. (1989). *The Lyotard Reader*. Ed. A. Benjamin. Oxford: Blackwell.
Marcuse, H. (1964). *One-Dimensional Man*. London: Routledge & Kegan Paul.

Index

anti-citizens 14, 15
art of sublimation 129, 147–148, 152–153
athleticism 111–112
auditory system 71, 73–75
Austin, John 16; felicity conditions 16
auto-methodologies 28; auto-ethnography 28–31; auto-hermeneutics 28–29, 31–32

Bachelard, Gaston 66–67
Baudelaire, Charles *see* flâneur
Baudrillard, Jean 45, 86–87, 104, 111–112, 123–124
Bauman, Zygmunt 5, 10, 14, 16–17, 27, 30, 33–34, 36, 42–47, 49–50, 52, 54, 76, 92, 95, 110, 121–125; legislators and interpreters 16–17, 27
Bech, Henning 34, 38
Beck, Ulrich 93, 107, 122; risk societies 93–94, 101
Becker, Ernest 123–125
Bedford, Bruce *see* kingdom of the dark
Benjamin, Walter 35–37
Bingham, Kevin 2, 5, 32, 34, 50, 68–70, 82, 89, 137
Blackshaw, Tony 5, 14, 17, 28, 32–33, 36, 45, 49, 81–82, 89, 105, 114–115, 121, 123, 151
Bridge Hall 77, 82, 84
British Speleological Association (BSA) 9
Bullpot Farm 64
Burke, Edmund 129, 136–137, 142–143, 152

Canetti, Elias 118–120
Cant, Sarah 8–9, 11
Casteret, Norbert 7
Castleton 115, 118, 123, 132
Cave Research Group (CRG) 9

Collins, Floyd 113, 126
community 14, 16–17, 52, 120–123; 'peg communities' 121–122
consumer capitalism 18–19, 34, 42, 45, 51–52, 60, 95, 104–105, 107, 111–112, 126, 130, 151–152
Corbin, Alain 82, 92
Crane, Ralph and Fletcher, Lisa 5, 7, 51

Daly, Jamie 132
Derrida, Jacques 130
Dickens, Charles 18, 36–38, 73, 151; The Uncommercial Traveller 18, 34, 36–38, 130, 151
disenchantment 42, 52, 60
Durham 1

edgework 18, 99–107, 146
Eshleman, Clayton 13
The Event Horizon 136, 140–141, 145, 147
existential insecurity 46–47, 49

fear avoidance 92–94, 99, 101, 107
Figg, Jim 132
Flâneur 34–37
Forster, E. M. 137–138
Foucault, Michel 5, 16, 18, 69, 102–108, 122, 125
Freud, Sigmund 49–51, 83, 119, 123

Gaping Gill 7
Gemeinschaft 121; *see also* community
Gesellschaft 121; *see also* community
Giant's Hole 96–97, 100, 105–107; Garland's Pot 97–99, 127; Giant's Windpipe 98, 100, 104, 107
Giddens, Anthony 32–33, 46, 88, 111
the Graveyard Series 79–80, 82–83, 85, 87

Index

Heap, David 6, 28, 52–53
Hellewell, Luke 96
hermeneutics 17, 31–32; hermeneutic
   sociology 18, 28, 32–34, 151;
   sociological hermeneutics 18, 28,
   32–34, 151
heterotopia 5, 69; heterotopic social
   space 5
Hull, John 71, 88, 151
Hunt, Will 13

imagination 3–4, 13, 28, 34–36, 39, 42,
   44, 50–53, 57–58, 66–67, 69–70, 73–75,
   80, 88, 99, 115, 121, 129–132, 134, 146,
   151–152
intimacy 18–19, 34, 60, 64, 66–68, 71, 88,
   110, 148

Jackpot 115, 118–119, 122–125, 127

Kant, Immanuel 129–131, 152
kingdom of the dark 3–5, 38, 52, 60,
   63, 88, 110, 118, 126, 130, 134, 150,
   152–153
Knock Fell Caverns 19, 153, 155; The
   Maze Cave 153

Lancaster Hole 64–65, 67, 70, 74–75, 77
limit experience 19, 102–108, 110, 131,
   148, 152
liquid modernity 45
Lyng, Stephen 18, 99–104, 106–107, 146
Lyotard, Jean-François 19, 129–131, 134,
   136–137, 139, 143–144, 146–147, 152;
   the differend 19, 129–132, 134–137,
   139, 142, 144, 147–148, 152–153; the
   sublime 19, 129–131, 135–137, 139,
   142–144, 146–147

Marcuse, Herbert 45, 60, 151
Marshall, Des 6, 8
Martel, Édouard-Alfred 7–8
Mathiesen, Thomas 94, 106; silent
   silencing 94, 106, 152
Matless, David 14–15, 73
Mattes, Johannes 8–9, 11–12
Mayhem, Ford 5, 23–24, 26, 43, 47–49,
   54–58, 74, 77–78, 80, 82–83,
   85–87, 115–118, 120, 122–125, 127,
   132–135, 138–141, 144–145, 147–148,
   153–156
McLuhan, Marshall 58, 73, 138

Mcnally, James 43, 47–50, 55–58, 65–66,
   71–72, 74, 77–78, 80, 82–83, 85–88,
   115–117, 120, 122–125, 127
Middridge Quarry 2
Mossdale Caverns Disaster 113

Newton Aycliffe 1–2
Nietzsche, Friedrich 63
nostalgia 69–70, 76–77, 80, 84, 88,
   143, 146

Odin Mine 42, 45, 49–50, 54, 56–58
olfactory system 76–77, 81–82
ontological security 46, 50, 111–112;
   ontological insecurity 46

Peak District 95–96, 120, 127, 132
Pérez, María 8, 10–12
Photographs 38–39, 56
phryneism 111–112
The Poetics of Space see Bachelard,
   Gaston
Project of the Hero 123, 125; being-a-
   caver 118, 124–125

rational recreation 14, 27, 44; field sport 8;
   sporting-science 8–9
Rorty, Richard 17, 29

Sand Cave 113
Sawyer, Dylan 134, 136, 142, 144, 146
Scotopia 18–19, 68–71, 75, 82–84, 88,
   151; scotopic experience 68–70, 76, 81,
   83–85, 88, 110
silence 134–139, 152–153
silencing of fear 18, 92, 95, 99–103, 107
Simmel, Georg 74
Simpson, Eli 11
Sleets Gill Cave 23, 26; Hydrophobia
   Series 23, 26
Sloterdijk, Peter 28, 30; anthropoetechnics
   28; art of living 28; foam 30
speleology 8–13; speleologist 9–11, 14–16,
   27, 39, 113, 151
Spracklen, Karl 53, 114
sublimation see art of sublimation

tactile system 84–87
Taylor, Michael Ray 6, 8, 14–15, 25, 27–28
Tham Luang cave rescue 52
thanatological pleasure 19, 112, 126
Titan 132–145

traumatic sublime 144, 146–147
Turkle, Sherry 54, 57–58

uncommercial traveller *see* Dickens,
  Charles
urban exploration 2, 5, 38; urban explorers
  4, 19, 23, 43, 132; urbex 2, 4, 26, 38

The Vice 97, 100, 105, 107

Weber, Max 94–95
whole-body seer *see* Hull, John
WildBoyz 4–5
Wordsworth, William 143

Yorkshire Dales 51, 64

Žižek, Slavoj 131
Zurita, María 11–12